# Equality for Contingent Faculty

D1384127

# Equality for Contingent Faculty

Overcoming the Two-Tier System

*Edited by Keith Hoeller*

Vanderbilt University Press | Nashville

© 2014 by Vanderbilt University Press
Nashville, Tennessee 37235
All rights reserved
First printing 2014
Second printing 2014

This book is printed on acid-free paper.
Manufactured in the United States of America

Library of Congress Cataloging-in-Publication Data on file
LC control number   2013031628
LC classification number   LB2334.E59 2014
Dewey class number   378.1'2—dc23

ISBN 978-0-8265-1951-1 (paper)
ISBN 978-0-8265-1950-4 (cloth)
ISBN 978-0-8265-1952-8 (ebook)

*This book is dedicated to the millions of women and men who spent many years and tens of thousands of dollars to earn graduate degrees and then found themselves toiling like migrant workers in our nation's academic fields.*

# Contents

# Preface

*Keith Hoeller*

It has long been assumed that a college education is just the ticket for admittance into the middle and upper classes. High school students are routinely advised to apply to several colleges, and to choose the one with the most prestige. While financial aid is important, students are told they should go to the best college they can, and to go into debt, if necessary, to make it happen. Government statistics have regularly confirmed the wisdom of this advice. College graduates earn several hundred thousands more over their lifetimes than high school dropouts, and earnings rise the higher the degree.

This advice has remained sound even though the Arab oil embargo of 1973 and the consequent recession of 1974–1975 halted the consistent economic growth that followed World War II. The mid-1970s mark the beginning of income stagnation in America, with globalization, downsizing, outsourcing, the steady decline in union membership and the middle class, and within higher education, the erosion of reliance on the tenured professor.

Yet the concomitant changes in higher education have rarely been mentioned in the mainstream press. Only since the great recession of 2007–2009 has there been any questioning of both the value and cost of a college degree. Attention has been paid to whether a degree should take so long, and whether online education will replace the traditional brick-and-mortar campus, with the traditional college professor giving lectures to large numbers of students or leading small graduate seminars. But most of this mainstream discussion has focused on students and parents, tuition, and student loans.

The major changes in the *professoriate* have been missing from the debate over the future of higher education in America. The public still retains the positive image of the college professor as well paid and well treated, with low teaching loads, plenty of funding, a lot of time free for research, and students devoted to learning. During the 2012 presidential campaign, Vice President Joe Biden, himself married to a community college professor, blamed high tuition on the high salaries of college professors.[1]

## From "Mobile Professors" to "Freeway Fliers"

Yet during the past four decades academe has gone from an overwhelming majority of professors holding tenure and tenure-track jobs in the 1960s to a minority today. In the past forty years, there has been a near reversal of the three-to-one ratio between the number of professors who teach on and off the tenure track, with part-time faculty now holding over 50 percent of all college appointments.

In "The Case of the Vanishing Full-Time Professor," Samantha Stainburn of the *New York Times* says: "In 1960, 75 percent of college instructors were full-time tenured or tenure-track professors; today only 27 percent are. The rest are graduate students or adjunct and contingent faculty."[2] Tenure-stream professors now find themselves adrift in a small, leaky lifeboat surrounded by an ocean brimming with contingent faculty who, prevented from climbing into the tenure boat, are forced either to tread water or drown. Even the American Association of University Professors (AAUP), the National Education Association (NEA), and the American Federation of Teachers (AFT) have begun to speak of tenure in apocalyptic terms.

"Today that system [of tenure] has all but collapsed," says the AAUP.[3] Former AAUP president Cary Nelson says, "Now the average college teacher is no longer eligible for tenure, and the good ship humanities is already partly under water."[4]

It was not always this way. In *The Mobile Professors* (1967), published by the American Council on Education, David Brown decried the lack of college professors to fill the ranks of the tenured:

*Academic labor markets serve the tremendously important role of allocating a resource (qualified manpower) which is not only scarce but vital to the social production function.* If professors are poorly placed, the quality of education will suffer. So also will the standard of living and the quality of life. Almost each individual professor is a scarce resource whose optimal placement is severely restricted and whose marginal product would be conspicuous by its absence. (italics in original)[5]

The resulting shortage in the 1960s led to a system of musical chairs for "mobile professors," who could and did move from one college to another in order to advance their careers. Colleges had trouble both finding professors to fill tenure and tenure-track positions and retaining them. In one study, nearly 80 percent of colleges predicted larger shortages in the future, with some analysts predicting they could only last for at least another decade.

The 1960s "mobile professor" turned into the 1970s "freeway flier," tackling part-time jobs at several colleges in order to eke out the financial existence offered to fast-food workers. Contingent professors have been compared to migrant farm workers and indentured servants, and the two-track system has been compared to the Jim Crow laws of the old South and the former racial apartheid system of South Africa.

Students have graduated with MAs and PhDs, and tens of thousands of dollars in debt, only to find few tenure-track jobs in their fields. Those not lucky enough to land a scarce tenure-track job have faced a stark choice: accept a part-time job, accept a one-year appointment, or leave academe altogether. These part-time teaching jobs pay only half the rate of full-timers, have few or no benefits, have no job security, and usually do not provide offices for the teachers in question.

## The Two-Tier System and "Inside-Out Sourcing"

Under economic duress, unions have sometimes agreed to two-tiered compensation systems. In 2007, the United Auto Workers agreed to a two-tier system where the new hires, doing the same work as the old-timers, are paid at half the rate, earning only $14 an hour.

But higher education has remained a growth industry and the origins of the two-tiered system were different. The statewide community college systems, expanded in the 1960s, led the change away from full-time staffing, often relying on "moonlighters"—that is, experts in the community—to teach courses. As Michael Dubson writes in *Ghosts in the Classroom*, "The use of adjunct faculty began innocently enough, as bad things often do. Members of the business community were initially brought in to teach highly specialized classes that academic faculty could not teach. The remuneration offered for this was minimal. The business person was successful in his/her field and didn't need the money. Instead, the primary gain for their efforts was a certain amount of prestige. The adjunct phenomenon was born."[6]

The community colleges expanded on this two-track system, transforming it in the process, and the four-year and research universities quickly followed suit. In order to meet the growing number of students in the 1970s, colleges decided to keep costs low by minimizing the expansion of tenure-track positions. Since graduate students were cheap and were not paid benefits, research universities began to expand their use. Teaching assistants were used more often to grade papers and lead discussion groups so as to allow for the increased use of large lecture classes with hundreds of students. More graduate students were assigned to teach their own classes.

As a result, tenure-stream professors discovered they could shift the repetitive teaching of lower-level introductory courses onto their students (or former students) and the growing ranks of non-tenure-track professors of all types. This allowed the tenure-stream professors to teach the more advanced and specialized courses they really wanted to teach and to keep their class sizes small to boot. And with reduced classloads, it also freed up more time for research.

Ron Swift, an adjunct instructor of communication studies for forty years, has called this new system "inside-out sourcing" to explain how the colleges have managed to keep the revolution secret from the public.[7] To the outside world, everything still looks normal. Colleges still hold classes, and teachers still teach them. The fact that three-fourths of the professors are treated in an inferior way is not advertised.

## Academic Unions

With a few notable exceptions, academic unions have adopted the two-tiered system, which generally has a negative effect on union solidarity. The full-timers tend to think that the part-timers drag their wages down; the part-timers tend to believe that the full-timers are neglecting them in favor of their own interests.

Whereas generally unions have been shown to increase wages, benefits, and job security for their members, the "union advantage" for contingent faculty has not been borne out, if it exists at all. Research has shown there is no union premium for full-time faculty, and there is virtually no research at all on contingent faculty.

The AAUP, the AFT, and the NEA have been and continue to be controlled by tenure-stream faculty who continue to elect the leaders and hand-pick the few adjuncts who will represent the contingent faculty within the unions. At the same time, no national adjunct union has been formed to specifically focus on the plight of contingent faculty.

As the Selected Bibliography makes clear, there have been other books on the topic of contingent faculty. What makes this book different is its focus on *equality* and the *two-tier system*. The latter makes equality nearly impossible to achieve. The book also gives examples of major changes that have already been accomplished, analyzes the structural problems, and lays out several solutions.

Part I, Case Studies of Progressive Change, shows how contingent faculty have worked to transform a large, mixed union to share power with, and advocate for, adjuncts. It also describes the fight to extend tenure to contingent faculty. And it exhibits how adjunct activism can even be extended to the burgeoning online network of courses.

Part II, The Two-Tier System in Academe, explains the structure of the two-tier system, how it came into being, and how it functions. One article points out the very real conflicts of interest between the two tiers. And another asks if all teachers should be judged primarily on their scholarly output.

Part III, Roadmaps for Achieving Equality, gives two blueprints for abolishing the two-tier system. One article tells exactly how to do it in the California community colleges. The other showcases how one community college actually replaced the two-tier system with a one-tier system.

*Equality for Contingent Faculty: Overcoming the Two-Tier System* has been written by some of the leading academic theorists of the contingent faculty movement. It is designed to provide concrete examples of how change has already happened, and how it can continue to happen.

## NOTES

1. "Faculty Groups Try to Educate Biden on Salaries," *Inside Higher Ed*, 12 January 2012, *insidehighered.com*.
2. Samantha Stainburn, "The Case of the Vanishing Full-Time Professor," *New York Times*, 3 January 2010.
3. AAUP, *Conversion of Appointments to the Tenure Track* (Washington, DC: AAUP, 2009), *aaup.org*.
4. Cary Nelson, "Playing Mozart on the Titanic," *Inside Higher Ed*, 4 January 2010, *insidehighered.com*.
5. David G. Brown, *The Mobile Professors* (Washington, DC: American Council on Education, 1967), 3.
6. Michael Dubson, ed., *Ghosts in the Classroom: Stories of College Adjunct Faculty—and the Price We All Pay* (Boston: Camel's Back, 2001), iv.
7. Ron Swift, "Adjunct Educators Need Full-Time Respect," *Green River Community College Current*, 13 November 2012, 11.

# PART I

## Case Studies of Progressive Change

# 1

# Organizing for Equality within the Two-Tier System

## The Experience of the California Faculty Association

*Elizabeth Hoffman and John Hess*

On November 15, 2006, a sunny day in Long Beach, California, 1,500 faculty and students marched across a bridge and assembled in front of the entrance to the chancellor's headquarters on Golden Shores. We had come to harass the California State University (CSU) chancellor and board of trustees, and that is what we did. The marchers carried banners large and small and even an enormous puppet of the chancellor. The crowd became more and more boisterous, students banged on the outside of the windows and held up banners to the windows so the trustees could see them, and a group of the protesters went inside the board of trustees' meeting room. Eventually, twenty-one faculty leaders sat down in the middle of the room and locked arms. Seven of these faculty were lecturers, people with little or no job security. They all began chanting, supported by other faculty and students inside and outside the trustees' chambers. Finally, the chancellor and the trustees fled the room and the CSU became what we had long been calling it: The People's University.[1] When the faculty and students went back to their campuses, they began to make preparations to go on strike. The faculty eventually voted overwhelmingly to do so. Had this happened, it would have been the largest faculty strike in the United States. The chancellor, however, threw in the towel and conceded nearly everything we had been asking for at the bargaining table.

How did this happen? What does it mean? How is it that CSU lecturers played an important role in this fight with the chancellor? We hope to answer these and other pertinent questions in this article from our special perspective as contingent faculty activists. To begin, step back with us to another time.

"Throw the lecturers out of the union," shouted one of the leaders of the California Faculty Association (CFA). To the two lecturers in the room, hearing this was a low point in their union experience and proof of the contingent faculty axiom that one is never more than fifteen seconds away from total humiliation. The setting was a retreat held by the CFA in the early 1990s, and the hired facilitator had directed the participants to brainstorm as honestly as possible about what the CFA should do to build a strong and effective union. This comment was certainly honest, and it brought out into the open some depressing realities. Although the CFA was the legal representative for all the faculty in the California State University, the union did not well represent almost half the faculty members—those with full-time or part-time temporary appointments. These faculty, the lecturers, were marginalized in their teaching positions and marginalized—even rejected—in their own union.

Now, some twenty years later, the CFA has become a very different union, far more democratic and inclusive and committed to protecting the needs of all the constituents in the bargaining unit. It's not perfect and certainly the university itself remains a status conscious and exclusionary environment. And despite improvements in job security provisions, lecturers still lead insecure lives. However, the mean-spirited "throw the lecturers out" comment is unimaginable in today's CFA. We're a big union, representing more than twenty-three thousand faculty at twenty-three campuses, and there is a clear understanding that we need every hand on board, not only to protect our own interests, but to protect the institution of higher education itself.

Higher education is the key both to producing the innovative professionals needed for the twenty-first century and to rebuilding a middle class whose members can expect respect for their contributions, job security, a livable wage with health benefits, and a retirement with dignity. It's a cruel irony that the majority of the faculty preparing this workforce of the future have few of these benefits themselves. The contingent, temporary nature of their faculty appointments undermines not only their working conditions but also academic freedom that ensures the integrity of the profession. This labor system results in an academic workforce with over half the faculty members marginalized from democratic decision-making and governance processes. The contingent nature of these appointments does not just negatively impact the faculty holding such positions. In a 2008 issue of *Academe* devoted solely to contingent issues, Gary Rhoades, general secretary of the American Association of University Professors (AAUP), writes, "The future of the academic profession is connected to the working conditions of contingent faculty. So is the Academy's future."[2] Rhoades concludes his article by arguing that we must do more than just improve job security and working conditions:

> For faculty associations, one of the most important goals is to secure for
> contingent faculty improved safeguards of academic due process. But it is

also worth questioning the discursive logic that influences the academy's direction and the working conditions and lives of contingent faculty. And it is worth challenging our current directions in ways that speak to a larger vision of professors and of higher education and its role in our society.[3]

The AAUP had already set out such an approach—one that is both visionary and pragmatic—in its 2003 policy statement *Contingent Appointments and the Academic Profession*. This landmark statement, the result of several years' work by a committee of both tenure-line and contingent faculty, states that its recommendations are "necessary for the well-being of the profession and the public good" and offers guidelines for "gradual transitions to a higher proportion of tenurable positions" while developing "intermediate, ameliorative measures by which the academic freedom and professional integration of faculty currently appointed to contingent positions can be enhanced by academic due process and assurances of continued employment."[4]

The CFA has supplied the model for what Rhoades says a faculty association must be by directly confronting contingency, making concrete plans to increase access to tenurable positions, and developing "intermediate, ameliorative measures" to improve the job security and working conditions of those faculty off the tenure line. Progress has been slow, hampered by the administrative demand for managerial flexibility and by recurring state budget crises. We have made progress, however, and it's worth examining how the CFA changed into an organization that can work in a unified way, challenge its direction, and develop Rhoades's "larger vision of professors and of higher education and its role in society."

The two of us, John Hess and Elizabeth Hoffman, share a long history in higher education. We have been graduate assistants, part-time and full-time contingent faculty members in community colleges and universities (in both collective-bargaining and noncollective environments), and union activists. John has worked as a tenure-line faculty member and as a union staff person. Elizabeth taught briefly in K-12 and spent time in the corporate world. But for both of us, CFA has been the place where we had an opportunity to participate in changing a union, a process that has enriched our lives and, we believe, benefited others. We have a story to tell about that process.

## Unionization of the Faculty in the CSU

The CFA has a history that has cast a long shadow on the lecturers in the California State University system. In 1978, after a long fight involving faculty activists, the California Legislature passed the Higher Education

Employer-Employee Relations Act, which enabled faculty to pursue collective bargaining. Prior to 1978, the CSU faculty had formed two groups: One was the Congress of Faculty Associations, known by the same acronym (CFA) as the current California Faculty Association but a very different organization. The other was the United Professors of California (UPC), an affiliate of the American Federation of Teachers (AFT) in which many lecturers were active. Elections were held in 1982, with 85 percent of the faculty voting for collective bargaining. By fewer than one hundred votes, the Congress of Faculty Associations was elected the exclusive bargaining agent.

The California Public Employees Relations Board (PERB), in their unit determination, had put both tenure-track and non-tenure-track faculty in the same unit, arguing that all CSU faculty share a "community of interests" and "perform functionally related services or work toward established common goals."[5]

The lecturers became part of the new union, renamed the California Faculty Association, which legally represented all CSU faculty. It would be some years, however, before there was much recognition of the shared "community of interests" that the PERB had identified. Lecturer issues had a low priority, and lecturers were generally ignored or made to feel unwelcome, both at the statewide level and the local chapters at each campus.

Many UPC members were reluctant to join the new CFA, but with the PERB's ruling and the election, the CFA was now the only game in town. Former UPC activists did become active in the CFA, including lecturers who were an important voice in making sure that their fellow contingent faculty were represented in provisions of the first contract and in the structures of the new union.

From 1983, when the CFA bargained its first contract, to the late 1990s, progress was slow for lecturers in the California State University system; they made few gains at the bargaining table. However, some rights already existed in the California Education Code, and these were mostly retained in the early contracts:

- Lecturers had access to the grievance procedure.
- Lecturers on full-year appointments who taught half-time or above and were eligible for health insurance could also qualify for the CalPERS retirement program.
- All faculty were on the same salary schedule; thus, a form of pro rata pay already existed.

The first CFA-CSU contract laid the foundation for lecturer appointments, with the following provisions:

- A lecturer appointed to a similar assignment in the same department in consecutive academic years must receive the same or higher salary as previously.
- Departments must maintain lists (or pools) of lecturers who have been evaluated previously and provide these lecturers with "careful consideration" for subsequent appointments.

These two provisions were the first steps in a long and continuing struggle to make lecturer work less piecemeal and less capricious. The "similar assignment" language is the basis of the notion that lecturers have an "entitlement" to a certain time base when they are rehired. The "careful consideration" language is the basis of the notion that faculty on temporary appointments should not be just churned; instead, incumbents with proven success at CSU should have some preference for work. Some strong arbitration decisions made "careful consideration" for rehiring a meaningful concept. A department at least had to make a careful review of the record and could not hire obviously less qualified, less experienced new lecturers just to get cheaper labor. This is the most often grieved article in the whole contract because it challenges the most prized managerial concept: the power and flexibility to hire whomever the administration wishes.[6] Courageous lecturers came forward to file grievances, and lecturer activists pushed the union to pursue them. One early and important arbitration defined "careful consideration" in a way that at least begins to sound like the deliberative process the profession uses for tenure-track faculty appointments:

> "Careful consideration" means exactly that, cautious, accurate, thorough and concerned thought, attention and deliberation to the task at hand. In a sense, on behalf of applicants, it can be viewed as a benefit to guarantee that special attention be given to persons who have already devoted effort and gained experience within the system and especially the department where the "new" position exists.[7]

Despite these and other contract protections, lecturers, on the whole, still had a marginalized and precarious status. Even the provision for "careful consideration" just forced the administration to go through a careful process. The provision made it easier to say yes than to say no to incumbent employees—no small thing when dealing with administrators—but the provision did not guarantee reappointment to lecturers. One particularly depressing development in the early 1990s was the union leadership's decision to settle a contract by abandoning a provision that gave some lecturers two-year appointments.

The progress, however slight, that was made on lecturer issues in these early years of CFA happened because lecturers had a guaranteed presence in the structure of the union. The CFA bylaws call for specific lecturer representation at the CFA Assembly (which functions as the statewide governing body and direct representative of members), on the board of directors (which oversees the governance and carries out the policies of the CFA), and on key committees, including the bargaining committee. At the campus level, a CFA executive committee or board must include a lecturer representative, and the representative serves at a delegate at the assembly. The statewide Lecturers' Council, which meets at every assembly, consists of these chapter delegates.[8]

Sadly, through the 1990s the Lecturers' Council was a pretty dispirited group. Sometimes fewer than a third of the campuses had representatives at the council meetings, and the meetings were often little more than a group gripe session. The meetings did provide, however, some opportunity to share information and build a base of lecturer solidarity, and there were some successes.

At statewide council meetings, we discovered just how little even the elected lecturer representatives knew about contract rights and lecturer benefits, and we started to improve the communications between the CFA and the lecturers, and among the lecturers on each campus. We put out information, for example, on the eligibility of most lecturers for unemployment benefits. A small group of CSU lecturers had been working on the issue of unemployment benefits since the 1970s; community college contingent faculty activists had also been working on the issue. Thanks to their efforts in challenging denial of benefits, the *Cervisi v. California Unemployment Insurance Appeals Board* decision in 1989 established that an assignment that is contingent on enrollment, funding, or program changes does not provide a "reasonable assurance" of reemployment.[9]

The unemployment issue provided the Lecturers' Council with some interesting insights. First, we had contingent allies outside the CSU, who though perhaps even more marginalized than we were, had fought back against a denial of rights and achieved a big win. Second, we had solid information, backed by law, that the university administration could not argue with, and the information meant money in the pockets of eligible lecturers. Third, the administration would never disseminate information about unemployment benefits. It was our responsibility to get the information out, talk with lecturers who had questions, and push lecturers to do something the employer did not want them to do. Some chapter lecturer representatives gave workshops on how to apply for unemployment benefits, and these workshops were usually very popular.

## The Mario Savio Effect

Getting out better information was a beginning of some action and organizing, but lecturer representatives were still generally lone wolves in the union. In the mid-1990s, meeting Mario Savio, a hero of the 1964 free speech movement at Berkeley, pushed the Lecturers' Council toward more collective action. Savio, a lecturer at Sonoma State University and delegate to the CFA Assembly, walked into the small room where the council was meeting. "There are a lot of lecturers in the CSU," Savio commented. Then he asked, "How many lecturers are usually at the bargaining table?"

"One," someone answered.

"There always has to be at least two of you if anything is going to change," Savio responded. That was a revelation to most of us in that room, but by the end of that Lecturers' Council meeting, we understood that getting more representation for lecturers was part of a broader organizing strategy and we did ask for—and get—another lecturer on the bargaining team, the beginning of significantly improved representation in years to come.

Our request for an additional lecturer on the bargaining team was met with some initial hostility, but we learned that being proactive rather than reactive can bring gains and that acting collectively gives the group the strength to stand up to hostility while making each individual lecturer in the group a stronger leader. In this environment, the Lecturers' Council elected a new and dynamic associate vice president for lecturers—the person who chairs the council and is an officer of the union. Jane Kerlinger, a born organizer, pushed the Lecturers' Council to move beyond complaining in order to focus on planning, goal setting, and tracking of results. Kerlinger saw lecturers as equal colleagues with tenure-track faculty and helped the Lecturers' Council think beyond an "us vs. them" approach between contingent and tenure-track faculty.

In a 1998 article, Kerlinger and coauthor Scott Sibary point out that the PERB had earlier determined that all CSU faculty share a "community of interests," but that fifteen years after PERB's determination, "the CSU central administration was still trying to undermine that community of interests and divide the faculty."[10] The authors state that conflict between different groups of faculty is "senseless," given our commonality of interest, and that improving job security for lecturers is in the interest of all faculty. "Or," Kerlinger and Sibary warn, "tenure-track faculty may see that what happens to lecturers may later happen to all faculty."[11]

Having a Lecturers' Council leader who encouraged lecturers to take a broader perspective and think strategically about the faculty workforce was empowering, but at that time the council was not able to sustain that level of energy. From a practical point of view, not much had changed for lecturers since the first contract in 1983. It must be added that tenure-line faculty did not make great gains in the first fifteen years of collective bargaining either. And tenure-line faculty lost steadily in numbers and in the percentage they represented of the total faculty. During bad budget times, the percentage of tenure-track faculty would make a slight recovery as the temporary faculty were "disappeared" from the campuses. With each budget improvement, the newly hired faculty were likely to be non-tenure track, and by 1990, over half of the CSU faculty by headcount, and a third of the full-time equivalent positions, were temporary.[12]

## A New Union

Then in the late 1990s, everything changed. First, in 1999 a new CFA president, Susan Meisenhelder, was elected in a contested election after a contract was voted down by the membership. Prior to becoming a tenure-track faculty member, Meisenhelder had taught as a lecturer in the CSU system, and she definitely "got it" regarding lecturer issues. Serving as CFA vice president was Jane Kerlinger, a lecturer and the previous Lecturers' Council chair. The new president then hired as general manager a very experienced union staffer who had extensive experience outside academic unionism. Finally, the passage of the "fair share" agency fee bill meant that the CFA had a lot more money to work with. It could hire more staff and consultants, and could provide more training and resources for rank-and-file activists, including many lecturers. A concrete result of these changes was the contract settled in 2002, which contained significant advances for lecturers in the CSU system.

The new president and general manager had a very different vision of what a union was and what a faculty union could be. Looking back on what had been accomplished from 1999 to 2002, Meisenhelder points out that the 2002 contract affected not just the faculty but the 450,000 students, many of whom were first-generation college students. According to Meisenhelder, the CFA "struggled to articulate a new vision for higher education based upon the democratic role that professors must play in assuring the highest quality of education for all of America's citizens."[13] Meisenhelder further defines the CFA's struggle and the union's new vision: "Our struggle is distinct in that it attempts to create one big union that can address concerns faced by a broad range of employees. We have also tried to move beyond contract negotiations by bringing our message to California's citizens more broadly. We do this because we are convinced that we stand at an opportune moment in history—a time when a democratic vision of higher education must be articulated by academic labor activists."[14] In this new vision, the stakes are much higher. Taking our campaign to the broader community means more has been asked of faculty, including of lecturers. But the focus on "the highest quality of education" also means that lecturer issues must become a central focus of bargaining. Having a workforce with more than half the faculty in fragmented, insecure positions undermines the quality of education, regardless of the commitment and dedication of the individual lecturers.

Since 1999, the CFA has become a more democratic and unified union, and the rights of lecturers have been significantly protected and expanded. The CFA was successful in getting the legislature to mandate a plan to increase the percentage of tenure-line positions in the CSU system without disadvantaging incumbent lecturers. We got enabling legislation that allowed us to bargain greatly expanded health benefits—full benefits for lecturers with a 40 percent time base and a one-semester appointment. In the 2002 contract, we bargained preference for work provisions for incumbent lecturers with accrual of work up to a full load, automatic three-year appointments after six years of service (with subsequent automatic rollover appointments), and salary range movement. The general trend in the contract is to move lecturers into longer-term, more secure appointments with a higher time base so they have a livable wage at one campus, with more time for students and more time to be part of the campus academic community.[15]

In 2005, bargaining began on a successor contract, setting the stage for a real test of the CFA's unity. The CSU administration, in their bargaining positions for a new contract, proposed takeaways in virtually every previous contract advance for lecturers. After two years of struggle, culminating in a 94 percent strike vote by the faculty, the CSU and the CFA settled in 2007, with a contract that was good for all the constituents in the bargaining unit. Lecturers played a key role in this contract fight, a story we tell in the next section.

Despite improvements in lecturer due process, benefits, and working conditions, over half of the faculty in the CSU are on temporary appointments and are always vulnerable. When there is a budget crisis, the administration does not have to seek hard solutions or more resources but instead slashes lecturer jobs. A smaller number of faculty is left to teach larger and larger numbers of students, undermining the quality of the teaching. The only solution is to return to the CFA's vision of all the faculty working with the students and the community to build the power necessary to protect public higher education for California.

## Organizing Lecturers in the CSU

The CFA could not have defeated a recalcitrant CSU administration and brought real change to the university without involving the "other half of the faculty": the lecturers. That meant organizing! In 2000, John Hess was the first former faculty member (in this case a former CFA lecturer activist) to be hired by the CFA and the first staff person ever assigned directly to work with the CFA Lecturers' Council. In 2001, Elizabeth Hoffman was elected as one of the statewide CFA officers, in the position representing the lecturers.

In the process of lecturer organizing since 2000, we could say that we developed what we thought of as an inside-outside strategy. This means that we organized within the CFA with all the resources available to us and, at the same time, we went outside the traditional CFA statewide and campus-based lines of command to confront our campus administrations, to develop parallel forms of lobbying, and to reach out to other contingent faculty.

## Inside Organizing

Because some already know the terms and because others will come upon them, we feel a need to make a brief distinction between our concept of "inside-outside" organizing and what Joe Berry calls the "inside-outside" strategy. Berry's discussion is rooted in his study of labor history and the debate over dual unionism. Contingent faculty have a variety of unions competing for their dues money, particularly the AAUP, the AFT, and the National Education Association, as well as the United Auto Workers, the Service Employees International Union, and the Communication Workers of America. Berry argues that the issue is not competition or no competition—at certain times each model has been good for workers and also bad for workers—but what kind of unionism the competition produces. "The principle is therefore not one of unitary mechanical formal solidarity," he argues, "but rather a flexible vision of solidarity that strives to unite all who can be united in practice while isolating those who are fundamentally enemies. This has been termed the 'inside-outside' strategy."[16]

Our situation in the CFA was positional; that is, the lecturer base was in the Lecturers' Council, which was basically an official caucus in the union. So long as that caucus had little or no access to resources, staff support, encouragement from the union leadership, or training, the council had little or no power and no reasonable way to get it. The lamentable situation of the Lecturers' Council that we described earlier was just that: a caucus without resources. So long as the union was run as a service organization and not as a union, there was little lecturers could do. In what was and is an all-too-common situation at universities, the union leadership served those with the most power in the union, the tenure-track faculty, and ignored the lecturers. The new vision that President Meisenhelder brought to the CFA was designed to change the CFA from a business/service union to one operated on an organizing/social movement model. With this change, it became essential to organize the lecturers, and the only way to do that was to give the Lecturers' Council resources and then give the lecturers their head. For the CFA lecturers, inside organizing was organizing for power within the union itself, turning the council into a power base in which we could train lecturers to organize their contingent colleagues—and by example, teach other CFA faculty how to do organizing as well. Outside organizing, for lecturers, meant going out from our base to meet and learn from other contingent faculty who were doing what we were trying to do.

As described earlier, in the CFA's structure there is one lecturer representative from each campus on the statewide Lecturers' Council. Traditionally the Lecturers' Council met twice a year, at the semiannual CFA Assembly meeting. There were often representatives from only a few of the campuses. There was little continuity from meeting to meeting and little contact among the lecturer reps during the rest of the year. The group was essentially powerless within the union and even more so on the campuses.

To begin to change this situation, we added two additional lecturer meetings a year, in early September and late January (i.e., early in the fall and spring semesters), and shifted the focus of the meetings to organizing, leadership development, and training in such things as faculty rights and political lobbying: training, training, training! These additional meetings were scheduled on Friday evenings and Saturdays. At each Friday evening session, we had dinner together and then heard a featured speaker, usually someone active in the contingent faculty moment or labor movement. These talks represented a great infusion of new ideas into our work.

We worked hard to increase the number of lecturer activists involved at the statewide level, relentlessly seeking resources so that at least three lecturers from each campus could attend the statewide lecturer meetings and asking campuses to send extra lecturer faculty to the CFA assemblies and leadership meetings. The CFA provided resources for monthly statewide conference calls. We developed an electronic mailing list of two hundred activists who have attended a statewide event, and we keep the list updated with regular e-mails. A lecturer team significantly expanded the *Lecturers' Handbook*, and we had a statewide campaign to deliver a hard copy to every lecturer in the system.[17]

We wanted to develop the Lecturers' Council as a center of power within the union so that it would not just articulate lecturer needs but have the will and ability to get them met. It was only after this, we thought, that lecturers could take their rightful place alongside the noncontingent faculty in the fight not only to change the CSU, but even to save it from itself.

One of our first successful campaigns was to get as many lecturers as possible to fill out the bargaining surveys used to determine what the key issues would be for the bargaining that got underway in 2001. We asked lecturers (no hard sell here) to give the highest priority to "lecturer job security." As a result, job security for lecturers became the second highest priority, giving us a way to engage lecturers in the ensuing contract campaign. This campaign is a good example of the sort of organizing we did in the early years. We found an issue that would appeal to lecturers; then we reached out to them and asked them to join the campaign by, in this case, filling out the survey. At the same time, we were working hard to build and expand lecturer networks on each campus. Key was getting people involved at the statewide and local level. We also pushed people to work on the campaign. Soon people who wanted to do work began to replace people who were less willing to work, less interested in organizing. Part of this process was also gathering results and publicizing them: announcing that so many surveys had come in from this campus and so many from that campus.

The CFA has provided resources to help lecturers do this work through a lecturer stipend program in which lecturer reps can apply for stipends to work on CFA organizing projects on their campuses. Traditionally, CFA officers, chapter presidents, and some committee chairs receive compensated "release time" or "reassigned time" for their work in the CFA. Because lecturers don't usually teach full time (officially, anyway), it has been difficult to get the university to implement such reassigned time for them. The stipend fills the gap and helps lecturers pay their bills and perhaps teach less and have more time for organizing.

As a result of our organizing and training, more and more lecturers came forward to take on positions of responsibility within the CFA, both statewide and on the campuses, including positions lecturers had rarely or never held, such as on campus faculty rights committees and as members and even chairs of key statewide committees. Lecturers began to serve the CFA not as lecturers but as the most energetic, competent, eager members available.

A review of the agenda for the January 2007 Lecturers' Council meeting shows the results of this inside organizing:

- Friday night joint dinner with the CFA Council on Affirmative Action (which includes Lecturer members), presentation by a representative of the state Legislature, update by former CFA president and current head of Political Action, John Travis, and outline of the CFA spring campaign by Lillian Taiz, current CFA president—and a former contingent faculty member
- Update on Re-opener Bargaining from Chris Haynes, Chair of Contract Development Committee. Chris is the first lecturer to serve as chair of this key CFA committee

- Introduction of the seven lecturers on the current bargaining team and another lecturer from a Bargaining Implementation Committee
- A presentation on faculty demographics by CFA Research Director, with data in hard copy and electronically so that lecturers can make similar presentations at the campus
- A workshop on building organization capacity through membership, run by one CFA staff person and two lecturers, who have done workshops at several campuses
- Panel presentations of campus models of building local capacity done by five newer lecturer Reps, representing the San Diego, Monterey Bay, San Francisco, Bakersfield, and Sacramento
- Action plans by all lecturers detailing next steps when they return to the campuses (all twenty-three campuses were represented by a group of activists)
- Lecturer Nuts and Bolts Workshop—a presentation of a model workshop on benefits and contract rights by a campus Lecturer Rep who is also on the statewide Representation Committee. The Lecturer Reps can use the power point (available electronically) to do a similar workshop on their campus or can have the Lecturer presenter come to their campus. (CFA has provided resources to support this on-campus workshop program.)[18]

The resources put into lecturer organizing and the climate of inclusion since 1999 have transformed these meetings from those of a small group of marginalized lecturers to those of a large group of activists central to the work of the union. Just how central is evident in the popularity of a retirement workshop put on by Jonathan Karpf, the lecturer who conducted the "Nuts and Bolts" workshop described on the agenda. Chapter presidents from most of the twenty-three CSU campuses have asked Jonathan to come to their campuses and do the workshop; the audience for these sessions has consisted mostly of tenure-track faculty who see Jonathan not as a lecturer but as an informed faculty colleague. Further recognition of lecturers' involvement in the union is seen in the 2008 board of directors' unanimous approval of a proposal to change the CFA bylaws to add another lecturer as a CFA officer and as a board member.

In the early years of this lecturer organizing, the CFA president and the general manager came to all the lecturer meetings and sat through the entirety of each meeting without speaking unless asked to. In retrospect, we realized that this is how they offered their support to the lecturers. They wanted us to succeed, because they understood that the union would not succeed unless we did. And they believed we could succeed. When we asked Susan Meisenhelder one time why she sat through these meetings, she responded,

"They were the most hopeful thing going on in the union."[19] Think about it. This is an unheard-of experience for contingent faculty. Without organizing contingent faculty in this way, no union is going to win or to be able to rescue its university. If the issue is described as helping the contingents, supporting the contingents, or improving the contingents' working conditions, a union is bound to fail. The issue has to be organizing contingents to become a power base within the union. Then the union has a fighting chance.

## Outside Organizing

It should come as no surprise to anyone that these increasingly active lecturers needed and sought more intellectual, political, and emotional support than they could get from the tenure track and tenured faculty—even those active in the CFA. The CFA president and the general manager understood this need and therefore did not try to tell the lecturers what to do. They understood that the lecturers, with whatever help they could each provide, had to and would organize themselves. These active lecturers needed to find engaged, positive collegiality, and active, stimulating solidarity.

We first developed an association with the California Part-Time Faculty Association (CPFA), which had just organized A2K (Action 2000: really the first Campus Equity Week). Margaret Quan, Robert Yoshioka, Mary Ellen Goodwin, and Chris Storer have all spoken at our meetings, and their wit, intelligence, and especially their irreverence were very refreshing and stimulating. Through this association we learned about the Coalition of Contingent Academic Labor (COCAL), and a group of CFA lecturers attended and spoke at the COCAL meeting in San Jose, California, in January 2001. We have continued this involvement in COCAL, sending large delegations of CFA lecturers to COCAL conferences in Montreal, Chicago, and Vancouver. The CFA cosponsored, along with the CPFA, COCAL 2008 at San Diego State University and sent a large delegation of lecturers. Any union that claims to represent contingent faculty but does not send contingent activists to COCAL meetings is not really representing those contingent faculty.

The CFA is affiliated with the AAUP, and Elizabeth sat on the AAUP Committee on Contingent Faculty and the Profession; through this connection we got to know Rich Moser and invited him to speak and work with us. He was at that time, if anyone was, the key theoretician of the contingent faculty movement. We also heard from Canadians Linda Sperling (from the College Institute Educators' Association of British Columbia) and Tom Friedman (from the University College of the Cariboo, also in BC). We had Gary Zabel from Boston COCAL and Linda Collins, president of the California Community Colleges Academic Senate, come to speak at our statewide lecturer meetings. Enrique Ochoa, of the Universidad de Baja California in Mexico, whom we had met at the COCAL conference in Chicago in August 2004, came to speak to the Lecturers' Council. Joe Berry, a visiting labor education specialist at the University of Illinois at Urbana-Champaign and chair of Chicago COCAL, spoke to us in 2006 and sat in on our council training. More recently, our Friday night dinners have featured important figures from the California labor movement, such as Kent Wong, director of the UCLA Labor Center, and Maria Elena Durazo, head of the Los Angeles County Federation of Labor, as well as national figures such as Cary Nelson from the AAUP. These labor leaders recognize that the increasing numbers of marginalized, at-will faculty in this country, most working at low salaries and without benefits, are symptomatic of what is happening in the rest of the workforce. These labor leaders also understand that access to quality higher education must be available for the good of working families and the community as a whole.

## Inside + Outside = Making a Ruckus

We often asked at the end of our Lecturers' Council meetings, in the space left to talk about "next steps," what it would take for the representatives to gather ten people and occupy their campus president's office. Our colleagues seemed to like the idea, but were nonetheless happy that we weren't asking them to act on it right then. However, it became increasingly apparent to us that the CFA needed to become more militant in order to win our struggle with the chancellor. We needed to move toward direct action.[20] In the early 2000s, most of the chapter presidents resisted the idea of being "trained." Many seemed to think that they knew all they needed to know about organizing, while others opposed getting involved in the "undignified" and the "unprofessional" aspects of our fight with the chancellor.

Still thinking about direct action, we decided that at a Lecturers' Council meeting in January 2005, we would show a video clip on the lunch counter sit-ins in Nashville in the 1960s.[21] We showed the video of the civil rights protesters not to suggest a link between their plight and ours, but to focus on their methods of organizing and preparing. The video brought home the idea that these movements don't just happen, but are planned. James Lawson, who had met Martin Luther King and studied nonviolence in India, had organized these early sit-ins and explains on the video how that was done. The sit-ins were not spontaneous; they were, in fact, well-planned direct actions.

There was some resistance among the lecturers as to where this focus on direct action might be going. Others, however, encouraged us to continue. John contacted the Ruckus Society in Berkeley, an organization of young activists that trains groups in direct action.[22] We arranged to have them teach direct action during our Lecturers' Council meeting in January 2006. This training was not to everyone's liking because it emphasized direct confrontation. Some of the exercises were designed to help a group figure out who would and who would not participate in direct action (although there were also many supporting roles people could play).

Since the lecturer meetings were the place to be, several of the union's officers were at the training and were very impressed with the trainer and interested in what was being taught. They instantly realized that this tactic had to be the CFA's next step. The Ruckus Society came back to do more training and began as well to consult with the union on effective demonstrations—showing us, for example, the benefit of using very large banners or seas of banners, both of which the press and passersby could not miss.

The Ruckus Society's training culminated in the November 15, 2006, demonstration and sit-in at the chancellor's office in Long Beach. As we described at the beginning of our story, many lecturers were part of the 1,500 faculty and students from all over the state who had gathered for the board of trustees' meeting. Seven lecturers were part of the faculty group of twenty-one who took over the board of trustees' meeting and were prepared to be arrested. And in January 2007, lecturers from all twenty-three campuses signed pledges committing to vote for a strike; a message to that effect was posted on the CFA website, along with a group picture.[23] The lecturers' unity and willingness to take action reinforced the two slogans of the contract campaign: "Unite to Win" and "I Don't Want to Strike, but I Will." The CFA stayed united, and just days before rolling strikes were to begin sweeping across the state, we settled in May 2007, with the best contract the CFA has ever bargained—a contract good for all the union's constituents and a contract that helped build the more stable workforce that best meets student needs.

The union has stayed unified during the years following the 2007 contract, even in a difficult and uncertain economic environment that resulted in devastating cuts to public higher education in California. In the CSU, contingent faculty did lose work because of budget cuts, but many lecturer jobs were saved because a majority of CSU faculty—both contingent and tenure-line—voted to approve a furlough of two days per month for the 2009–2010 academic year (the equivalent of a 10 percent pay cut). Then in 2010, the 2007 contract expired and bargaining began on a successor contract. The CSU administration, following the management adage "a crisis is a terrible thing to waste," went after not just economic issues but once again made proposals that would have completely undermined the contingent faculty job security provisions our union had worked so hard to get and protect.

Once again the faculty stayed united. In November 2011, CSU East Bay in Northern California and CSU Dominguez Hills in Southern California each pulled off a successful one-day strike, with CSU faculty from across the state—both contingent and tenure-line—joining the picket lines at the striking campuses and shutting down the two campuses. The following spring, CSU faculty voted by 95 percent to approve rolling strikes at all twenty-three campuses. That vote was announced at a May 2012 press conference, and finally in July 2012, the CSU administration and the CFA reached an agreement that continued the contractual rights for contingent faculty, and even more importantly, protected the stable faculty workforce our students need.

## Conclusions

What conclusions can one draw from the California Faculty Association's experience?

1. Beginning with the new CFA president in 1999, and continuing with the next two CFA presidents, John Travis and Lillian Taiz, we had strong support from the CFA's elected and staff leadership and considerable resources to carry out the project. Knowing this support was there emboldened us in our work. In the first fifteen years of the CFA's history as a bargaining agent, that support was not there (nor of course were the resources) and lecturers did not have the organizational power to move or change the union very much. This grand experiment demonstrates without a doubt that contingent faculty can be organized and can come to play major, positive roles in their unions.

2. Contingent faculty, whatever their circumstances, must organize themselves in their own interests. If they are able to do that, they will end up leading the way, showing the rest of the faculty how to organize. The evidence is in the numbers: our statewide Lecturers' Council meetings now have sixty or more lecturers in attendance, representing all twenty-three of the CSU campuses. Increasingly in the CFA, other groups and committees want to do things "the way the lecturers do it."

3. The shift that has taken place in the CFA in the last twelve years is the shift from business or service unionism to organizing unionism.

4. Protecting the profession and higher education is a difficult fight that will take all faculty as well as alliances with staff, students, the labor movement, community groups, and politicians.[24] However, we have observed that it is the contingent faculty, the most marginalized and exploited faculty in higher education, who are fighting to save the university from the privatizers and dismantlers long after many of the tenured and tenure-track faculty have given up. It is the contingent fac-

ulty who seem to understand best what is happening to the university. Bertolt Brecht once said something to the effect that exile makes one a wonderful dialectician. So does academic contingency.

## NOTES

1.  For pictures of the CFA Board of Trustees Action, see "November 15 Rally," *California Faculty* 11, no. 1 (Winter 2007): 12–13, *www.calfac.org*.
2.  Gary Rhoades, "The Centrality of Contingent Faculty to Academe's Future," *Academe*, November-December 2008, 12.
3.  Ibid., 15.
4.  AAUP, *Contingent Appointments and the Academic Profession* (Washington, DC: AAUP, 2003), *aaup.org*.
5.  California Gov. Code, section 3579 (a) (1).
6.  The current collective bargaining agreement between the California Faculty Association (CFA) and the California State University is online at the CFA website, *www.calfac.org*.
7.  In the Matter of Bryant Creel: Arbitration between the Board of Trustees of the California State University and the California Faculty Association, American Arbitration Association Case No. 72 390 0028 85 under Impartial Arbitrator Philip Tamoush, Torrance, California. Hearing held in Long Beach, California, April 26, 1985. Award Issued June 15, 1985. Supplemental Decision issued October 1, 1985. For an electronic copy of this arbitration, please send the name, case number, and date to Representation Department, California Faculty Association, at gro@calfac.org.
8.  The CFA bylaws are available at the CFA website: *www.calfac.org*.
9.  This principle was established in California Unemployment Insurance Code 1253.3(g) and Cervisi v. California Unemployment Insurance Appeals Board (1989), 208 Cal.App.3d 635, 256 Cal.Rptr. 142.
10. Jane Kerlinger and Scott Sibary, "Protecting Common Interests of Full- and Part-Time Faculty," *Thought and Action: The NEA Higher Education Journal* 14:91.
11. Ibid., 96.
12. Data on CSU faculty demographics is from *Research Report to CFA Lecturers' Council* (January 2009) and *Accompanying Handout* (January 2009), both available at the CFA website, *www.calfac.org/lecturers-council-lecturers-archive*.
13. Susan Meisenhelder, with Kevin Mattson, "Renewing Academic Unions and Democracy at the Same Time," in *Steal This University*, ed. Benjamin Johnson, Patrick Kavanagh, and Kevin Mattson (New York: Routledge, 2003), 221.
14. Ibid., 222.
15. For a complete list of lecturer contract provisions, see the *California Faculty Association Lecturers' Handbook, 2012–2014* (Los Angeles: CFA, 2012), 10, at *www.calfac.org*.
16. Joe Berry, *Reclaiming the Ivory Tower: Organizing Adjuncts to Change Higher Education* (New York: Monthly Review Press, 2005), 36.
17. The handbook is also available electronically on the CFA website (*www.calfac.org*).

18. This agenda is archived in Elizabeth Hoffman's personal collection.
19. Interview with Susan Meisenhelder at the CFA Assembly in Los Angeles, California, April 21, 2007.
20. It is not our topic here, but it should be noted that the CFA put considerable resources into organizing students, and our students ended up playing an important role in our struggles with the CSU chancellor and board of trustees. The students understood that they were paying more and getting less, in the form of increased fees, larger classes, and delays in graduation because classes were not available. Every campus had one or two student organizers working under the supervision of young staff members. Organizing students added great energy and diversity to our efforts.
21. The video clip was from the documentary *A Force More Powerful: A Century of Nonviolent Conflict* (Washington, DC: York Zimmerman, 2000).
22. For more information, see the Ruckus Society website (*www.ruckus.org*).
23. The lecturer pledge to vote for a strike and the picture of those pledging is at *www.calfac.org/lecturers-council-lecturers-archive*.
24. The CFA faces continuing and relentless challenges, especially in times of budget crises, but the lessons of unity and inclusiveness from the lecturer organizing struggles helped move the CFA toward a recognition that only the broadest alliance possible, the Alliance for the CSU, will build the power necessary to protect public higher education in California. See Irv Muchnick, "Alliance for the CSU," *California Faculty* 12, no. 2 (Spring 2008): 3–4, *www. calfac.org/post/spring-2008*.

# 2

# The Case for Instructor Tenure

## Solving Contingency and Protecting Academic Freedom in Colorado

*Don Eron*

Beginning in the late 1970s, university administrations at Colorado and else-where began waging what can be seen, with the benefit of hindsight, as a revolution against the academic freedom protections of higher education faculty. In order to achieve a more flexible workforce in times of budgetary constraints and curricular change, they began replacing retiring tenured faculty with contingent faculty—defined by the American Association of University Professors (AAUP) as faculty who teach off the tenure track—because these faculty will teach for less money and require little commitment from the universities. Thirty-five years later, roughly 70 percent of all higher education faculty are contingent.[1] This revolution has been a triumph for administrators, who can now exercise unprecedented control over faculties, increasing their class sizes and course loads while decreasing their benefits and wages and summarily dismissing those who dare to complain or otherwise challenge the status quo. However, the consequence of employing faculty who teach without even a modicum of job security has been the corrosion of undergraduate education. Another consequence—this one stemming not from administrators but tenured faculty who have neglected to ensure academic freedom for their contingent colleagues—may well be the elimination of tenure altogether, at least in any form that current tenured faculty are liable to find palatable.

## Section 1: The War to Eliminate Tenure

In 1975, the landscape of higher education was much different than it is today. According to data from the AAUP, 57 percent of all faculty were on a tenure track.[2] If this meant that a full 43 percent were off the tenure track, most employed at will—meaning that they could be fired at any time, for any reason (including, by definition, for expressing their opinions), or for no reason at all—the circumstance struck few as particularly onerous. This may be because many of these contingent faculty had little pretense of participating in university culture, and as such were invisible to their tenured colleagues. These marginal faculty tended to fall into three categories—true adjuncts, spouses of tenured faculty, and part-time teachers who had finished their graduate coursework but not their dissertations (a status known as "All But Dissertation," or ABD).[3]

As a generality, the true adjuncts were experts in "practice" who could augment the education of students by drawing on firsthand clinical knowledge. If they pushed the envelope in the classroom or otherwise alienated administrators with their opinions and lost their contingent positions as a result, they had their regular employment to fall back on. The lack of academic freedom for such faculty was not a particular deterrent to teaching. What's more, most, while perhaps pleased to enjoy the professional imprimatur (and market value) implicit in teaching a course at the local university, hardly considered themselves central to, or even part of, the mission of the university. Similarly, the spouses of tenured faculty, many of whom returned to teaching on a part-time basis after taking time out to raise families, often considered themselves to have foregone professional academic careers, at least in the way their spouses engaged their career ambitions. The academic back seat was part of the social contract; many felt they had no standing to complain, even were they inclined. By the same token, many faculty in the third category, part-timers who were ABD, regarded themselves as being in academic limbo, at least until they finished their dissertations and landed tenure-track positions elsewhere. Most had little interest in the cultural life of the institution—per academic custom, they wouldn't be considered for tenure-track employment at the institution where they had received their professional credentials; they would have to pursue their careers elsewhere. They didn't covet inclusion; indeed, many would have considered any expectation of participation in faculty business an imposition.

When one finds invisibility desirable, which was typical of faculty in the three contingent categories, others can't be fully faulted for failing to see them. Still, while it would be an overstatement to suggest that these contingent faculty were denied meaningful access to academic freedom by mutual agreement (in fact, the AAUP issued a cautious statement addressing the lack of due process for contingent faculty as far back as 1980), it was easy for contingent faculty to view the status quo as an unfortunate but largely tolerable fact of life.[4] It was easy as well for the few tenured faculty who may have been troubled by their contingent colleagues' treatment to view their own projects as far higher priorities—after all, nobody was complaining. It was also easy for other tenured faculty, who seldom if ever crossed paths with their marginalized colleagues, to view most contingents as second-rate scholars and failed academics, and thus not warranting protections.

In retrospect, such stances, understandable in the context of the era, can be seen as miscalculations.

## A Neat Solution

In the late 1970s, hiring contingent rather than tenure-track faculty must have seemed a reasonable solution to a pressing problem. According to the AAUP's 2003 report, *Contingent Appointments and the Academic Profession*, full-time appointments off the tenure track were almost unknown a generation ago. In 1969, they amounted to 3.3 percent of all full-time faculty positions.[5] However, as the "greatest generation" began retiring, state governments were cutting appropriations to higher education and the production costs of higher education were rising. Attracting students while charging higher tuitions to offset reduced appropriations posed a crucial, continuous challenge to university administrators. As a measure to combat this challenge, according to the 2003 report, "Many institutions chose to allocate proportionately less to their instructional budgets, and instead to increase spending on physical plant, new technologies and technology upgrades, and administrative costs."[6] In other words, administrators were required by market forces to produce new recreational facilities, dormitories with the latest in comforts, and classrooms with dazzling new technologies, all to attract out-of-state students. In many instances, these measures were afforded by replacing retiring tenured faculty with contingent faculty who would teach more courses for far less money and for whom no long-term commitment on the part of the universities was necessary. Thus began the revolution.

Thirty-five years ago, university administrations, responding to an immediate crisis, probably could not have anticipated the extent to which their quest to change the composition of higher education faculty would succeed as a permanent solution. One thing they could not have anticipated was that they would receive virtually no resistance from university faculties, or from the professional organizations charged with protecting the academic freedom of all faculty. For example, the AAUP long equivocated about whether contingent faculty warranted academic freedom protections. In 2008, Cary Nelson, then president of the AAUP, conceded that the nation's foremost watchdog of academic freedom had its "head buried in the sand" on the academic freedom protections for what by now had become the vast majority of higher education faculty.[7]

Today, over 70 percent of all faculty at our colleges and universities are off the tenure track. Most are employed at will. As a practical matter, they cannot teach without fear of retaliation from students, or argue positions at faculty meetings without fear of retaliation from tenured colleagues or administrators who may feel inconvenienced not only by their opinions but even by the necessity of having to reply to their opinions at all. What's more, while some still belong to one of the three contingent categories discussed earlier, most teach for a living. Most faculty in higher education today are fully credentialed professionals who suffer the indignities of working without academic freedom for the sin of seeking careers in academia at the precise point in history when tenure has all but disappeared. According to longtime academic labor activist John Hess, "No contingent faculty is ever more than 15 seconds away from total humiliation."[8]

At-will employment stands as a towering institutional disincentive against faculty fulfilling their professional responsibilities. Certainly among this vast majority are some who, despite their at-will status, teach rigorous, demanding courses and evaluate students honestly. No doubt a larger group does its best within the parameters of at-will employment. But the reality is this: if one is more likely to get fired for teaching a rigorous, demanding course in which students are evaluated honestly, than for teaching a less demanding course that's "lots of fun" for students, one will likely teach the latter. Similarly, if one is more likely to get fired for trying to contribute one's expertise on curricular or pedagogical matters at faculty meetings than one is for keeping one's head down, for not attending faculty meetings at all, or for vigorously praising whatever views issue forth from the department chair, one is more likely to lapse into survival mode than to challenge department orthodoxy. When every move that contingent faculty make is a negotiation with the parameters of at-will employment, and when they constitute the vast majority of higher education faculty, the ramifications for the quality of the higher education that all students deserve is obvious.

The boons that university administrators have reaped from their own negotiation with the quality of undergraduate education are threefold: flexibility, increased revenue, and the silence of the vast majority of the faculty. When administrations can impose policy across the spectrum without having to deal with 70 percent of their faculty, the other 30 percent—many of whom, in the academic tradition, champion themselves as existing above the prosaic considerations of university politics—quickly fall into step. Faculties pose no impediment to corporate imperatives. Today, meaningful shared governance—the guarantee that education experts, rather than administrators subject to the political and economic pressures of the marketplace, are in charge of the educational product—has all but disappeared from the higher education landscape.

## Deadwood

If there is any cause for optimism, however, it can be found in the views of the general public, who are invariably unaware of academia's dirty little secret. After all, universities never mention in their brochures that the vast majority of their faculty can be fired at any time, for any reason, and therefore hold students to rigorous standards and offer ideas at faculty meetings at their peril. Some in the general public have held the unexamined view that the problem with higher education lies with the institution of tenure—that it is tenure that gives license to faculty to teach without standards, to remove themselves from the intellectual mix, and eventually to become deadwood. But as Annette Kolodny, professor of comparative culture and literary studies at the University of Arizona, notes, "If abuses in the tenure system sometimes protected 'deadwood' in the senior ranks, the characteristics of non-tenured employment guarantee 'deadwood' at a far earlier age."[9]

*Deadwood at a far earlier age.* I have never spoken of these issues with anybody—state legislators, parents, students, citizens with an interest in the future of a viable and vigorous society, or tenured colleagues emerging from decades of their heads in the sand—who thinks that's a good thing.

## Section 2: Solving Contingency

In 2007, Suzanne Hudson and I, both longtime contingent faculty at the University of Colorado (CU), Boulder, and officers in the CU chapter of the AAUP, created the Instructor Tenure Project as a correction to the deleterious effects of the trend that had begun thirty years earlier. The concept was simple—that CU implement the AAUP's *Recommended Institutional Regulations on Academic Freedom and Tenure* (RIR).[10] Under this plan, after a probationary period not to exceed seven years, and a final review similar to previous reviews, faculty members will be tenured in their current position—same rank, same pay scale, same teaching load. What these faculty gain is not just job security; it is academic freedom—the freedom to teach without fear of retaliation from students and to argue positions without fear of retaliation from the administration and tenured colleagues.

### The Backdrop at Colorado

While much of the academic world considered academic freedom at Colorado in light of the controversial plight of Ward Churchill, numerous other events occurred, more or less simultaneously, that made it clear that academic freedom at Colorado, at least for contingent faculty, existed entirely at the discretion of the administration.[11]

First, Adrienne Anderson, an environmental studies instructor whose students, as part of a field study, used the Colorado Open Records Act to investigate industrial pollution, was not reappointed, ostensibly because her unit decided to discontinue her course, one of the most popular offered by the Environmental Studies Program. Many of Anderson's students rallied to her defense and—employing the Colorado Open Records Act, a skill they'd learned in her class—discovered a string of e-mails from corporate donors (whose environmental practices her students had criticized) and conservative politicians demanding that the CU administration fire Anderson. The evidence of political pressure gave Anderson grounds to protest her nonrenewal to CU's Faculty Senate Committee on Privilege and Tenure (P&T). According to the *Colorado Daily*, P&T unanimously agreed that the administration had violated her right to a "fair and unbiased appeal" of the nonrenewal of her contract. The *Daily* further reported that CU's then-chancellor Phil DiStefano rejected the P&T finding, in large part because (in his words) he wanted to defend the authority "of the departments on this campus to make decisions about instructors."[12] In other words, while instructors had the right (according to published policy) to appeal their terminations, the right of departments to terminate instructors without being second-guessed by an appeal process was the greater right. Worn down by her Kafkaesque experience of navigating the university's appeal system, Anderson left academia.

If the Anderson case spoke volumes about the meaninglessness of due process protections without legal backing, the nonrenewal of Phil Mitchell, a history instructor who had taught at CU for twenty years while accumulating some of the most prestigious teaching awards and highest student evaluations in the history of the university, was equally disturbing. Mitchell, an evangelical conservative, had taken to occasionally voicing political opinions against affirmative action during faculty meetings. In 2004, he wasn't reappointed. Mitchell used his political and media contacts to raise a firestorm of publicity, claiming he was fired as retaliation for his political and religious views. Because Mitchell was an at-will employee, administrators weren't required to provide a reason for his dismissal or documentation to support their claims. In the face of the publicity onslaught, they were therefore unprepared to answer inquiries; on the defensive, the administrators offered numerous reasons, their rationales shifting as each was proven improbable. Finally, the CU administration claimed it was all a misunderstanding and rehired Mitchell. Two years later, however, they fired him again. This time the administration was ready. As extensively documented in a report by the CU-Boulder chapter of the AAUP, Mitchell's peer reviews, heretofore superlative, suddenly noted egregious inadequacies.[13] He was also cited by his program director for not meeting course goals (though there was no evidence he had failed to do so) and for completely disregarding the required writing text (though, in fact, his syllabus assigned the writing text). He was even investigated by his department to uncover an alleged history of homophobic remarks. (No evidence of any such remarks was uncovered.) Despite the AAUP report, the media response this time was far more tepid. Unlike Anderson, Mitchell eventually found work at another university.

Finally, there was the unfortunate fate of the Instructor Bill of Rights, legislation passed by the faculty government and approved by the administration. IBOR, as it was known, not only described the professional responsibilities of lecturers and instructors, but called for the promotion of lecturers to instructors (that is, full-time non-tenure-track faculty) after three years of service. As ever, faculty protections that lack the force of legal standing are only as good as the willingness of the administration to honor them. The dean who was most involved with IBOR honored the three-year clause. By 2001, however, he had moved to another university. His successor, with nothing vested in the initiative, refused to honor IBOR, citing restricted flexibility and budgetary constraints. Soon, several instructors who had been promoted under IBOR found themselves demoted back to lecturer.

### The Unit Level

I became involved in the movement to restore academic freedom inadvertently, when Suzanne Hudson became aware of discrepancies between principles of shared governance and our program's bylaws, which essentially gave all the power of decision-making to the director. We set out to change the bylaws and soon found that challenging the governance practices of our program was an entirely different matter than complaining about office space or classroom assignments, issues about which contingent faculty are usually free to complain without risking their careers. We met with intense resistance, so we started looking into things—reading the CU Laws of the Regents and college and university policies—which led us toward understanding how vast were the ways in which our rights to shared governance and due process, granted to instructors by the laws and published policies of the university, were either violated or disregarded by administrators. Still, we felt invigorated by the published laws, and felt that our combined thirty years of demonstrated teaching excellence at the university, as well as our significant publication records, qualified us to speak out. Soon thereafter, the three tenured authors of the internal review report for our unit's periodic program review recommended that contingent faculty "dissatisfied" with the leadership, bylaws, and/or pedagogical direction of the program be terminated, before the end of their contracts if necessary. Clearly, that the regulations of the university "guaranteed" academic freedom (as a matter of policy but not law) would not be seen as a deterrent to our getting fired for expressing our opinions when they weren't welcome. Needless to say, the director of the program, validated by her tenured colleagues in her determination to stifle her critics, heartily endorsed the recommendation.[14]

Stories such as these are a dime a dozen at Colorado and elsewhere. That there are even more egregious instances can't be doubted, in part because most terminated faculty stagger away in humiliation, with no legal recourse and no stomach to relive their shame. Since Suzanne and I began the Instructor Tenure Project, we have been stunned by the volume of similar stories we've heard. At CU, one instructor writes that "years of being underpaid, underappreciated, and frankly, abused, have clouded my vision." Another says she can't join the AAUP because she's "up for reappointment"—code for "Must lie low, remain invisible." Another suggests that, by conducting an e-mail survey subject to the Colorado Open Records Act, we jeopardize the employment of instructors who make unflattering comments about their administrators. Similarly, dozens of times we have heard our colleagues say they would speak up about various initiatives to improve their franchise within the university, but they "need this job."

Often when instructors complain to us of circumstances within their programs or departments that they believe are exploitative, we explain to them their rights, as published in the policies or laws of the university, and urge them to advise their department chair of these laws, or at least permit us to do so, either as individuals or as officers of the local AAUP. But to complain, or to cite "guaranteed" rights that might inconvenience their department chairs—rights that may exist in policy but not in practice—is always too great a risk for these faculty. Rights that depend entirely on the good faith of someone who has already denied you those rights are worse than no rights at all, because the denial of such rights forces on these faculty tests of character in which to win the existential battle may well be to lose their livelihoods.

Greater than the damage to their self-respect, however, is the loss to the university of their ideas. The AAUP's 2003 report, *Contingent Appointments and the Academic Profession*, generalizes the impact of this situation on higher education:

> Contingent faculty may be less likely to take risks in the classroom or in scholarly and service work. The free exchange of ideas may be hampered by the specter of potential dismissal or nonrenewal for unpopular utterances. In this chilling atmosphere, students may be deprived of the robust debate essential to citizenship. They may be deprived of rigorous and honest evaluations of their work. . . . Perhaps most important, institutions may lose the opportunity to receive constructive criticism of academic policies and practices from a significant portion of the academic community.[15]

### The Solution to Contingency
According to the US Department of Education Integrative Post Education Data System (IPED), as reported in the 2006 *AAUP Contingent Faculty In-*

*dex*, in 2005 CU-Boulder had 705 tenured professors, as well as another 248 on the tenure track. The data also reported 162 full-time instructors, as well as 959 part-time instructors (instructors with one-year appointments; lecturers, many of whom taught full loads; and adjuncts), for a total of 1,121 professional faculty with teaching responsibilities who taught off the tenure track. In other words, out of 2,074 professional faculty with teaching responsibilities, 1,121, or 54 percent, served CU without access to meaningful protections of their academic freedom. If research faculty and graduate students with faculty responsibilities were added to the data, 83 percent of all faculty at CU were off the tenure track.[16] According to data provided by CU and reported to the *Rocky Mountain News*, instructors and part-time faculty taught 60 percent of the credit hours.[17]

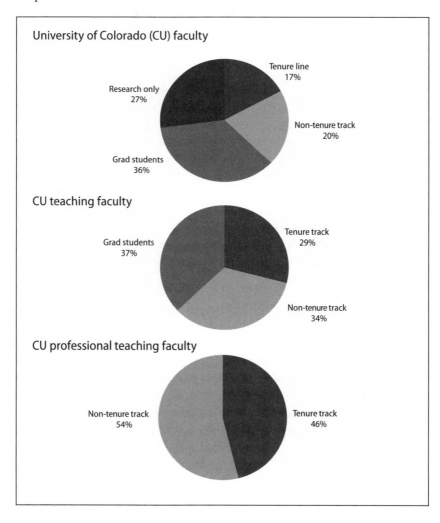

How reliable are these data? As Joe Berry, who teaches at Roosevelt University in Chicago and is an expert in academic labor, points out, "The statistics from government sources on contingent faculty rely upon self-reporting by administrators. This source has a strong self-interest. Therefore these numbers are generally of poor quality and reliability," given the interest of administrators in "downplaying the numbers."[18] If Berry's assumptions are applicable to CU, then a more reliable way to consider the data is this: *at least* 54 percent of the professional teaching faculty were at-will employees, and thus not entitled to legal protection of their academic freedom.

At Colorado, as of this writing, lecturers (faculty on one-semester appointments, though many teach full-time loads year after year, barring complaints from students about their standards or from tenured faculty about their opinions) typically earn $4,000 per course. Full-time instructor salaries start at about $36,500 annually; after an initial one-year "contract," typically instructors receive a three-year "contract." (The quotation marks are well warranted. These "contracts" are not binding on either party; indeed, the at-will clause is prominently displayed. In essence, these contracts say, "You can teach here for three years, unless you decide otherwise, or we decide otherwise.")

Few contingent faculty have a scholarship component in their workload formula (typically 75 percent teaching / 25 percent service for instructors; 100 percent teaching for lecturers). But contingent faculty often perform scholarship as assiduously as their tenured colleagues. The CU Office of Faculty Affairs found that about two-thirds of instructors with at-will contracts reported research or creative work on their 2004 Faculty Report of Professional Activities (FRPA), compared to 80 percent of tenured faculty. The actual numbers, however, may be even more comparable: given that for contingent faculty this research and creative work is performed outside the parameters of their workload formula, and thus, in the view of the administration, is not part of their job, it is reasonable to imagine that many instructors simply do not bother to report their research or creative work.

Even though contingent faculty may be temporary and unrewarded for their nonteaching academic work, according to CU's Laws of the Regents they are faculty in every sense of the word, and entitled to all the same privileges of academic freedom as tenured faculty. Nonetheless, Colorado state law nullified this claim. Colorado state law dictated that there are only two kinds of faculty: tenured and at will; there was no third option—no possibility for a middle category that could provide contingent faculty with any kind of academic freedom at all.[19] Legally, these two conditions—having academic freedom and being at will—cannot coexist. Academic freedom includes the freedom to express an opinion. "At will" means you can be fired for expressing an opinion. The two, by definition, are mutually exclusive.

In December 2006, Suzanne Hudson and I were contacted by a reporter from the *Boulder Daily Camera* about the AAUP's recently released *Contingent Faculty Index*. On a bright Monday afternoon, we met in Suzanne's office and discussed with the reporter the institutional disincentives that come from at-will employment, and the fear and fatalism these disincentives breed in professional teachers who have the tools to deliver excellence in the classroom but are constrained by the need of the administration to maintain maximum flexibility over what was—according to the *Index*—83 percent of the workforce. We spoke of the disagreeable habits of mind one cultivates in order to secure a livelihood under such conditions—of the necessity to please students, to please administrators, to please tenured colleagues (to please, to please, to please) in a profession where such attitudes are anathema to excellence, to the vigorous exchange of ideas that is essential to the pursuit of knowledge. The reporter nodded agreeably. Tuesday morning, when the article appeared, it was clear that what she'd heard from us wasn't what we'd intended—that at-will employment creates conditions in which excellence in the classroom becomes largely unattainable—but, instead, that untenured faculty were, by and large, cowardly, second-rate educators. A valued colleague, Donald Wilkerson, scolded us for "failing to control the message." That Saturday, the *Camera* ran an op-ed piece by Wilkerson calling for instructor tenure.[20] The next day, our op-ed piece, "University Excellence at Risk," appeared in the *Camera*.[21] We called on the chancellor to create a task force to study the possibility of instructor tenure. Until that week, the notion of pushing for tenure for contingent faculty had never crossed our minds; within a month (since we knew it could be a very long wait before the chancellor got back to us on that task force suggestion), we wrote *The Problem and Solution to Contingency at the University of Colorado*.[22] Though the concept—that, after a probationary period, faculty would receive tenure in their current positions, with the same pay rank and same responsibilities—could not have been more obvious, we believed it was the first comprehensive tenure plan for contingent faculty at a major research university in America.[23]

In essence, at CU there would be two tenure tracks: one for professors and one for instructors, each with distinct ladders. In either case, tenure would be considered after a probationary period not to exceed seven years, as stipulated by the AAUP. In further accordance with AAUP recommendations, instructors who had already exceeded the probationary period and thus established a record of commitment to undergraduate education at the university would be immediately tenured.[24] For contingent faculty who had not yet completed their probationary period, their tenure clocks would be set retroactive to their time of hiring. Part-time contingent faculty would also be tenurable, at levels commensurate with their current positions, after the probationary period and a final performance review; the final review would have to be similar to previous reviews as a measure against administrators raising the bar as faculty approach the tenure mark.

The proposed system would involve very little change in procedure during the first seven years of employment beyond intensified efforts on the part of some departments and programs to implement rigorous hiring procedures and to provide the training, mentoring, and supervision necessary for probationary faculty to succeed on the path to instructor tenure. The only substantive change would be that, after the probationary period and a final review similar to previous reviews, an instructor would be offered instructor tenure. They would be relieved of their at-will status, of the constraints of teaching without academic freedom, and of the need to reapply for their jobs every one to four years, a process guaranteed to render most faculty docile and silent.

Like all tenured faculty, tenured instructors would be evaluated for purposes of salary increases every year and they would undergo a post-tenure performance review every five years. They could still lose their jobs, for legitimate cause, financial exigency, or the discontinuation of their academic unit. But the job would be theirs, as would the tools to pursue excellence that only come with the legal assurance of academic freedom. After seven years, proven faculty could not be fired at any time, for any reason or for no reason, their careers dependent on the promises of an administration free to change its mind at any time, or to deny, legally, that there was ever the presumption of a promise. In other words, the only real difference to the university, under the system of instructor tenure, would be that academic freedom would be a legal right for faculty who had taught more than seven years.

On several occasions, over the next few months, Suzanne and I were asked by contingent faculty: Why the focus on academic freedom? Why not instead pursue more money, reduced course loads, greater benefits? In response, we'd make an obvious point—that our time and energy are limited, that we can't accomplish everything at once. Still, we'd say, "We're in favor of more money, reduced course loads, greater benefits. Very much so! Why don't you pursue them? We'll support your efforts." In each instance, the response was the same: They couldn't do that. They'd be fired.

After all, they are at-will employees. They must be good boys and girls.

On other occasions, contingent faculty advised us that, rather than pursue tenure, we'd do better to go after collective bargaining, as if the two goals were mutually exclusive. (Indeed, if faculty had the freedom to agitate for causes without risking their careers, collective bargaining might well rank among those causes.) Still, while collective bargaining has provided real gains for some contingent faculties, by and large academic freedom has not been among them. As Joe Berry and Elizabeth Hoffman note in "Including Contingent Faculty in Governance," most contingent faculties, where unions exist, are "virtually 'at-will' employees. This means that disagreement with our tenure-track and tenured colleagues is expressed publicly (or even privately) at great risk."[25]

### The Campaign
Once the implications of at-will employment for the vast majority of higher education faculty are understood, the issues clarify.

For example, is it fair to students that those who teach most of their classes are deprived of access to academic freedom, but that some professors, safe in their labs from the obligations of teaching undergraduates, have those protections? Is that a tolerable double standard? Or is it fair to society that a minority of researchers and scholars, who happen to have a research component in their contracts, are protected in their pursuit of knowledge, while the vast majority of faculty who perform research and scholarship (but do so outside the parameters of their contracts) are entitled to no protections? As a society, can we be so certain of what ideas may prove to be valuable in the future, and what is mere self-indulgence?

But these are practical considerations. After all, students need the ideas and honest evaluation that faculty are professionally obligated to provide for them, but are discouraged from doing so by the realities of at-will employment. Similarly, society requires the contributions of the vast majority of faculty to issues of pedagogy and curriculum, and whatever they may have within them to contribute to the stock of available knowledge but, again, are discouraged from contributing by the administration's need to maintain maximum flexibility over the work force. But what of the more esoteric dimensions, of the kind tenured faculty must face when they engage the moral complexities of a system where the vast majority of their colleagues are deprived of academic freedom? They, the tenured faculty—who, after all, possess the power to change the status quo—are complicit in an exploitation not only of their colleagues but of students and society, mostly because they also possess the very real human desire to maintain status over the vast majority of their colleagues. They may also possess the desire to browbeat colleagues— or to savor the joys of acting highhanded!—with impunity. For many such tenured faculty, their shame when confronted with their culpability would be palpable.

Perhaps that's why, at least in my experience, there's nobody less willing, nobody slower, to comprehend the implications of at-will employment on our students and on our society than that shrinking percentage of faculty who are not employed at will.

But also consider the shame of contingent faculty, who, after all, possess the sheer numbers to change the status quo, but also may possess habits of thought that prohibit the demonstration of collective will. Their shame when, in order to face their spouses and children, they must persuade themselves they've acted honorably when they know they've acted dishonorably. And consider the shame of many administrators, faculty themselves, who understand that the unique responsibilities of university faculty require unique protections, that the primacy of flexibility over the faculty ought not be the ultimate ethic in higher education, but who make so much more money than they did as faculty that they cannot, realistically, afford to break ranks with higher-up administrators and risk a forced return to the academic fold. Consider their shame in proclaiming to the press that all faculty have academic freedom, while knowing that any faculty who take them at their word (while making so much less money) risk their livelihoods.

It can be difficult establishing traction on an issue that so many people, from each side of the equation, are so reluctant to consider. But it's not impossible. Over the next five months, we sent the chancellor our proposal, met with the provost to inform him of the proposal, held two campus-wide meetings (with the generous assistance of the CU chapter of the AAUP) to discuss the proposal with contingent faculty, and wrote numerous letters to the editor and op-ed pieces about the issue. Suzanne Hudson identified all 889 contingent faculty listed in the faculty directory with e-mail addresses and e-mailed them several times—on one occasion, she e-mailed each of the 889 individually. Several stories about the proposal appeared in the local press. We enlisted "point people" in every department and program where we could find people willing to help. Faculties in numerous programs met to discuss the initiative. We submitted the proposal to the Boulder Faculty Assembly (BFA), the faculty government. To supplement the proposal, we wrote and widely distributed a list of Frequently Asked Questions (FAQ).[26] We founded an organization, the Association of Teaching Faculty, that included all contingent teaching faculty at CU. We wrote a resolution for passage by the BFA, and held a secret-ballot referendum on the resolution during the week of April 22–27, 2007, sponsored by the CU AAUP, in which all contingent teaching faculty were eligible to vote.[27]

Throughout our campaign, most of the apprehension from contingent faculty addressed retaliation scenarios. Some of these scenarios—typically of wholesale firings that occurred at other institutions when instructors tried to implement tenure systems—were floated by administrators, others by tenured faculty who claimed to have the best interests of contingent faculty at heart. Because there was no plausible reason for contingent faculty to oppose our initiative, other than that they feared for their jobs, we took these rumors seriously. In each instance, as we tracked them down, the cited examples proved to be either wildly inflated, or, most often, nonexistent. In our FAQ, four questions addressed the issue of administration retaliation against faculty for seeking academic freedom, and related instructor anxieties:

*What will prevent administrators from firing us in retaliation?*
Nothing, just as nothing prevented them from firing us last year or yesterday and nothing is to prevent them from firing us tomorrow. Tenure is the only protection we can have against such capricious action.

Still, as a practical matter, the era when firing contingent faculty was a solution to the problem of contingency has passed. We are the majority of the faculty now, and we teach most of the classes, including those identified as most essential by the University. It is possible, of course, that the administration will choose to undertake the time and expense of firing most of CU's faculty, restructuring the University, weathering the public relations nightmare, watching CU's ratings plummet, jeopardizing relationships with current and potential donors who do not want their names associated with controversy, and risking AAUP censure. Or, as another possibility, they can implement instructor tenure and formalize the system already in place, at no additional personnel cost to the University.

*What has happened when this has been tried before?*
While rumors exist of steps taken by administrations at other institutions to subvert tenure for instructors, these rumors—typically of wholesale firings—are the academic equivalent of urban myths. This will be the first time a college or university has implemented the AAUP's *Recommended Institutional Regulations on Academic Freedom and Tenure* or any equivalent instructor tenure system.

*Will instructor tenure precipitate systematic non-renewal of our contracts as we approach tenure eligibility in order to prevent us from having it?*
No. Final review prior to tenure must be similar to previous reviews. Also, denying tenure to qualified candidates runs contrary to the interests of the departments. Such a practice would not only diminish the purchase of a department within the University structure but would acknowledge that the department has (1) failed to prepare the instructor to receive tenure and (2) has provided students with inferior teaching over the past seven years (assuming seven years constitutes the probationary period). It is similarly not in the University's interest to deny tenure to eligible instructors. To do so would acknowledge that the University has offered inferior instruction. Additionally, if CU were to acquire a reputation for denying tenure, few instructors would apply for CU positions. Conversely, a great strength of instructor tenure would be that CU's commitment to its teaching faculty will attract the most outstanding teachers in the country.

*Nothing's perfect. I may not have real academic freedom, but nobody pays too much attention to me if I keep my head down, the chair likes me, and students don't complain. I fear that the proposal will invite increased scrutiny of my teaching. Why should I support instructor tenure?*

Assuming your unit has performance procedures already in place, your performance will warrant no more scrutiny than that to which it is already subject. On a further note, someday you may be moved to contribute your expertise to the University, and if your expert opinion runs contrary to the current orthodoxy, you might want to express it without fear of being fired. Someday you may wish to be taken seriously as a professional.

As for tenured faculty who discouraged contingent colleagues from supporting instructor tenure out of concern that instructors would be fired by the university to avoid commitment, Suzanne Hudson addressed the issue in a speech to the faculty on April 19, 2007:

> Tenured faculty, we need your help. I've heard several well-meaning tenured faculty express fear and caution on instructors' behalf. "I'm afraid," they say, "that if CU tries to implement a system of instructor tenure, you'll all be dismissed before you reach the tenure mark." And I don't doubt your sincerity. You truly fear for us. But you know what we need from you? We need you to stand up for us. Rather than advise us to go back, slow down, don't ask for anything lest we get fired, we need you to turn around, face those people who threaten us, and tell them to stop it. Rather than encourage us to fear for our livelihoods, see to it that no instructor who is an asset to your department will be executed the moment he or she reaches the tenure mark. Say out loud and publicly that you will not stand for it.[28]

The fears of contingent faculty were real. However, as became clear from documents leaked to us by sympathetic tenured faculty, contingent faculty were not the only faculty who feared consequences from instructor tenure. Jeffrey Cox, the associate vice chancellor for Faculty Affairs, warned the Faculty Affairs Committee of the BFA that at least one high-ranking administrator at CU was skeptical of tenure, as were many members of the board of regents. There was a risk that the instructor tenure proposal would not result in expanded tenure rights for faculty, but rather a "weakening of tenure for everyone." Cox went on to caution the committee that, when he was in Texas, a similar initiative led to "mass dismissals" of instructors.[29] In another email, the president of the BFA, Gerald Hauser, echoed similar fears. As he saw it, Eron and Hudson had oversimplified a complex issue. Hauser agreed that enhanced due process protections for instructors against unwarranted dismissal might be necessary, but that instructor tenure was "irresponsible";

it might backfire by provoking the regents or the legislature to reexamine the institution of tenure, and thus could damage the "tenure status of faculty." Interestingly, after implying a distinction between faculty and those who teach most of the courses at CU, the president of the faculty government went on to declare that the proposal represented the views of only a minority of one unit on campus and did not enjoy much support among instructors in other units.[30]

In other words, according to Associate Vice Chancellor Cox and faculty government president Hauser, the proposal would lead to mass firings, most of the instructors on campus opposed it, and it was "irresponsible" because it could call into question the legitimacy of their own tenure. In March 2007, the instructor tenure proposal was killed in committee. According to the tenured committee chair, instructor tenure wasn't in the best interest of the university. He also claimed, based on conversations he'd conducted with colleagues around campus, that it was unclear if instructors themselves favored instructor tenure.[31] During the week of April 22–27, contingent faculty endorsed the resolution asking that the BFA approve the instructor tenure proposal, 279–29. With 308 voters, the turnout for the referendum was more than twice that of the BFA election, held the previous week. We weren't surprised that the resolution passed overwhelmingly. However, many tenured faculty had thought the resolution would fail because, in conversations with contingent faculty, they had been assured that contingent faculty vigorously opposed the measure. Anyone who has tried to improve the circumstances of contingent faculty eventually learns that a major impediment to progress can be other contingent faculty. As a survival strategy, we learn to keep our heads down, our voices (and ideas) muffled, and to tell tenured faculty exactly what they want to hear. At Colorado we tell tenured faculty we're thrilled with our jobs, especially when we compare our paychecks and benefits to those of adjunct faculty at Front Range Community College or Metro State College of Denver. Even as we're mistreated, we declare that we get along swimmingly with the tenured faculty in our departments. Under the circumstances of contingency, one would have to be reckless indeed to proclaim anything other than that one adores the status quo. As Steve Street, a writer who often published on contingent issues, sardonically observed in "Don't Be Kind to Adjuncts," "[We] are too scared for our jobs not to be happy."[32] But the claim that one is satisfied, when one can be fired simply for being dissatisfied, is *prima facie* cause for skepticism.

However, even were these contingent faculty not merely placating tenured colleagues, but genuinely against the measure, instructor tenure would not be invalidated. The truth is that not all university teachers require the protection of academic freedom. There are teachers, contingent and tenured alike, who are satisfied not to challenge students in the classroom, and would not dream of speaking up at a faculty meeting to take a position on an important matter that may be contrary to the position of their department head. These teachers do not require protection because, always keeping their heads down, except to endorse the edicts of the powers-that-be, they will never give anybody cause to fire them. For many years, I was such a teacher myself. But, as I often tell parents, alumni, legislators, and other interested citizens when I discuss these issues, it is the teachers that you most want teaching your children who need academic freedom.

On May 2, 2007, the Boulder Faculty Assembly, taking into consideration that the instructors had spoken, called for a task force to study the AAUP proposal for instructor tenure.

## Section 3: The Task Force

As a generality, within academia and elsewhere, task forces are stacked one way or the other, their results predetermined by who's assigned to the committee and who isn't, and by the specific nature of the charge. Even so, the co-opting of the Contingent Faculty Task Force at the University of Colorado, convened in September 2007, was remarkable. But first, a brief analysis of shared governance, as practiced at Colorado and elsewhere, may be useful.

### You Can't Make This Stuff Up

The concept of shared governance between a university's administration and its faculty, as envisioned by the AAUP in numerous statements since 1920 that led to its classic 1966 *Statement on Government of Colleges and Universities*, is that the faculty takes the lead on matters of curriculum, pedagogy, and personnel, in which they are the experts, while the administration runs the business end, its forte.[33] As is typical of many colleges and universities today, the University of Colorado's Laws of the Regents concur with the AAUP's concept of shared governance.[34]

However, if shared governance ever existed in such a crystalline form, it certainly doesn't today. Today, at Colorado, as elsewhere, the administration hands down edicts to which, occasionally, faculty assemblies such as the BFA are free to offer suggestions, which in turn may be considered by the administration before the edicts become policy. Perhaps the most accurate way to view the transaction of shared governance today is through the concept of buy-in. The administration hands down the edict to the faculty assembly, and the faculty assembly, in the name of buy-in, may have the opportunity to comment. If, hypothetically, the faculty refused to buy in, then the edicts become policy without faculty buy-in.

But what if, again hypothetically, a faculty governing body were to take a stand in the name of shared governance? For example, in 2008 the BFA voted 41-4 against the appointment of Bruce Benson, a well-connected political functionary and wealthy oilman with no experience in higher education, as the president of the University of Colorado—a vote that the board of regents duly disregarded. What if, however, instead of shrugging and mumbling and bemoaning the erosion of shared governance before dipping their heads back in the sand, a faculty were to stand up and say no? No, we will not accept Bruce Benson as our president. If you appoint him against our emphatic wishes, we will advise donors not to contribute. We will caution students not to enroll. We will tell the truth about the University of Colorado.

The question is rhetorical in that such a response by a faculty governing body, in today's reality, is beyond comprehension. After all, at least for the minority of the faculty who run faculty governments—safe in their academic freedom, tending to their projects, leaving the actual teaching to the "second-rate, failed academics"—the erosion of shared governance means that much less to worry over. Occasionally they may sense something amiss, and then demonstrate their moral superiority by writing op-ed pieces decrying the situation in Iraq, or railing against the pettiness of academic politics. Through such permutations, some tenured faculty may resolve any dissonance they may feel over the role they've played in the corrosion of higher education. The historical notion that the oppressed, when they're in the majority, are complicit in their oppression is debatable. But what's not debatable is that if faculty governments run by tenured faculty, in what they perceive as their self-interest, took an occasional stand on behalf of their right to determine the policies that shape the education product, students would profit.

In effect, shared governance at many universities today is a dumb show. But is this state of affairs a reality that one must accept, making the best of the diminished circumstance? Such is the stance of many faculty governments, taking the view that, since the game is already lost, faculties can salvage more scraps if administrations view them as accommodating. Or is this state of affairs merely the result of an assumption that—in the name of quaint ideals such as the free exchange of ideas—one might consider entirely unacceptable? That one might, in fact, resist in the name of those quaint ideals? In either event, the oppressed are not relieved of the ethical charge of striving for legitimacy. What if a faculty government were to act in the interest of all faculty, including the vast majority who teach the classes, who do so without academic freedom and who are denied—by these tenured faculty, in what they perceive as the university's interest—voting rights in faculty deliberations? What if the tenured minority were to undergo a slight alteration in perspective? What if they were to see their subjugation of their colleagues not as high-minded, not as symbolic of the standards a university must maintain and of the achievement they believe themselves to manifest, but rather as corrosive, as greedy, as selfish, as small?

These questions are rhetorical, for such acts and perspectives in today's reality are implausible.

### The Task Force Deliberates

Membership in the BFA task force to study instructor tenure was not assigned by the BFA, but by the provost, who had already made his opposition to the proposal clear. What's more, according to BFA president Hauser (in response to my request that he clarify for me what the procedures had been for appointment to the task force), the provost only wanted faculty who were opposed to, or who had distanced themselves from, a "specific proposal."[35] Since the only specific proposal was for instructor tenure, Provost DiStefano's stance was unambiguous. Still, the provost must have feared that members of the task force who had already made up their minds to oppose the proposal, as a requirement of their appointment, might change their minds. In what he must have hoped would be the final stake in the heart, DiStefano declined to put the instructor tenure proposal on the charge of the task force that was formed, in part, for the purpose of studying the instructor tenure proposal. As a result, Jeffrey Mitton, chair of the task force, announced that the task force assigned by the faculty government to consider instructor tenure was not going to consider instructor tenure.

In an e-mail addressed jointly to the current and past presidents of the BFA, the task force chair, and the provost, I wrote:

> Please find attached the Provost's charge to the BFA Task Force on Instructors and Research Faculty. I assume you all have in your possession the BFA motion to form a Contingent Faculty Task Force, approved by the BFA May 3, 2007. From the motion, I quote the following sentence: "The task force should consider the instructor tenure proposal advanced by the CU chapter of the AAUP, among other policy options."
>
> According to Jeff Mitton, chair of the TFIRF, the task force will not consider the instructor tenure proposal because it is not included in the Provost's charge to the task force.
>
> I'll refrain from drawing—and disseminating—any conclusions until you get back to me (I hope by Friday) with your plan of action to address this schism between the BFA motion and the assignment of the task force. Until then, though, I must say that this entire process has been extremely peculiar.[36]

I went on to trace the peculiarities, as I saw them: that the provost's charge was at such variance from the request of the faculty that in effect it nullified the will of the faculty, and that giving the provost the authority to appoint the members of a faculty task force was an abdication of shared governance. What's more, the notion that if prospective task force members favored a particular proposal they were, according to the logic of the provost and implicitly endorsed by BFA president Hauser, biased, whereas if they were "on record as opposed to a particular proposal," they were objective, was not only bizarre but disturbing. On these grounds, I concluded, "It's extremely difficult to imagine how any such committee, given this basis for appointment, could have any credibility. Any action of such a committee promises to be, in effect, fixed."

But that was precisely the point. Still, even by the rules of the dumb show the original charge of the BFA was difficult to dispute. Two days later, the current president of the BFA, who had been instrumental in killing instructor tenure in committee because the administration was opposed, replied to my e-mail. A directive to study the instructor tenure proposal would be added to the provost's charge.

We went through the paces. At 10 a.m. on a Tuesday morning in September, Suzanne Hudson and I, along with several other instructors, met with the task force. I had cancelled a class to appear, made that quite clear to Chair Mitton, and had been assured by Mitton that as the coauthor of the proposal, I would have an opportunity to speak. But it would have to be fast; the ground rules were that each instructor would be given ten minutes. I was scheduled to speak second. Another instructor spoke first. She addressed the issue of office space for contingent faculty in her department, and as she prattled on for fifty minutes, Mitton smiled wanly. I hadn't arranged for a sub for my class at 11, so at 10:55 I left, reluctantly. Later, Suzanne spoke, voicing her concerns for the record about the objectivity of the panel. If the task force had questions for the authors about the proposal that they had been formed to study, perhaps about its specifics, such questions apparently weren't on their minds that morning. We assumed they'd get back to us if any questions came up. We're still waiting.

### The Aftermath

Provost DiStefano's manipulations were probably overkill. A member of the task force, a longtime contingent faculty who had a knack for getting appointed to any committee that the administration felt required non-tenure-track representation, later wrote to Suzanne about the task force's rejection of instructor tenure: Everybody feared backlash. In fact, backlash against instructors had been "barely avoided" in the wake of the proposal.[37]

Since the issue of backlash against faculty for expressing their opinions was the reason for instructor tenure, Suzanne wrote back, asking what she meant.[38] The instructor, who had been supportive behind the scenes, recalled the hostilities of the previous spring, when "normally genial faculty" expressed their outrage over the proposal. For example, one member of the BFA had angrily declared that if the proposal passed, no instructors in his unit would get tenure. Everybody she talked to thought the idea was "untenable." She said she'd tried different versions before the task force, but none of them were seen as "acceptable."[39]

Unacceptable. Untenable. An issue about which normally mild-mannered faculty went ballistic. Diffident before the administration, against contingent faculty their righteous indignation knows no bounds.

While it was a foregone conclusion that the task force was not going to recommend instructor tenure, the Mitton task force made several commendable recommendations. Included among these, perhaps to demonstrate that the academic freedom concerns of the 279 faculty who asked the faculty government to endorse the AAUP proposal for instructor tenure were not being ignored, was the following: "All employees at the University of Colorado Boulder are guaranteed academic freedom. Contract renewal should not be jeopardized by exercise of that freedom."[40] The laws of the university already guaranteed academic freedom. But based on that recommendation, the provost established a fast-track grievance policy for instructors. The instructor grievance policy, exemplary from several perspectives, stipulates: "Where an instructor feels that s/he has not been renewed due to procedural violations or due to an unfair (i.e. arbitrary, capricious, retaliatory, based on personal malice, and/or inconsistent with treatment accorded to the instructor's peers in similar circumstances) recommendation, s/he should use the grievance procedure mentioned above."[41]

By most measures, this procedure is a considerable advancement for contingent faculty at Colorado. It's also unenforceable because, legally, at-will employees can be fired any time, for no reason at all. These "guarantees" exist entirely at the discretion of the administration. For example, if a grievance board makes a recommendation that the administration doesn't like, the administration can simply disregard the recommendation, which is exactly how the system worked before this new policy was put into place, as Adrienne Anderson could have attested. Still, that the administration is legally free to disregard the recommendations of the grievance board, or the policy altogether, does not mean that they will.

So why not trust the administration? It had taken an extraordinary step, in writing. It appeared to have come a long way in the two years since Provost DiStefano's unabashed imperative, when contingent faculty were fired, to defend the authority "of the departments on this campus to make decisions about instructors."

Why not trust? Perhaps this question was on the mind of Jeff Mitton the day after he met with the BFA's Benefits and Compensation Committee

(BCC), and later with its Executive Committee, in October 2008. Reading from a statement that would be published on the BFA website, he explained to the BCC that his task force had rejected instructor tenure on the grounds that tenured and tenure-track faculty have the right to choose their colleagues, that the intensities of scrutiny applied to non-tenure-track faculty (NTTF) and tenure-track faculty (TTF) are not comparable, and that their respective hiring processes are not comparable, nor are their activities and evaluations. Mitton also made the curious statement that, according to the task force, the proposal that instructors who have already exceeded the probationary period of seven years and thus established a record of commitment to the University should be immediately tenured was a "non-sequitur." According to his task force, he explained, "NTTF have contractual agreements lasting from one semester to four years. But completion of a contract means that the obligation of the University and the NTTF come to an end."[42] In other words, when you begin a new contract, the first year of that contract is, by definition, the first year of your service to the university. Thus, the seven-year probationary period was a non sequitur. Finally, tenure-track faculty, according to the findings of the task force, did not want to see the standards of tenure diminished.

In his statement to the BCC, Professor Mitton also wrote, "It has been asserted that for NTTF, reappointment demonstrates excellence. The committee discussed this and concluded that at CU it is more the norm that satisfactory performance is rewarded with reappointment."[43] This notion of Professor Mitton and his task force—that the norm for contingent faculty is not "excellence" but merely "satisfactory performance"—is one widely shared among tenured faculty. It's also quite curious. I'm not sure how Professor Mitton or the task force would have any idea whether these faculty are satisfactory, excellent, or incompetent. Perhaps Professor Mitton's view is reasonable: if he sees faculty who never voice opinions except in agreement, and who, obsessed with keeping their heads down, appear altogether detached from faculty business, what other inference is he to draw? Personally, I find it remarkable that so many contingent faculty do not allow the institutional disincentive of at-will employment to prevent them from trying to fulfill their professional responsibilities with high degrees of excellence.

However, let us assume for the sake of argument that the task force's assessment is accurate. As discussed earlier, at-will employment creates conditions for faculty in which "satisfactory" performance is all but inevitable. In rejecting instructor tenure on the basis that contingent faculty are not excellent but merely "satisfactory," Mitton and his task force had used mere "satisfactory performance" as justification for the conditions that create it.

In 2008, I was a member of the BCC. Suzanne attended the meeting at which Mitton provided the task force rationale. The BCC also had—not coincidentally—a new chair, Margaret LeCompte, the president of the local AAUP chapter, who served on the BFA Executive Committee. In essence, our response to his report was this: Fine, the standards are higher for professor tenure than they would be for instructor tenure. Nobody disputes that. But what of the at-will clause? After all, state law requires that faculty be either tenured or at will. What of the disincentive? What of the cost to higher education when the vast majority of the faculty cannot teach without fear of retaliation from students, or argue positions at faculty meetings without fear of retaliation from the administration or tenured colleagues who may feel inconvenienced by their arguments, or even by the very obligation to respond to their arguments?

To his credit, Mitton admitted at the meeting that the task force would have acted differently if we could have called it "something other than tenure." Still, he was apparently nonplussed when I wouldn't agree that his grievance process, with no legal obligation on the administration's part to abide by a grievance board decision that favored an instructor, adequately addressed job security. He also seemed taken aback that—despite the recommendation of the task force—the proposal for instructor tenure would be returning to the BFA, and that the topic was not the dead issue that his task force had painstakingly declared it to be when it decided that tenure was not necessary in order to protect academic freedom.

In an e-mail sent the next day to several members of the executive committee, Jeff Mitton reflected on his meeting with the BCC. He recalled my argument that academic freedom is necessary in order to pursue excellence in the classroom. However, Mitton wrote, assistant professors don't have tenure, and nobody would suggest that assistant professors are placed in situations where they cannot pursue excellence. Therefore, tenure is not necessary in order to strive for excellence.

As for ways other than tenure to protect academic freedom, Mitton told these members of the BFA executive committee that I had been assured by the institution at several levels—the dean, the BFA, Mitton's own task force, and the provost—that academic freedom is protected at the University of Colorado. Furthermore, his task force had called for a fast-track grievance process that would "prohibit" any instructor from being "punished" for expressing his or her views. Nonetheless, Mitton noted, these institutional assurances of academic freedom weren't good enough for me; it was clear that I don't trust people. But a research institution, Mitton concluded, cannot redesign tenure just because people like Don Eron are "cynical."[44]

Whatever the accuracy of his characterization (disclosure: there's something to it), Margaret LeCompte, the local AAUP chapter president and a new member of the BFA executive committee, emphasized, in her response to Mitton, the large disparity that often exists between tenured faculty and their contingent colleagues regarding their perceptions of due process procedures for contingent faculty. "Whether we agree with [Don Eron] or not, his feelings are shared by many instructors, lecturers and assistant professors, and there have been some recent cases where their distrust of procedures at CU have been warranted, in that procedures guaranteed were not followed." LeCompte then addressed a common misunderstanding among tenured faculty and administrators when contingent faculty advocate to improve the working conditions of their colleagues. "Thus," she wrote to Mitton, "Don Eron is representing his constituency, not just expressing his own feelings."[45]

But Mitton's ideas are instructive. His views toward the relationship between academic freedom and tenure are held by many other tenured faculty, especially—although by no means exclusively—professors of long standing who tend to dominate faculty governments today. I sometimes wonder if these professors, secure in their decades of academic freedom protected by tenure, suffer from a form of mass amnesia. Or possibly, having come of age in a time when tenure-track jobs were widely available, they're unacquainted with the anxieties that many assistant professors today face constantly, lest they not be awarded tenure and be forced to join the ranks of the contingent majority, or abandon their careers altogether. Today, for example, you'd be hard pressed to find an assistant professor who feels he has any academic freedom at all. As Gabriel Kaplan, an assistant professor in the Graduate School of Public Affairs at the University of Colorado, Denver, has observed, "Few assistant professors, knowing they will come before a tenure committee comprised of senior and tenured peers, are likely to voice strong opposition to the positions of tenured faculty."[46] In academia today, assistant professors are renowned for playing it safe in the classroom, giving high grades, and never, under any circumstances, challenging anybody's views at faculty meetings. I doubt that anyone would consider that to be a prescription for excellence.

More troubling, however, than not recognizing the disincentives under which many assistant professors labor, is Professor Mitton's view that a grievance board can provide meaningful protection for academic freedom—indeed, that to suggest otherwise is to disrespect the faculty government, the task force, the dean, and the provost, because each has provided assurances. In other words, what Professor Mitton argues is that, philosophically speaking, tenure is not necessary; he understands the need for academic freedom, but believes academic freedom can be protected just as well by other means, such as a grievance board.

So casual is the dismissal of the academic freedom justification for tenure that I wonder if Mitton and colleagues have any idea that academic freedom is the original justification for tenure. That without the argument that university faculties, as the pursuers and transmitters of knowledge, play a unique role in the survival of democracy and therefore require unique protections—

namely, academic freedom backed by legally enforceable due process—tenure has no reliable rationale. Without the academic freedom argument, Mitton himself would not enjoy the security of tenure today. I wonder if one day he'll appreciate the fact that, in so cavalierly giving up tenure's central justification—because the word itself was such a sticking point—he helped pave the way for his own loss of tenure.

Or perhaps Mitton and colleagues aren't acting unwittingly against their own interests, but really don't believe in tenure. Possibly these tenured faculty understand that the very existence of tenure implies that institutions cannot be trusted to observe academic freedom when it might be inconvenient or financially painful for them to do so, but that they nonetheless wish to live in a world where trust trumps cynicism. As Suzanne and I pursue academic freedom for instructors, some tenured professors have told us that they would support us, but that they are opposed to tenure as an institution. Whenever we've encountered such a response, we've asked these tenured faculty, as a matter of ethics—in that they are denying others protections they themselves enjoy—to renounce their own tenure. Give it up. Send it back to the shop. Become at-will employees themselves. Trust. To date, none have taken us up on our suggestion.

Apparently, like Bartleby, though without the scrivener's stubborn integrity in the face of despair, they would prefer not to.

## Section 4: Why Should Contingent University Teachers Get Tenure When the Private Sector Doesn't?

The irony of the campaign waged by university administrations to eliminate academic freedom for university teachers, in the name of reduced wages and greater flexibility over the workforce, is that in so doing they are depriving faculty of the very protections that empowered the "greatest generation" to achieve its postwar potential.

The underlying philosophy that justifies academic freedom—as well as providing the basis for the 1925 Supreme Court decision (*Gitlow v. New York*) that freedom of speech is protected by the due process clause of the Fourteenth Amendment—stems from the premise that our knowledge is imperfect. Thus, certainty cannot exist, although—as formulated by Louis Menand in *The Metaphysical Club*, which won the 2002 Pulitzer Prize for nonfiction, and which culminates in the founding of the AAUP—there are countless people who claim certainty.[47] Furthermore, according to the pragmatist philosophy that informs both academic freedom and freedom of speech, history demonstrates that the fundamental characteristic of modern life is social change. Unfortunately, there are no guarantees that society will advance onward and upward, or that social change will prove to be for the good. The only guarantee is that social change is inevitable.

Ideas, or at least any ideas potent enough to acquire social currency, are fundamentally social expressions, according to the instrumentalist philosopher John Dewey. As expressions of social conditions, ideas are essentially tools—or strategies—that people use to solve their problems. Within a social group most people have the same problems—how to live humanely with each other in a civil society, how to conduct their affairs with the dignity and integrity they would wish to find in others, how to improve the quality of human life within their reach. Differing ideas, then, while perhaps defined by their opposition to each other, are, pragmatically speaking, competing strategies toward the attainment of a mutual goal.

For this reason, unpopular ideas, which express social conditions that are inconvenient to think about, must nonetheless be expressed, understood, confronted, and sometimes accommodated to ensure the survival of the group. Likewise, students must have access to unpopular ideas, posited by faculty as strategies of education, because the articulation of such ideas and their confrontation and accommodation by competing ideas are the best assurance we have for the survival of democracy.

As the pursuers and transmitters of knowledge, university teachers play a central role in the survival of democracy. Because they are obligated by their profession to pose unpopular ideas, they carry responsibilities and require protections necessary in few other professions. Suppose, for example, that rather than being a university teacher, I am a construction worker, employed by Mr. X, who in turn is employed as a general contractor to build a house for Mr. Y. In the course of helping to build Mr. Y's house, let's say that I had a number of suggestions that I believed would help us to achieve our goal more efficiently. Let us further suppose that, rather than acting on my suggestions, Mr. X found them to be inconvenient—a nuisance—and chose to fire me instead. In that I was employed at will, he'd be under no obligation to furnish a reason why he was firing me (though I might have a pretty good idea, and resolve to keep my mouth shut the next time), and Mr. X certainly wouldn't be obliged to defend that reason, which he would be under no obligation to furnish, in a court of law, were I to press the issue of my capricious dismissal. I would be out of luck. Similarly, assuming that my ideas had been good ones from which Mr. X might have benefited had he been more receptive, Mr. X would be out of luck, as would Mr. Y, whose house might have been built more efficiently. But while we'd all be out of luck, society wouldn't be, for there's no societal interest in whether Mr. Y's house is built as efficiently as it might be. Indeed, the sole purpose of Mr. X's business is to make money for Mr. X. That's where the imperatives of business and education differ: there is a central societal interest in providing students with the best possible education to prepare them to face the challenges of our collective future.

While the unique protections required by university teachers have always infuriated segments of the population, society as a whole has tolerated this arrangement because, as Menand notes, it is in the self-interest of society to do so. Indeed, this self-interest was borne out by America's ubiquitous contributions to twentieth century knowledge. Thus, it is paramount that university teachers not be beholden to the ephemeral interests of the state, the trustees of the university, or taxpayers. It is similarly paramount that university teachers not fear reprisals from students or dismissal from the university for challenging students' worldviews or "comfort zones" within the classroom. University teachers should not have to fear administrators or colleagues who may have little tolerance for unpopular ideas, even as educational gambits, or for the occasional complaints of students uncomfortable with the character of a viable education.

As advanced by the AAUP in the early twentieth century, so unique is the role of university teachers to the survival of the group that their only obligation is to serve the good of society as they see it, within parameters determined not by administrators, trustees of the university, or even the taxpayers, but by others within their profession. That's how tenure, as the workable protection for the expression of ideas within and outside the classroom, empowered the "greatest generation" to construct a more humane world. It's also how our universities, backwaters at the beginning of the twentieth century, had become the envy of the world by the 1980s.

These fundamental assumptions are at the core of the only protection university teachers have when they are threatened for their ideas either directly or through administrator or student retaliation—the protection of legally enforceable due process. If knowledge is imperfect, then due process cannot attain legitimacy on the basis of whether we believe a teacher's opinions are right or wrong, or whether these opinions correspond to a metaphysical truth. In order to obtain legitimacy, decisions or outcomes must derive from processes and procedures that are themselves legitimate. To be legitimate, these processes must be a matter of continuous, demonstrable practice, and not mere theory. They must be enforceable as a matter of law, rather than as a matter of discretion or the caprice of administrators who are not philosophically opposed to the good of society, but have more pressing concerns or don't wish to be bothered.

In truth, we cannot expect the actions of university faculty (though they may speak in their classes of noble ideals) to be any more courageous or altruistic than we can the actions of university administrators, or of Mr. X. We cannot expect them to act as if they don't have financial obligations, children, elderly parents, the need for health insurance, or the desire to avoid the humiliation and emotional battering that comes from losing one's career. When the vast majority can be fired simply for offering their strategies, vastly fewer strategies are offered.

We should hope that the pragmatists had it wrong—that our knowledge is perfect, that we don't require access to competing strategies in order to ensure our survival, and that society is unchanging.

## Section 5: The End of Tenure

The AAUP's seminal *1915 Declaration of Principles on Academic Freedom and Tenure*, which furnished the philosophical basis for tenure as it would be practiced in America's colleges and universities, argued two justifications. The first was the necessity of academic freedom to the pursuit and the transmission of knowledge. The second justification was the lure of job security—if administrations were required to present cause before terminating faculty, and if that cause could be legally contested, more of the best minds might be attracted to academia than to other professions that offer greater material incentives but less security.[48]

Since then, however, tenure has acquired additional significances that in the understanding of many tenured faculty and administrators, as well as to many task forces assigned with studying the relevance of tenure in today's society, have taken precedence over the original justifications. Among these is that tenure is essentially a reward for significant accomplishment—an acknowledgment of hard work. Another is that if a university were to take the precipitous step of abolishing tenure, the best faculty would flee. A final significance, often voiced by tenured faculty at universities charged with research missions as an argument against tenure for teaching faculty who lack research components in their contracts, is that tenure symbolizes the research mission of the university.

Unless our universities embrace a fundamental rethinking of what tenure means—in other words, unless faculties return to the original academic freedom justification—within fifteen years it is doubtful that tenure will exist at all, at least in any way that today's tenured faculties might find to be palatable. But returning to the academic freedom justification requires tenured faculty to insist that academic freedom cannot be protected by grievance boards or assurances. It requires that access to tenure be made available to all proven faculty. It requires that tenured faculty act in their self-interest, for either tenure is necessary to protect academic freedom, or it is not necessary. And if tenure is not essential for academic freedom, then all that will remain to justify tenure are the subsequent, easily demolished arguments.

Here's a scenario far more plausible than the survival of tenure: within a few years, a state legislature—citing budget constraints, the disappearance of tenure altogether at numerous community, technical and liberal arts colleges, and the de facto disappearance of tenure-track positions at public research universities such as Colorado—will once again examine the viability of tenure as an institution. And it will find that, as Gertrude Stein famously said of Oakland, "There's no there there."

For example, why should the accomplishments and hard work of those in academia be acknowledged differently from the accomplishments and hard work of those in the private sector, who are either employed at will or run their own businesses without legally guaranteed job security, and whose livelihoods are always subject to the interface of individual ingenuity and the caprice of market forces?

Perhaps, the legislators may acknowledge, faculty have unique responsibilities and, for the good of society, require protections for their academic freedom, but—as tenured faculty themselves have insisted, through their subjugation of the rights of the vast majority of their colleagues—academic freedom can be more than adequately protected by, for example, a fast-track grievance process backed by the assurances of the administration. Thus, while a societal interest remains in the academic freedom of faculty, there is no longer a societal interest in the existence of tenure. Still, hard work and significant accomplishment are laudable for their own sake, and deserve recognition; perhaps, the legislators might suggest, as a more proportional response than guaranteed job security, somebody should schedule an annual parade.

A corollary of the significant achievement justification, one that was often posed by Colorado officials to defuse criticism of tenure in the wake of the Ward Churchill controversy, is the argument that critics of tenure need not be disturbed at the prospect of professors running amok because, contrary to public perception, only the very best faculty receive tenure. Typically, when this "defense" is advanced, it will be accompanied by data showing, for example, that out of two-hundred applicants for tenure-track positions at CU, only one will ever receive tenure at Colorado. If this reasoning mollifies some critics, it may be because it is not a justification for tenure but an argument that supports the abolition of tenure. If the only faculty who receive tenure are the ones who have already demonstrated that tenure isn't necessary for significant achievement, then there's really no societal interest in the existence of tenure. It's simply not necessary for significant achievement.

Next, let's look at the argument that if a major research university were to abolish tenure in favor of term contracts for all faculty and not just the majority, the best faculty will flee to Cal Tech or Iowa State. Interestingly, this "brain drain" assumption has proven somewhat persuasive to groups or individuals not otherwise inclined to support tenure. For example, the chair of a task force assigned by the Colorado legislature to study the viability of tenure, in the wake of the Ward Churchill controversy, concluded that if Colorado were to abolish tenure, the consequences of a massive brain drain would devastate the university.[49]

Similarly, in October 2008, Bruce Benson—the wealthy oilman and political functionary who had been appointed CU president (despite, as mentioned earlier, the 41-4 vote of the faculty government rejecting his candidacy)—assured the faculty that he supported tenure because without it there would be "a massive brain drain." When President Benson offered this view to the BFA, I asked him a question. "What if," I said, "in a few years a state legislature decided to challenge your assumption that there would be a brain drain? What if they decided to see if the best faculty might enjoy their lab facilities and be secure enough with their government funding, and the research overhead their funding brings to the university general fund, that they can't conceive of their own positions being threatened, with or without tenure. What if the state legislature guesses right and there is no brain drain? Then every other state legislature will follow suit. If the 'brain drain' argument is the best we can do, soon there may be no tenure anywhere."

"Well," President Benson said, "help me out then. What other arguments are there?"

"How about academic freedom," I said, "so that faculty can teach without fear of retaliation from students, and argue positions at faculty meetings without fear of retaliation from administrators? It's important to the quality of undergraduate education."

President Benson looked puzzled.

In fairness to President Benson, I don't think he accepted my premise that state legislatures might altogether abolish tenure. He may be right. But here is what is far more plausible, if the brain drain argument remains the primary justification for tenure. A state legislature, given all the considerations discussed earlier, will pose this question: where can we afford a brain drain, and where can't we afford a brain drain? The answer will be self-evident to anybody familiar with the funding of higher education. In some pockets of the hard sciences and the social sciences, which can be counted on to generate revenue, tenure might remain essential. Elsewhere, tenure will quickly disappear. The state legislature will answer its own question by concluding that in the humanities, we can afford a brain drain. Most faculty teaching those classes already don't have access to tenure, and the truth is, students can't tell the difference.

However, many faculty in the hard sciences will not find themselves bulletproof. Once the academic freedom justification disappears, once certain questions begin to be asked, there is a slippery slope. For example, research in the hard sciences may be privileged over scholarship in English or research in sociology, where the brain drain is affordable, but can't we make distinctions between types of research in the hard sciences? Yes, CU is a research university, the state legislature may conclude, but at CU three thousand research faculty are already off the tenure track. Of teaching faculty, with no research or scholarship components in their contracts, 60 percent report scholarship or research activity on their FRPAs. So it's not as if distinctions aren't already being drawn between what research is valued, and what isn't. "What should be valued?" the legislature might wonder. Then it will ask more questions, zeroing in. Should those doing general research, far less likely to be funded than more specific projects, be entitled to tenure? Shouldn't we strip their tenure and place them on term contracts, thus gaining flexibility? They're not so likely to be poached by Cal Tech. If one were to point out, in response to the legislature's incessant questioning, that many of the great discoveries emerge from general research, it would be the rhetorical equivalent of serving up a softball. But the pursuit of knowledge is not jeopardized, it might respond. As a society we won't suffer. There is a fast-track grievance procedure that faculty insist is just as good as tenure.

One final consideration may contribute to the end of tenure, once state legislators become involved with the kinds of distinctions tenured faculty so love to draw between themselves and the vast majority of their colleagues, at the expense of the education product and at great risk to knowledge: when they see the sense of self-importance of so many faculty, these legislators may have a very human reaction. They may decide this: it'll be fun to stick it to 'em.

## A Personal Coda: For the Good of Society

The war to eliminate academic freedom will invariably take its toll on the second justification for tenure cited by the AAUP in its 1915 statement: that the job security that comes with tenure might attract the best minds to the profession.[50] When the vast majority are at-will employees, even the best minds cannot enter the profession and assume they will command job security. Indeed, it may require a grandiose sense of self to bank one's future on the expectation that one will be the exception to the rule and be permitted the tools that are necessary to achieve excellence, or even be treated with respect by colleagues and administrations. If administrations and complicit tenured faculty prove victorious in their war to eliminate tenure, it would be difficult to imagine anybody entering the profession who doesn't have a deep passion for teaching, and a sizable trust fund. Aspiring to work in academia will become akin to aspiring to be a poet: totally irresponsible, and slightly admirable.

If the day comes that tenure is finally abolished, in all but the few pockets that generate revenue, it will be a happy day for me. Not only for the right to boast, "I told you so," though that will be satisfying. I will think of all those once-tenured faculty who treated me with such high-minded disdain when I asked for academic freedom, who cut me off, who dismissed me as foolish and untutored in the realities of academia, who shouted out, "Can't you get it through your thick skull that we're a research university!" or "But it could erode the tenure of faculty!" I will picture them as at-will employees who would like to evaluate students honestly but can't because it could mean career suicide, and who wish to speak up, to contribute their expertise at faculty meetings because they believe they have a better idea, but must now swallow their words, their dignity. The happiness I feel as I picture this is almost unbearable.

But then I think of the profession. I think it's not just their profession, but also the profession of my father, who was a full professor for over forty years, and whom I think of more and more as I write these pages. It's my profession, and that of my contingent colleagues who stand courageously for excellence, and of many tenured colleagues who, despite my unpleasant generalities in these pages, have stood with us. I think of my students, who deserve better, and of a society that needs the best that we can give it, and not merely the best we can give it subject to the greater imperative of university administrations—that is, their drive for maximum flexibility over the cheapest possible workforce. I think of the grand notion that as academics it is the good of society that we serve—the good as we see it, and not the ephemeral interests of administrators or voters or taxpayers or radio jocks. If academic freedom could once again flourish, then our society might have all it could ever need: a fighting chance.

Instructor tenure is the natural correction to the trend that began forty years ago of replacing retiring tenured faculty with less expensive contingent faculty in order to achieve a more flexible workforce in times of budgetary constraints and curricular change. The unintended consequence of employing faculty who specialize in teaching, but do so without academic freedom protected by due process, plausible avenues for participating in shared governance, or an appreciable commitment to their professionalism, has been the corrosion of undergraduate education.

Let us hold true to this assumption: that faculty, staff, administrators, and trustees of our colleges and universities all share a mutual goal, to deliver an education that vitalizes our graduates with the knowledge and skills necessary to better shape our collective future across the spectrum of American life. If success, as defined by George Will, implies an "enterprise in which benefits exceed cost," then the experiment of contingency for university teachers is an abject failure.[51] Yet the mutual goal we all share remains attainable. It is never too late to replace failed strategies with better ideas.

## NOTES

1.  AAUP, *Trends in Instructional Staff Employment Status, 1975–2011* (Washington, DC: AAUP, 2013), *aaup.org/sites/default/files/files/AAUP_Report_InstrStaff-75-11_apr2013.pdf* [hereinafter *Trends 1975–2011*]. Because my discussion centers on academic freedom, professional responsibility, and tenure, I have calculated this most recent data to exclude graduate students with teaching responsibilities. When graduate students, who may teach under the supervision of faculty advisors, are included, about 76 percent of college and university teachers today fulfill their responsibilities off the tenure track.

2.  John W. Curtis and Monica F. Jacobe, *AAUP Contingent Faculty Index 2006* (Washington, DC: AAUP, 2006), *aaup.org*. This study, when calculating the percentage of tenured and tenure-track faculty among all faculty in 1975, did not categorize graduate students with teaching responsibilities as faculty. For that reason, I consider it to be the most reliable source regarding faculty percentages in 1975. Relative percentages of faculty categories, even when compiled from the same source, will vary depending on whether these graduate students are considered as faculty. However, when the data from *Trends 1975–2011* is adjusted to exclude graduate students as a faculty category, the results of the two studies are consistent within one-half of a percentage point.

3.  There was a fourth category, instructors who were ABD from other institutions, who were hired with the understanding that upon finishing their dissertations they'd be promoted to assistant professor positions on the tenure track. They were employed at will, and would remain at will until achieving tenure, but didn't qualify as contingent faculty, given their employment assumptions, and so will be excluded from this discussion. There was also a fifth category of adjunct: graduate teaching assistants, who, at that time and regardless of their actual faculty responsibilities, were considered to be students working under the supervision of their faculty supervisors, and as such didn't warrant the protections of academic freedom.

4.  AAUP, *The Status of Part-Time Faculty* (Washington, DC: AAUP, 1980), *aaup.org*.

5.  AAUP, *Contingent Appointments and the Academic Profession* (Washington, DC: AAUP, 2003), *aaup.org*.

6.  Ibid.

7.  Alison Schneider, "To Many Adjunct Professors, Academic Freedom Is a Myth," *Chronicle of Higher Education*, 10 December 1999, 6, *chronicle.com*.

8.  Quoted in Peter Schmidt, "Use of Part-Time Instructors Tied to Lower Student Success," *Chronicle of Higher Education*, 14 November 2008.

9.   Annette Kolodny, "'60 Minutes' at the University of Arizona: The Polemic against Tenure," *New Literary History* 27, no. 4 (1996): 699.

10.  AAUP, *Recommended Institutional Regulations on Academic Freedom and Tenure* (Washington, DC: AAUP, 2009; first formulated in 1957), *aaup.org*.

11.  Ward Churchill was a tenured ethnic studies professor and Native American activist who was fired for research misconduct—allegations that, not coincidentally, arose after the governor and state legislature demanded his ouster for sentiments he expressed in a polemic written in the aftermath of 9/11. For a comprehensive account of the Churchill case, please read "Report on the Termination of Ward Churchill," *AAUP Journal of Academic Freedom* 3 (June 2012), *www.academicfreedomjournal.org*. (Disclosure: I am one of the authors of the report.)

12.  Quoted in Paula Pant, "Committee Finds Prof's Rights Violated," *Colorado Daily*, 20 September 2006, 4–5.

13.  Don Eron and Suzanne Hudson, *Report on the Termination of Phil Mitchell* (Boulder: AAUP CU Chapter, 2007; revised edition, Colorado Conference AAUP, 2 November 2011), *www.cu-aaup.org*.

14.  Indeed, the director did try to terminate Suzanne at the end of the 2007–2008 academic year, but her method was so blatantly unethical that the dean intervened.

15.  AAUP, *Contingent Appointments*.

16.  Curtis and Jacobe, *AAUP Contingent Faculty Index*.

17.  Berny Morson, "Adjunct College Faculty Growing in State, Nation," *Rocky Mountain News* (Denver, CO), 22 January 2007, *rockymountainnews.com*.

18.  Joe Berry, *Contingent Higher Education Faculty and their Unions in the USA: A Very Brief Summary* (Chicago, IL: COCAL, n.d.), *www.chicagococal.org*.

19.  Subsequent to this account, the ongoing Instructor Tenure Project has led to changes in Colorado state law that give public institutions the right to engage in binding term contracts with contingent faculty. This legislation (HB 12-1144) is an important step toward academic freedom, but falls significantly short (for reasons discussed elsewhere in this essay) of the academic freedom protections of tenure.

20.  Donald Wilkerson, "Grant Tenure to Teachers," *Boulder Daily Camera*, 16 December 2006, *dailycamera.com*.

21.  Don Eron and Suzanne Hudson, "University Excellence at Risk," *Boulder Daily Camera*, 18 December 2006, *dailycamera.com*.

22.  Don Eron and Suzanne Hudson, *The Problem and Solution to Contingency at the University of Colorado* (Boulder: AAUP CU Chapter, 2007), *www.cu-aaup.org*.

23.  As it happens, a similar proposal was being advanced by a group of contingent faculty at Rutgers. Please read *Teaching at Rutgers: A Proposal to Convert Part-time to Full-time Appointments and Instructor Full-time Non-tenure-track Appointments to Tenure-track Appointments*, by Zoran Gajic, Karen Thompson, and Richard Moser, 5 May 2008, *www.rutgersaaup.org/misc/13_Teaching_at_RU_Proposal_Revised_5May08.pdf*.

24.  AAUP, *Contingent Appointments*.

25. Joe Berry and Elizabeth Hoffman, "Including Contingent Faculty in Governance," *Academe*, November-December 2008, 30.

26. Don Eron and Suzanne Hudson, *Frequently Asked Questions Regarding the Implementation of the AAUP's "Recommended Institutional Regulations on Academic Freedom and Tenure" for Instructors at the University of Colorado*, 31 March 2007, *www.cu-aaup.org*.

27. Don Eron and Suzanne Hudson, *Resolution of the Association of Teaching Faculty at CU to Implement an Instructor Tenure System at the University of Colorado*, 2 April 2007, 21–24, *www.cu-aaup.org*.

28. Suzanne Hudson, *Academic Freedom and Tenure: You Can't Have One without the Other*, 19 April 2007, *www.cu-aaup.org*.

29. Jeffrey Cox, e-mail to Faculty Affairs Committee, 22 February 2007.

30. Gerald Hauser, e-mail to Paul Levitt, 19 February 2007.

31. The Faculty Affairs Committee originally passed the proposal. The president of the BFA, Gerald Hauser, then sent it to the Benefits and Compensation Committee (BCC), of which I was a member. The BCC passed the proposal 4–3. At a subsequent meeting, with one of the proposal's supporters absent, the chair of the committee, who would soon become the new president of the BFA, called for a revote. The tally was 3–3. Invoking his privileges as chair, he cast the deciding vote to kill the proposal.

32. Steve Street, "Don't Be Kind to Adjuncts," *Chronicle of Higher Education*, 24 October 2008, *chronicle.com*.

33. AAUP, *1966 Statement on Government of Colleges and Universities* (Washington, DC: AAUP, 1966), *aaup.org*. This statement was revised in 1990 to edit gender-specific references.

34. University of Colorado, Laws of the Regents, Article 5.E.5, *www.cu.edu* (Article 5 last amended 21 August 2008).

35. Gerald Hauser, e-mail to Don Eron, 9 September 2007.

36. Don Eron, e-mail to Uriel Nauenberg, Gerald Hauser, Jeffrey Mitton, and Phil DiStefano, 11 September 2007.

37. Cathy Comstock, e-mail to Suzanne Hudson, 18 September 2008.

38. Suzanne Hudson, e-mail to Cathy Comstock, 18 September 2008.

39. Cathy Comstock, e-mail to Suzanne Hudson, 18 September 2008.

40. *Recommendations from the Task Force on Instructors*, n.d., accessed 17 May 2013, *www.colorado.edu/FacultyGovernance/resources/Instructors_Task_Force_Recommendations.pdf*.

41. Phil DiStefano, "Memo to Boulder Campus Instructional Faculty," 9 December 2008; reissued as "Academic Affairs Takes Action on BFA Instructor Task Force Recommendations," 13 August 2009, *www.colorado.edu*.

42. Jeffrey Mitton, "The Task Force on Instructors Rejected the Proposal of Tenure for Instructors" (statement to BFA Benefits and Compensation Committee), 18 October 2008, *www.colorado.edu*.

43. Ibid.

44. Jeffrey Mitton, e-mail to members of BFA Executive Committee, 21 October 2008.

45. Margaret LeCompte, e-mail to members of BFA Executive Committee, 22 October 2008. Quoted with permission.

46. Gabriel Kaplan, "Tenure More than Academic Freedom," *Denver Post*, 7 May 2006.

47. Louis Menand. *The Metaphysical Club: A Story of Ideas in America* (New York: Farrar, Straus and Giroux, 2002).

48. AAUP, *1915 Declaration of Principles on Academic Freedom and Academic Tenure* (Washington, DC: AAUP, 1915), *aaup.org*.

49. Howell Estes (chair, Advisory Committee on Tenure-Related Processes at the University of Colorado), statement at a Boulder Faculty Assembly meeting, 4 May 2006.

50. AAUP, *1915 Declaration*.

51. George Will, "McArthur's Two Words," *Newsweek*, 15 January 2007, 72.

# 3

# Online Teaching and the Deskilling of Academic Labor in Canada

*Natalie Sharpe and Dougal MacDonald*

Athabasca University (AU) is an accredited research university founded in 1970 as the first open distance education university in Alberta, Canada. It was modeled on the prestigious British Open University, founded in 1969, which offered each registered student an assigned academic instructor called a "tutor." AU aimed from the start to offer "open entry" to affordable quality university education to those wishing to pursue higher education on a part-time or distance basis—that is, students lacking access to traditional institutions. AU reaches remote aboriginal communities, mothers working at home, students with disabilities, workers studying part time, incarcerated learners, and other marginalized groups. It provides a variety of online undergraduate, graduate, and certificate courses in areas such as anthropology, chemistry, education, and business. Each year, thirty-two thousand students attend the university. Students enroll online mainly from Canada but also from the rest of the world. Two hundred sixty thousand students have taken courses since the university was founded.

Athabasca University remains a virtual university that provides almost all of its educational offerings online, relying on computers and the Internet to distribute its courses through distance education. Other online universities across the globe are also offering all their courses online. At the same time, many traditional brick-and-mortar institutions, which previously conducted only face-to-face classes in classrooms, are also now offering online courses. One of the most recent innovations is MOOCs, or massive open online courses. MOOCs are free online courses for an unlimited number of students, aimed at achieving mass student participation through open access via the Internet. At the same time, such courses do not typically count for degree credit. The situation today is that there are now many institutions worldwide—private and public, nonprofit and for-profit—offering distance education courses, which run the gamut from the most basic instruction to the highest levels of degree and doctoral programs. This proliferation has created an unprecedented level of competition for online students on a global scale, a situation that did not exist at the time AU was founded over forty years ago.

As at other postsecondary institutions, both traditional and online, the 295 contracted tutors at Athabasca University do the bulk of the teaching. In 1980, with over one hundred tutors, AU separated the teaching staff into two kinds of academics: full-time tenured professors with university offices and contracted part-time tutors working from home. In 1983, the tutors formed their own association to improve wages and working conditions. The tutors had attempted to join the full-time tenured faculty association, but they had been rejected by that association's members and by the AU administration, which claimed that tutors were not academic staff. In response, tutors from this rather remote institution in western Canada unionized with the central Canada-based Canadian Union of Educational Workers (CUEW) as Local 11. In 1990, the first collective agreement was reached through arbitration. In 1993, Alberta's long-ruling Progressive Conservative government began massive cuts to education, leading to AU reducing tutor numbers from 250 to 150 and implementing a 5 percent wage rollback for three years. In 1994, the CUEW disintegrated and the AU tutors became Local 3911 of the Canadian Union of Public Employees (CUPE), Canada's largest union of public sector workers.

While the vast majority of AU tutors have master's and doctoral degrees and many years of teaching experience, they differ from full-time AU faculty in many important ways. Tutors can only be part-time workers; they are prohibited by the university from tutoring full time. However, tutors must still respond to any student request within forty-eight hours, including Saturday and Sunday, and so are constantly on call, unlike full-time faculty, who work a conventional thirty-five-hour work week. Tutors receive lower wages than full-time salaried faculty, with more and more of tutor pay calculated on a "piecework" basis. If tutors do the jobs of higher-paid staff such as course coordinators as temporary replacements, they receive no additional pay. Tutors go through a five-step process of pay rates based on seniority, "topping out" after nine years at a much lower pay level than full-time faculty and taking longer to reach the final level. Full-time faculty top out at a salary of $143,000 per year (plus annual cost of living adjustments) for 1.0 full-time equivalent (FTE).

Full-time AU faculty may also receive various additional salary benefits that are unavailable to tutors. Full-time faculty may augment their salary by overload payments, such as stipends for teaching during spring and summer. They may also receive additional market supplements of up to $15,000 annually, offered by AU to "attract and retain" certain individuals in the face of "competitive market pressures."[1] Full-time AU faculty are also eligible to receive yearly merit increments (one increment = 2.8 percent of a full-time faculty member's salary) for research or service, while tutors do not have this opportunity. At the same time, the university still asks tutors to submit documentation of their research and service in order to enhance the university's reputation.

Tutors receive fewer benefits than full-time faculty, including less medical, dental, and life insurance. Tutor benefits had to be fought for by the tutor union and have only been in place for the last few years, while full-time faculty benefits were granted at the time of the founding of the university. Tutor pensions are much smaller than those of full-time faculty, constituting only 2 percent of the tutor's final salary, compared to 5 percent for full-time faculty. Tutors receive only $300 per year in individual professional development funding, compared to the full-time faculty's $2,000 per year. Full-time faculty are given twenty-one working days of fully paid professional development leave per calendar year while tutors receive none. Full-time faculty also receive twenty-one days of fully paid annual research leave while tutors receive none. According to AU regulations, tutors, unlike faculty, do not have academic freedom but only "academic opinion," which means they are free to "reasonably" express their opinions in response to student queries but must also make such opinions known to the course coordinator.[2]

AU tutors are currently facing a serious attack from the administration, which is also a more veiled attack on full-time faculty because the ultimate aim is to compensate for provincial underfunding of postsecondary education by reducing employee salaries and wages. This goes back to the fact that AU was founded on a very successful model of teaching-learning called the "tutor-learner" model. In this model, students enroll in an AU course and are assigned to a personal tutor whom they consult with, send assignments to, and contact when they need a problem solved. In a sense, the model is an online version of the regular classroom. In the context of online education, the tutor-learner model works well because it provides relational learning, promotes healthy dialogue, and enforces academic rigor in teaching. The innovative tutor-learner model, which is still used in all of AU's schools except the Faculty of Business, is now again under attack by the administration and is on the chopping block as a "cost-saving" measure. This was foreshadowed by a recent cutting of allowed tutor marking time, which also meant a de facto cut in pay.

In the tutor-learner model, the group of students assigned to a tutor is divided up into what are called "blocks," each block averaging 28–40 students (like a classroom). The underlying pedagogical rationale of blocks is that tutors can contact their students directly, engage them in discussion, and carry out administrative work such as grading. Tutors are given a salary called "block pay" as compensation for each block of students they are assigned. Tutors are in addition paid for marking on a piecework basis, based on the

AU computer system's automatic recording of tutor-marked assignments and exams. Tutors long ago concluded from their own experience that online students favor the tutor-learner model, which is not only pedagogically sound but also develops the more personal relationships between tutors and their students that are so critical to quality education, a view supported by the 2012 student union's survey of its student members.[3]

AU now wants to replace the tutor-learner model in AU's Faculty of Humanities and Social Sciences (the faculty that the coauthors teach in) with what AU employees call the "call center" model but what AU now calls the "student support" model, obviously trying to give it a positive spin. The call center model was introduced into the AU Faculty of Business fifteen years ago, and the business tutors and their students have had many negative experiences with it. In the call center model, students are no longer assigned in blocks to a tutor but are left as isolated individuals. Individual students contact a generic call center when they need something or have a problem and are then redirected to whomever the call center respondent thinks is the appropriate person—perhaps an administrator, perhaps a course coordinator, perhaps a tutor. Providing increased support for student requests related to administrative matters in no way precludes retaining the tutor model, even though AU is making this fallacious argument.

The call center model not only eliminates the "electronic classroom" nature of the tutor-learner model but also the block pay salaried aspect of tutor compensation, turning everything tutors do into piecework. This is the real focus of AU's attack on the tutor model: to eliminate tutors' block pay. Under the call center model, tutors have no salaried portion of their wages but instead have to keep track of every minute they spend working—e.g., sending an e-mail, answering a phone call, marking an assignment, and so on—and then spend unpaid time compiling and sending a lengthy, detailed timesheet summarizing all activity to the payroll department. Four different levels of approval of the tutor timesheets are then required. Currently, in the Faculty of Business, there is a large backlog of tutor grievances concerning the denial of tutor timesheet claims by certain gatekeepers, these denials having resulted in the withholding of significant tutor pay.

It is not surprising that the call center model was first implemented in the AU Faculty of Business and is being primarily pushed by that faculty. Clearly, it is a very impersonal business model, not an interactive educational model. In fact, a whole new set of business terms is associated with it: students become "customers" or "clients," courses become "products of consumption," and workers become "knowledge advisors."

AU claims that the call center model is pedagogically better for students than the decades-old tutor-learner model but there is no objective research-based evidence for this. The last AU administration study to compare the two models, completed during 2008-2009, found little difference between the two models; moreover, the authors of the study openly admitted: "Most of the courses (note: taken by the study respondents) appear to have been taken from the Undergraduate Faculty of Business and this appears to have introduced a bias against the Tutor Model."[4] A comprehensive study completed by the AU Student Union in 2012 found that the majority of students preferred the tutor-learner model. This is backed up by the fact that, under the call center model, once students find out who their tutor is, many bypass the call center and contact their tutors directly, as in the older model! The model that is best supported by pedagogical reasons in the view of the tutors, based on their own direct experience and on consultations with students, is the tutor-learner model, and tutors see no reason for it to be replaced.

Tutors are convinced that the real reason AU wants to implement the call center model in the Faculty of Humanities and Social Sciences is mere cost cutting, to reduce AU's investments in the education of their students. Athabasca University is caught up in the capital-centered outlook that tutors are only a cost of production to the university. Its administrators put forth this false argument in order to rationalize the attack on the tutors' wages and benefits. In reality, the tutors are not a cost of production but are the actual producers of value through the teaching service they provide. Cutting tutor wages, under the hoax of "improving pedagogy," will not "save money," but it will degrade the quality of education.[5] Further, AU has no right to dictate the terms of tutor employment by arbitrarily cutting wages and benefits through imposing the call center model or through any other means. The tutors, organized into their defense collective, must be the final arbiter of their wages and benefits, which are their just claims on the added-value they produce through teaching.

## Table 1. A Comparison of the Models

| Tutor Model | Call Center Model |
| --- | --- |
| Education as process | Education as product |
| Teaching/learning | Product consumption |
| Satisfied learner | Unsatisfied customer |
| Academic as educator | Deskilled academic worker |
| Fair compensation | Cheap labor |
| Education as a right | Education for profit |
| Integrity of degree | Degree for sale |

In pushing their call center agenda, AU administrators attempted in June 2012, without consultation or warning, to mandate that the call center model be implemented in the Faculty of Humanities and Social Sciences starting in September 2012. The majority of academics, administrative and clerical workers, and students at Athabasca University immediately and vehemently protested this arbitrary decision. When confronted, the AU administration backed down but continues to argue very unconvincingly that the tutor-learner model is "broken," as one administrator put it, and that the call center model is pedagogically preferable, as well as a "cost saver" and a means of making tutors "more accountable."[6]

To placate the protests of the tutors and others, AU set up a special "consultative" committee in August 2012 to supposedly examine the issue of further instituting the call center model on an objective basis. This committee set up a rapid series of one-hour meetings in September and October 2012, inconveniently scheduled for tutor participation and too short for serious discussion. Also, the committee's terms of reference, as established by the then-VPA (Vice President, Academic), basically state that the committee already agrees that the tutor model is broken, which is an unacceptable, preset agenda. Three meetings of the consultative committee have been held at which tutor representatives and representatives of other groups, including faculty, have proactively opposed the administration's attempt to use the consultative committee meetings to sell the call center model under the ruse of concern for student engagement and retention. Currently, the tutors take the position that the committee is phony (one tutor refers to it as the "zombie committee") and that the General Faculties Council, which is the second highest AU decision-making body (below the board of governors) and includes representatives of faculty, tutors, nonacademic staff, graduate students, and students, as well as the administration, should be the venue for discussing the whole issue.

AU continues to put forth fake pedagogical arguments to cover up that the real reason for the call center model is mere cost cutting. The fact is that the whole impetus for the campaign comes from AU's Strategic Budgeting Committee, acting on a secret report by a well-known international accounting firm, which the AU administration refuses to make available. Like other postsecondary educational institutions in Alberta and most of the rest of the world, AU is under the gun because of the refusal of the Alberta provincial government (each Canadian province has jurisdiction over its education sector) to adequately fund postsecondary educational institutions, using the excuse of a need for "fiscal austerity." Instead of fighting back against underfunding, the AU administration, like the administrations of other Alberta postsecondary institutions, is caving in and perpetuating this underfunding by trying to shift the burden of the crisis onto the tutors and the students. In the summer of 2012, the AU administration was pathetically forced to publicly apologize for illegal donations to the long-ruling provincial Progressive Conservative party.[7]

While AU and other Alberta postsecondary educational institutions are facing funding cuts, which are being vehemently opposed by students, faculty, and staff, the international oil companies that rule Alberta are given billions of dollars by the government to exploit Alberta's huge oil resources and to make big profits. Imperial Oil, Alberta's largest oil company and a subsidiary of Exxon, was the tenth most profitable company in Canada in 2011, while oil sands giant Suncor Energy was fourth.[8] The energy companies are highly paid by the state through subsidies, royalty relief, tax credits, tax deductions, exploration "expenses," capital cost allowances, and special programs such as carbon storage and drilling incentives, while education is starved of funds. The ruling circles of Alberta keep saying that Alberta is a rich province, but if that is the case, then why is postsecondary education denied the funds that it requires?

Some of the key events so far in the struggle against deskilling at AU are:

- Initial and ongoing protests against the attempt to arbitrarily impose the call center model on the tutors
- Effective use of an open electronic mailing list for intensive, very free-wheeling discussion of the issue
- Demand for transparency in internal budget allocations
- Not falling into the trap of supporting "cost saving," which Albertans got caught by in the 1990s when a previous Conservative government made big and very damaging funding cuts to education and other social programs in the fraudulent name of "fiscal austerity," including blowing up a hospital!
- Developing the unity of the tutors, faculty, office workers, graduate students, and students to create a common front against the arbitrariness of the administration
- Rejecting the phony AU consultative committee that is supposedly being set up to objectively study the issue of the two models but has already predetermined its conclusions

The mailing list discussion and the various individual and joint meetings of the tutors, office employees, faculty, graduate students, and students have generated some of the following arguments against the call center model:

- There is no evidence that the call center model is pedagogically better than the tutor-learner model.

- There has been no objective or in-depth research and discussion to compare the two models, except by the AU student union, which has concluded that the tutor model is preferable.
- AU has used and bragged about the tutor-learner model for decades; it is very suspicious that in the face of underfunding it is now implied that this model is suddenly "pedagogically unsound."
- The call center model undermines the critically important pedagogical and professional relationships of tutors with their students, which are vital to learning.
- The call center model is an attack on the working conditions of tutors and specifically aims to turn tutors completely into pieceworkers.
- The call center model could also be used to keep surveillance on tutor activities.
- The call center model may be violating the tutors' collective agreement because removing block pay will be a de facto cut in tutor wages.
- The ultimate aim of implementing the call center model may be to globally outsource the call center work to locations where labor can be paid cheaper wages.

The tutors, their organization, and their allies at AU have already begun action against the arbitrary implementation of the call center model:

- A program of research of the pedagogical value of each of the two competing models is being planned.
- Unity with other employee groups such as faculty and students is being strengthened and will be further developed.
- Open electronic mailing list discussions and meetings and joint meetings with other employees, which have been extremely productive, will be continued. Many who work at AU are experienced political activists who are willing to stand up for their rights and the right to education.
- Pressure will be kept on the administration in various ways, not excluding protests and other forms of collective action.
- The broader issue of holding the Alberta provincial government accountable for guaranteeing the right of everyone in Alberta to post-secondary education will be kept firmly in mind.

The Athabasca tutors, led by their union, will continue to fight against the further implementation of the call center model. It is an arbitrary attack on the right to education, on tutor rights, and on the rights of students. Our students have a right to the best quality education and we as tutors at Athabasca University have the right to Canadian standard wages, Canadian standard working conditions, and job security. These constitute the necessary conditions for us to carry out the critically important job of educating our students to the very best of our abilities and preparing them to make a significant contribution to the future of society.

## NOTES

A version of this paper was presented at the 2012 COCAL Conference in Mexico City on August 10, 2012. The coauthors are both experienced tutors—that is, part-time continuing online teachers—at Athabasca University in Alberta, Canada, as well as contract instructors at several other Edmonton-area universities and colleges. They are also both executive members of Canadian Union of Public Employees Local 3911, the union local representing the AU tutors.

1.  Terry Anderson and Fathi Elloumi, eds., *Theory and Practice of Online Learning* (Athabasca, AB: Athabasca University, 2004).
2.  Athabasca University Governing Council and the Canadian Union of Public Employees, CUPE 3911, Collective Agreement, 2010–2012.
3.  Athabasca University Students' Union (AUSU), *2012 Instructional Model Survey* (Edmonton, AB: AUSU, 2012; *ed@ausu.org*).
4.  David Annand, Kerri Michalczuk, Edward Acquah, Jan Thiessen, Cammy Peden, Cindy Kilborn, and Pamela Quon, *Evaluation of the "Student Support Centre" and "Tutor" Models at Athabasca University* (Athabasca, AB: Athabasca University, 2010), 11–12.
5.  AUSU, *2012 Instructional Model Survey.*
6.  Conversations with Athabasca University administrators, June-July 2012.
7.  Charles Rusnell, "Alberta Colleges, Universities Made Illegal Donations to Tories," *CBC News*, 21 March 2012, *www.cbc.ca.*
8.  "Top 1000: 2011 Rankings of Canada's Top 1000 Public Companies by Profit," *Toronto Globe and Mail Report on Business*, 23 June 2011, 53.

# PART II

## The Two-Tier System in Academe

# 4

# Organizing the New Faculty Majority

The Struggle to Achieve Equality for
Contingent Faculty, Revive Our Unions,
and Democratize Higher Education

*Richard Moser*

The increasing exploitation of contingent faculty is one dimension of a new employment strategy sometimes called the "two-tiered" or "multitiered" labor system. This new labor system is firmly established in higher education and constitutes a threat to the teaching profession. If left unchecked, it will undermine the university's status as an institution of higher learning because the overuse of contingent appointments and their lowly status and compensation institutionalizes disincentives to quality education, threatens academic freedom and shared governance, and disqualifies the campus as an exemplar of democratic values. These new developments in academic labor are the most troubling expressions of the so-called corporatization of higher education.[1]

## Section 1: Revisions to the Academic Social Contract

The period 1972–1977 marked the first surge in the use of adjunct faculty.[2] We look back at the early 1970s as a time when society's existing economic assumptions, sometimes called "the mid-century social contract," underwent profound revision.[3] In higher education the changing times were, and still are, characterized by disinvestment in public education, the ascendancy of a corporate style of management, and the subsequent shifting of costs and risks to those who teach, research, and study.

Consequently, faculty have been slowly transformed into contingent and part-time employees without due process or economic security, with students increasingly forced to carry a greater burden of the costs of higher tuition by taking on debt and having to work to make ends meet. Contingent faculty and graduate assistants now number over one million and constitute the overwhelming majority of faculty appointments.

In the wake of World War II, America's unrivaled economic and political power allowed most Americans to enjoy a remarkable period of economic opportunity. Government promoted and sustained economic growth in part through investment in higher education. The GI Bill, the economic shift toward service industries, and demographic trends dramatically increased student enrollment and changed the character of the student body by making higher education available to working-class families. Higher education underwrote the scientific, technical, and theoretical knowledge necessary for postwar economic activity. Virtually free technology transfers from research universities and government laboratories enriched thousands of business enterprises of all descriptions.[4] Assured of government support and commanding unparalleled resources, business and administrative leaders upheld their end of the bargain by tolerating unions and permitting a rising standard of living for most working people. This social contract prevailed until the mid-1970s.

Despite the big budgets of the 1960s, equitable investments in faculty were not made. In 1959 there was 1 faculty member for every 9.6 students but by 1969 that proportion rose to 1 to 17.8, roughly the same ratio as today.[5] These increases in teaching loads were the first indication that the fate of the faculty was changing.

By the late 1960s the postwar social contract had begun to subvert itself as a result of the multiple crises that came to a head during the Vietnam War. Not only did the war era lead to a crisis of faith in political and cultural institutions but it spurred changes in America's economy.

By the mid-1970s, slower economic growth and heightened global and national competition were evoked to change popular expectations concerning living standards and public expenditures. In a broad historical sense, the accumulated costs of industry and war had become a significant obstacle to maximizing profits, and business leaders sought to shift or externalize those costs. In effect, the new contingent and low-wage workers began to subsidize enterprise with their cheap labor and to stabilize profit margins with their own precarious lives.

The strategy of shifting costs brought an end to the period of rising material wealth for most Americans even as corporate profits grew. As a result, calls for smaller government and lower taxes began to resonate with many and it was the beginning of funding cuts for higher education. As a consequence of these cutbacks, the full-time academic job market contracted, the use of contingent faculty rose sharply, and compensation stalled. Despite almost thirty years of economic growth, the purchasing power of the average full-time professor declined slightly between 1972 and 2000.[6]

The political influence of faculty also began to falter. Today faculty in over twenty states still do not have the basic human right to organize. A growing movement toward unionization among tenure-track faculty at private institutions was effectively quashed when the Supreme Court decided, in the infamous 1980 *Yeshiva* decision, that they were managers and therefore not eligible for collective bargaining rights.[7]

The remaining bonds of the mid-century social contract were torn apart when Ronald Reagan fired striking air traffic controllers and staffed the National Labor Relations Board with members hostile to workers' rights. Reagan's policies seemed to deny labor's role as a legitimate part of the social order.[8] During the same years, Republicans and Democrats passed new tax, budget, money, and debt policies that would lay the groundwork for an almost unprecedented redistribution of wealth from the vast majority of working people to the richest Americans, with the greatest gains being made by the top 1 percent. These changes weakened the political and economic leverage of professional associations, trade unions, and the people they represented.[9]

Most important for the topic at hand, the two-tiered or multitiered workforce, which had been taking shape in academia since the early 1970s, became one of the most effective strategies for realizing corporate and administrative goals. The government bailout of Chrysler in 1979–1980 gave official imprimatur and union approval to two-tiered arrangements.

In the typical two-tiered system, new or younger employees are not offered the same level of compensation or job security as existing staff. The body of teacher-scholars was fragmented and reworked into a system that included tenure and tenure-track faculty, full-time non-tenure-eligible faculty, part-time faculty, postdoctoral researchers, clinical faculty, a growing variety of academic professionals, and graduate student employees.

According to John W. Curtis, director of research and public policy for the AAUP, the change in faculty status has been nothing less than profound. In 1975, the number of contingent faculty (full- and part-time faculty, plus graduate teaching assistants) off the tenure track was 54.9 percent of the total profession. By 2009, the contingent faculty were 75.5 percent—the overwhelming majority of faculty appointments. When considered as a proportion of the total growth of faculty appointments, the seismic shift is starkly revealed. Between 1995 and 2009, 92.4 percent of the increase in faculty appointments can be attributed to the growth in contingent positions. Part-time faculty appointments went from 24 percent of all teaching positions in 1975 to 30 percent in 1989, 33 percent in 1995, 37 percent in 2003, and 41 percent as of fall 2009.[10]

In *The American Faculty: The Restructuring of Academic Work and Careers*, Jack H. Schuster and Martin J. Finkelstein have comprehensively documented this "unprecedented" change in higher education. Their definitive research is organized around the thesis that "change in higher education surely has never been so rapid or so pervasive."[11]

This multitiered approach succeeded, in part, because it blunted opposition by promising not to affect existing constituencies. In fact, if enough full-time positions were converted to contingent ones, an administration's total labor costs declined while allowing compensation for the top tier to improve, at least in the short run. The evil genius of the multitier system was that it enticed the tenured faculty with short-term benefits and lured contingent faculty with what seemed a reasonable expectation—that they would gain valuable experience in a highly competitive job market.

The faculty continue to cooperate in their own demise but rarely by formal decree. No faculty senate or union ever explicitly agreed to abolish tenure for the majority of future faculty so that departmental labor costs could be reduced for introductory courses or sabbaticals, but such complicity is rarely formalized. When faculty did assent to the creation of new non-tenure-track appointments, it usually had been sold to them as one small exception at a time, sweetened with administrative assurances of future restraint, and absent any discussion of the larger picture. At worst, faculty senates or union contracts yielded to demands for two-tiered arrangements or resisted attempts at reform. The good news about faculty complicity in the new system is that it depends on such complicity to continue. When the faculty decide that having easily exploitable labor on hand is not worth risking the destruction of the university and the profession along with it, then the system will at long last be reformed.

### The New Corporate Model of Education

"Corporatization" is the name sometimes given to what has happened to higher education since the mid-century social contract was overthrown. Corporatization is the reorganization of our great national resources, including higher education, in accordance with a shortsighted business model. Three decades of decline in public funding for higher education opened the door for increasing corporate influence and, since then, the work of the university has been redirected to suit the corporate vision.

The most striking symptoms of corporatization shift costs and risks downward and direct capital and authority upward. Rising tuition and debt loads for students limit access to education for working-class students. Faculty and many other campus workers suffer lower compensation as the number and pay for management rises sharply. Campus management concentrates resources on areas where wealth is created and new ideas and technologies developed at public cost become the entitlement of the corporate sector. The privatization and outsourcing of university functions and jobs from food service to bookstores to instruction enrich a few businessmen and create more low-wage non-union jobs. More authoritarian governance practices have become the "new normal."

The liberal arts and all areas of research not conducive to the creation of wealth are faced with austerity. It seems that the universities' internal budgets remain in perpetual crisis as funding declines and more demanding accounting devices are established, thereby making each department, program, or school reliant on their own self-generated resources. This new financial "rigor" in instruction and research has tended to starve the core liberal arts mission while promoting entertainment venues and real estate development.

The search for truth, critical thinking, intellectual creativity, academic standards, scientific invention, and the ideals of citizenship have been discounted in favor of maximizing profits, vocational training, career success, applied research, and bottom-line considerations.[12]

Three types of related issues—instructional, curricular, and professional—emerge from the increased use of contingent faculty in the context of corporatization.

Contingent faculty and graduate students often deliver excellent instruction, but I must emphasize that this is in spite of their working conditions. Most contingent faculty and graduate assistants are so poorly compensated and teach so many students that there are powerful disincentives to quality instruction.

To professionally evaluate and mentor adjuncts and graduate students would take an enormous resource commitment from full-time staff that would work against the fiscal imperatives responsible for the use of adjuncts in the first place. Instead, contingent faculty members often are forced to rely solely on students to evaluate their work. It is reasonable to expect that such a system of evaluation makes teachers vulnerable to student pressure for better grades, or reluctant to teach controversial subjects or engage in stressful disputes over plagiarism and cheating.[13]

Furthermore, when the job of teaching is separated from the job of establishing curriculum and developing programs, faculty become mere delivery systems of standardized content. People hired for the short term have no incentive to understand or question the long-term educational goals of the college. Similar disincentives exist for contingent faculty to develop long-term relationships with students. As a result, fewer faculty members will know students well and advising will suffer. As a multidisciplinary conference on part-time work concluded, the nature of "the terms and conditions of these appointments, in many cases, weakens our capacity to provide essential educational experiences and resources" and therefore "are inadequate to support responsible teaching or, by extension a career."[14]

Finally, and most important, the new academic labor system has fragmented the faculty, weakening their ability to act as a constituency. Tenure has lost support from both junior faculty and faculty on the lower tiers, rendering the profession less able to defend its central institution. Without due process and full access to governance, the professoriate loses its ability to govern in the conventional manner, hence the turn to unionization as an additional means of advancing professional standards and values.

The political aspect is decisive. The multitier personnel system has produced classic "divide and conquer" effects that can be addressed by demanding more tenured positions, and dramatically increasing the compensation and due process rights of the contingent faculty. Drawing the tiers closer together in status and standing would serve the long-term interest of the teaching profession. It is no coincidence that tenure-track compensation sagged and tenure requirements and review escalated as the profession fractured.

The fragmentation of the profession is driven by administrators; yet, faculty members are also often complicit in the transformation of tenure from a right into a privilege by allowing or even encouraging the escalation of the requirements for tenure. The traditional prerogatives of faculty, in terms of having a voice in the standing and status of 75 percent of the profession, have been lost; the 17 percent of faculty already with tenure compensate for this lost power by showing how tough they are on the remaining 8 percent eligible for tenure. Can we believe that the attacks on tenure or the increasingly unrealistic requirements for tenure are concerned with quality or accountability when there is almost no concern for the professional evaluation, recognition, and support of the 75 percent of the faculty off the tenure track?

The overuse and abuse of contingent faculty is a threat to academic freedom and intellectual innovation. Contingent faculty find their teaching constrained by fear of the uncontested right administrations have to "non-renewal."[15]

In an address to the American Council of Learned Societies, Clifford Geertz, one of our most influential scholars, recounted his own career, calling it "a charmed life, in a charmed time. An errant career, mercurial, various, free . . . and not all that badly paid." Geertz continued:

> The question is: Is such a life and such a career available now? In the Age of Adjuncts? When graduate students refer to themselves as "the pre-unemployed"? . . . Has the bubble burst? . . . It is difficult to be certain. . . . But there does seem to be a fair amount of malaise about, a sense that things are tight and growing tighter . . . and that it is probably not altogether wise just now to take unnecessary chances, strike new directions, or offend the powers. Tenure is harder to get (I understand it takes two books now, and God knows how many letters . . .), and the process has become so extended as to exhaust the energies and dampen the ambitions of those caught up in it. . . .

All I know is that, up until just a few years ago, I used . . . to tell students and younger colleagues . . . that they should stay loose, take risks, resist the cleared path, avoid careerism, go their own way, and that if they did so, if they kept at it and remained alert, optimistic, and loyal to the truth, my experience was that they could . . . have a valuable life, and nonetheless prosper. I don't do that any more.[16]

The struggle to reform the new academic labor system is a struggle about freedom. It is fundamentally a political issue and an invitation to citizenship that none of us can afford to refuse. As the number of administrators grows and that of full-time tenure-track faculty declines, the balance of power in the university shifts away from educators. Participation in governance has been based on the idea that dissenting opinion can be exercised without the fear of reprisals. But without the protections of tenure, are non-tenure-track faculty really free to engage in discussion or comment critically on administrative policy?

I am most deeply concerned about the example that the university itself is setting in regard to intellectual activity, citizenship, and democracy. What lessons are being taught to aspiring young academics when they realize that all of their foundational courses are being delivered by people who earn what they did at their summer jobs? What values are being learned when those who teach and research—who esteem the intellect and hold high the values of citizenship—are apparently held in low regard by society and by the university community itself? The lessons are all too clear: teaching and learning—the pursuit of the truth—are unworthy activities. We learn that it is acceptable to exploit someone if you can get away with it. We learn that it is acceptable to discriminate against someone based on the fact that they belong to a certain class of employees. We learn to pay lip service to art or science or history or literature, but that money is what really matters. Exploiting cheap labor to teach is teaching of the worst sort.

What to do about it? *The primary obstacle is, as usual, in our own minds.* Too many of us believe that these developments are the inevitable outcome of some juggernaut, usually the free market. Indeed, that is how corporatization is presented by its advocates.

In this context, the free market is primarily a cultural and political artifact; it is a rationale, a managerial tool, and a means to blunt resistance. Rather than apply our professional standards, or understand our history, we are supposed to shrug because the new standards of the market reign supreme. Market ideology now functions to foreclose other alternatives. But, history has its uses. History helps us to broaden our view with alternative understandings and suggests that our personal struggles have political meanings.

I look at higher education and I do not despair. Everywhere I see a growing consciousness about the new academic labor system and corporatization, and an increasing willingness to take action to defend higher education. Academic citizenship is on the rise, unionization continues, and the engaged citizen-scholar is emerging as a new model for academic life. There is, after all, no professional activity more important than the exercise of academic citizenship. Only activism, organizing, and effective shared governance can create and advance the conditions on which all of our teaching and research depend.

## Section 2: The Challenge of Organizing Contingent Faculty

Contingent workers are the second-class citizens of the workplace. While these workers are employed in a wide range of settings, from day laborers to college professors, they share precarious terms of employment, lacking job security, full benefits, or the expectation of continued employment. Contingent workers are usually considered among the most challenging segment of the workforce to organize and mobilize and that holds true for contingent faculty as well.

The obstacles confronting contingent activists and organizers pose important problems for the entire labor movement, but may also be sources of insight for the larger movement, particularly a movement intent on reinventing itself. The regenerative potential of organizing nonstandard workers is the flip side of the danger part-time and multitier employment practices pose.

The task of organizing contingent workers requires that the labor movement do things it must do to renew itself: develop new forms of solidarity, learn creative and innovative tactics and strategies, and commit significant resources to organizing. At the very least, contingent organizers must form coalitions that look beyond the individual workplace for allies and levers of power. Contingent organizing places the nagging question of union democracy and member initiative on the agenda. Contingent faculty issues challenge many of the existing cultural norms and assumptions of academic life and draw our attention to things we would rather forget: the transformation of the faculty role, the corporatization of higher education, and the need for faculty activism.

The problems facing union-minded contingent faculty are increasingly well understood by faculty activists, and a growing body of literature on the subject is emerging.[17] Let me start by discussing the union drive that aims to organize a unit composed solely of contingent faculty. The "stand-alone" unit deserves our attention not because it is necessarily preferable but because it highlights the problems and strengths inherent in contingent campaigns of all kinds.

The conventional view of organizing assumed that working people prepared themselves for unionization through the experience of common problems and were already organized as a collectivity by work itself. The spontaneous organizing function of the workplace can no longer be taken for granted, as the political power and mobility of capital, rapid transportation, and real-time global communications have enabled corporate elites to achieve flexibly by segmenting, moving, and dispersing the production of goods and services, and by churning the workforce.

On campus this has translated into the segmentation of the faculty into multiple tiers that are further fragmented by scores of titles and appointment types. Democratic shared governance in all its forms has been weakened and professional working conditions have been eroded for all but a shrinking elite.

Guided by a common set of managerial assumptions, financial restraints, and political priorities, campus managers have created a new academic labor system with international implications that nonetheless remains chaotic and arbitrary in local detail. Faculty unionists first engage these challenges as immediate and practical problems with organizing.

### The Organizing Drive

Contingent faculty face daunting obstacles to self-organization because the decentralized, fragmented, transitory, and insecure character of their jobs inhibits the development of a visible community of interest. Yet, it is precisely a visible community that organizers conventionally strive for. The lack of accountability and uniformity in the new labor arrangements means it is difficult for contingent faculty to identify, locate, and contact each other using standard institutional research methods. Contingent faculty often know few of their immediate colleagues personally, so information cannot easily flow along the lines of established networks.

Like other working people in the United States, contingent faculty are hamstrung by a legal system that favors the employer and limits workers' rights. By contrast, workers in Canada enjoy greater freedom and unionization has proceeded more rapidly. In both countries, however, contingent faculty remain fearful because they lack tenure and due process rights. Fear and insecurity make for rough going, and most successful union drives begin with long periods of covert preparation. During and sometimes even after a winning union drive, activists may shun public roles, and organizers must be aware that a few suspicious "non-renewals" can demobilize many potential activists.

Like social movement organizers outside the workplace, contingent faculty activists must invent their community as they go. Faculty activists strive to create community and solidarity by gathering information, establishing communications, reaching out to the broader community, and concentrating resources, all with an eye toward protecting the union's leadership from attack. Luckily, the contingent relationship does provide a certain amount of cover, allowing activists to use secrecy and anonymity to their best advantage.

Fear and isolation can be overcome, but take care in the early stages. Gather information without exposing activists to harm. Avoid chairs and deans. Since the best information exists on the departmental level, the usually sympathetic support staff can provide list of contingent faculty, but it is wise to acquire as much information as possible while the drive is still covert. Some institutional websites will list contingent faculty, but they are often inaccurate, incomplete, and can be taken down. Tenured faculty allies can get lists and are important sources of information about who is working where. The organizers must continually edit the list, using their growing contacts. List management is an essential skill in all organizing drives, but particularly so in drives among contingent workers.[18]

Make office visits if possible, but contingent faculty are often without private offices and are better contacted before or after class or at home. Phone banking has been a very successful means of reaching colleagues while maintaining confidentiality and minimizing risks. Calls work best on the heels of a mailing to the home address. Faculty may also be contacted by e-mail or through websites, although contingent faculty are understandably wary of using their campus accounts for sensitive communications.

Small group meetings and social events held off campus have also proven worthwhile. Happy hours in the local tavern or receptions with free food and drink are good ways for people to meet each other. Have a house party and ask students from music or other performing arts to provide the entertainment.

While public events have proven to be of very limited utility for initiating contacts with faculty, they are an excellent means of informing the campus community about the issues. Film showings of Barbara Wolf's *Degrees of Shame* or *A Simple Matter of Justice: Contingent Faculty Organize* are good ways to start building community support, and those events can be led by tenured faculty or student leaders.[19]

The political and technical problems that beset the early stages of organizing drives are balanced, however, by the deep grievances contingent faculty bear. Years of exploitation and abuse make union supporters of most adjuncts. To tap the positive potential of contingency, activists become comfortable with organizing techniques that fly in the face of long-established norms for faculty organizing. Mailings, phone calls, newsletters, and e-mail can all be used to great effect, while they are largely ineffective with tenure-stream faculty. Unlike their tenured colleagues, contingent faculty overwhelmingly vote to form unions. Despite relatively modest turnout for elections, very few union efforts among contingent faculty are lost. Successful organizers "file light," with the percentage of authorization cards just above the legal minimums, yet win with comfortable margins.

The true labor market for contingent faculty is often regional or metropolitan, with individuals working at multiple institutions. In Chicago and Boston, and more recently, the District of Columbia, organized unions have acted as hubs that seed neighboring campuses with experienced activists. This has commonly taken the form of individual organizers extending their political work to the second or third institutions at which they teach. Farsighted organizers swap duties, organizing at campuses that do not currently employ them. Contingent organizers dream of the day citywide or regional hiring halls or multiunion organizing centers can be established, but early attempts have failed for lack of sufficient resources, union density, and resolve.

Our inability to adjust organizing attempts to real metropolitan or regional labor markets result in a disconnection between the capacity of academic unions and the source of labor's potential power. Unions become powerful when they limit competition between workers by controlling the work itself. That control cannot be effectively achieved on an individual campus level unless the campus is geographically isolated. The metropolitan or regional organizing strategy remains high on the agenda of activists, but the current national leadership of the US academic labor movement has not had the commitment, daring, or vision to risk such a venture. Until such leadership emerges, individual unions are the best building blocks of a regional strategy and we are left little choice but to organize campus by campus.[20]

The advantages contingent faculty have early in the drive are converted into disadvantages once the contract campaign has begun, since successful elections often require only the bare minimum of self-organization. The real problem with contingent faculty organizing is not winning elections but creating dynamic, member-run unions.

Often, a new union is confronted with creating itself as an organization during the contract campaign. Experience suggests that contingent contract campaigns should be politicized early on, but many new unions lack the power to mobilize large numbers of their still-vulnerable members or to convince their affiliates to pursue labor-intensive and costly contract campaigns. Whatever limits exist, abandon hope that clever bargaining strategies or reason will prevail. Public and visible pressure should, however, produce results. Metropolitan and regional strategies, community campaigns, and coalition-building are valuable and perhaps indispensable means of addressing faculty fears and winning contracts with real benefits.[21]

Activist students are interested in labor issues and can help to provide the political muscle for contract campaigns. Student newspapers are essential forums for labor issues and student governments and activist organizations will rally to the side of their teachers. Support from student organizations (like United Students Against Sweatshops) or labor-community groups (such as Jobs with Justice, the Coalition of Contingent Academic Labor), or the New Faculty Majority) can be decisive. Outreach to parents, alumni, and other unions and activists may also be required.

Contingent faculty unions often have difficulty negotiating good contracts. Of all the things administrations are willing to concede, job security is the last, because job security strikes at the heart of the contingent status and begins to fundamentally alter the employment relation. Yet, without job security of some sort, everything else a union might win at the table will remain in jeopardy.

In the face of multiple political disadvantages, faculty unions are tempted to provide support in the form of staff members, and union members are inclined to accept such support. Despite the enormous progress made over the last decade, the question of whether or not contingent faculty can create their own vital and democratic unions—ones that do not overly rely on staff resources—remains an open question. Perhaps we are just approaching the threshold of rank-and-file-activism, but the answer to this question may well determine the fate of the contingent faculty movement.

While headcount is up, and victories are scored, the pace of organizing remains painfully slow. The number of contingent faculty activists, while growing, still falls far short of what is needed, and many leaders burn out or go on to other pursuits. Although unions of all descriptions sometimes suffer the same problems, many contingent faculty unions struggle simply to survive.

As a long-term professional staffer at both national and local levels, I am not trying to minimize the important, even sometimes decisive, role of professional staff. Nor am I suggesting that there are easy answers to our dilemmas. But the tendency to substitute money, technocratic expertise, or temporary staff organizers for rank-and-file activism will not, in the long run, produce either real solidarity or a movement capable of defending academic freedom rights or securing professional compensation. At the very least, here is what history suggests: every major upsurge in the labor movement has been based on the self-organization and initiative of working people, and I doubt that our time is that much different. Perhaps staff-run unions are the best we can manage for the time being, but our resort to emergency measures should be accompanied by a humility born of the awareness that, in truth, there are no shortcuts.

Staff members should carefully consider how they can best facilitate the development of local leadership and initiative. Social movement unionism can provide staff and leaders with a vision best suited to achieving the long-term goals of faculty organizing.

## Organizing across the Tiers

In campaigns that combine contingent and tenure-track faculty, many of the issues discussed in the previous section remain relevant, except that important synergies are more likely, even at the risk of intense internal divisions. Contingent faculty can provide the margin of victory in closely contested organizing drives, since many tenure-track faculty elections are decided by relatively few votes. Farsighted tenured faculty can shield contingent activists from reprisals and provide the political weight that adjuncts often lack in making their issues a top priority at the bargaining table.

The question of whether to organize jointly with tenured faculty or in stand-alone units is a perennial one, and the answer is specific to the political, cultural, and legal environment. Such decisions are made properly only after close examination of local conditions. Some states, such as New Jersey, forbid combined units. Ohio and Michigan effectively strip part-time faculty of the basic right to free association. The *Yeshiva* decision forces part-time faculty at private institutions into stand-alone units because it prohibits unionization by tenure-track faculty. To date, *Yeshiva*'s implications for full-time contingent faculty remains untested.

The history regarding stand-alone or combined units is a mixed one. Among graduate student employees, as well as some community college faculty, some instructors in Quebec, and full-time contingent faculty, conditions favor stand-alone units. Stand-alone unions can focus their time, energy, and attention on their own agenda and avoid having their interests ignored.

For the majority of contingent faculty, the best contracts and working conditions have been the result of combined bargaining units.[22] Combined unions allow faculty to share resources, to benefit from greater control over the work, and to fight out their differences prior to bargaining. Combined units can more effectively blunt divide-and-conquer management strategies. They also reinforce core union values such as solidarity and mutuality. The positive potential of combined units is not, however, automatic, and was often realized only after sustained political efforts by contingent faculty.

Perhaps the best arrangement is a best-of-both-worlds approach. At Rutgers, part-time lecturers have a separate union and bargaining unit; it has its own officers, bylaws, and contract but works cooperatively with full-time faculty and graduate employees in an umbrella organization styled the "Council of Chapters." This arrangement allows the contingent faculty to enjoy the resources and solidarity of the larger full-time unit, but the lecturers maintain independent leadership and control over their bargaining agenda.

When contingent faculty are included in the same union with the tenure-track faculty, they may well benefit from forming a rank-and-file caucus. The caucus is an organizational form long employed by marginalized people, minority groups, and dissidents to articulate their perspectives and help bolster their political power. Caucuses are interest groups inside the union that can pursue demands for negotiations, act as voting blocs, and educate the community regarding contingent faculty issues. Caucuses can also effectively lead membership drives or mobilization efforts. A caucus usually meets separately, develops its own priorities, and elects its own leadership before making its case before the entire union. Progressive tenured leaders support such efforts because rank-and-file caucuses help revive slumbering unions.

An alert union leadership will find that contingent issues resonate well with students, legislators, and the public. Similarly, the regional, community, and coalition strategies, and the desire to organize the unorganized that are necessary for contingent unionization, are also important for the wider labor movement. The California Faculty Association of the California State University system and the Professional Staff Congress of the City University of New York are leading examples of large unions that have reformed and rejuvenated themselves, in part, by paying close attention to contingent faculty issues and activists. The members of the Canadian Association of University Teachers have tasked themselves with the bold but achievable goal of the complete unionization of contingent faculty in Canada. The Campaign for the Future of Higher Education (CFHE) promises new directions in organizing across the tiers. Composed of tenure-track and contingent faculty from all kinds of institutions and drawn from all major unions, the CFHE is a grassroots attempt to assure access to affordable education and protect the quality of higher education. The experiences of these and other progressive organizations suggest that contingent faculty will step forward and become more active participants if their issues are taken seriously or their job security improves.

Overall, however, contingency has been an obstacle to local self-organization. While faculty activists exist in small numbers on almost every unorganized campus and have organized caucuses or played leadership roles in many unions, contingent faculty as a whole tend to lower levels of participation in union activity. Perhaps lower levels of activism are to be expected from people with precarious lives, but the ambivalent relationship and checkered history between unions and contingent faculty have made many people wary of sticking their neck out.

For three decades, union leaders and many full-time tenured faculty ignored contingent issues and treated adjuncts as second-class citizens or simply as invisible. Negative attitudes were often expressed as snobbery and bias, similar to other forms of prejudice. Contingent issues were viewed as special pleading, or unimportant, and traded away at the bargaining table in favor of issues that mattered to more powerful constituencies.

On the institutional level, the class bias against contingent faculty fits comfortably within the framework of conventional or business unionism.

Part-time and contingent faculty have low salaries, pay low dues, and require significant investments of union resources. A union with a business-oriented view or scarce resources sees contingent workers as bad investments. This shortsighted view has saved little and purchased only trouble. Avoidance, denial, and union practices corresponding to the lost world of the mid-twentieth century have encouraged administrations and corporations to increasingly turn toward the hard-to-organize contingent workforce. While there has been a promising shift in the attitudes of union leaders since 1998, mistrust and failure continue to haunt organizing efforts.

To compensate for the political and economic disadvantages faced by contingent faculty and the limitations of the unions, contingent faculty organizers devised a movement-building strategy that includes but is broader than unions.

### Community Organizing for Quality Education

Contingency increases the relative power of the administration by lopping off constituencies—rendering peripheral and powerless a significant proportion of the faculty. The marginalized segments of the workforce become subject to the wishes and whims of management rather than to good-faith negotiations or collegial relations. As a result, contingent faculty do not have to be treated as a constituency with its own interests or authority.

This more authoritarian style of campus governance devalues democratic practices and is a telling example of what higher education is becoming. "Fairness" or "equity" has emerged from the contingent faculty movement as the central rhetorical strategy to redress this imbalance of power and to reconstruct the campus body politic.

The first aspect of equity is: equal work deserves equal pay. Equal compensation for equivalent work has a time-honored appeal to fairness and justice that people can connect to their own lives and is very popular among contingent faculty. While equal compensation will relieve the financial strain many teachers suffer and discourage the overuse of contingent appointments, it does not address the insecurity inherent to contingent appointments.

Recent breakthroughs in the United States and Canada have emphasized the non-monetary aspects of equity: equal work deserves equal rights. Equality in rights assumes that all faculty work demands the same kinds of safeguards to protect academic freedom because all faculty work is essential to the educational mission and should be respected as such. The concept of equal rights simply means first-class citizenship with access to due process and job security or tenure.

Increasingly contingent faculty contracts recognize some principle of job security, be it a form of seniority, multiyear contracts, assumption of continuing employment, or establishing standards for just cause for dismissal. The California Faculty Association's contract is widely considered a model for job security provisions in the United States. The Lecturer Employee Organization at the University of Michigan and the Lecturers' Union at the University of California, both AFT locals and both stand-alone unions, have also made significant breakthroughs on job security. In a few rare but notable cases, such as at Western Michigan University, the San Francisco Art Institute, and Vancouver Community College, tenure eligibility or its equivalent has been achieved, essentially solving the problems of contingent work.

Equity in compensation and rights are the essential goals of the movement, but they will not be achieved without placing another, more unconventional form of equity at the forefront: teachers' working conditions are equivalent to the conditions under which students learn.

Faculty and students have a shared fate. Just try to imagine how the quality of education can be advanced while the educational practitioner is being degraded. Every accommodation that faculty must make in face of insecurity, overwork, and lack of resources and office space diminishes the material conditions of the students' educational experience. The curriculum will lose its vitality as its authorship slips from the hands of teachers. The energy, freedom, and careful attention that good teaching and research require have already been compromised.

Union campaigns must focus on the student-teacher relationship because it lies at the heart of our mission as educators and is our connection to the broader community, the common good, and grassroots political power.

Academic unions will achieve justice only by creating a broad and energetic movement that reaches beyond the faculty to include our students, their parents, and other campus workers, as well as allies in other unions, the general public, and government.[23] In order to build political strength, unions must address issues of concern to the public—access to quality education and everything it implies for critical thinking, citizenship, and economic well-being. In other words, we must speak not just for the interests of the faculty but for the common good. We can introduce our message by demonstrating how working conditions for teachers are also learning conditions for students.

Coalition-building and public education is being undertaken by two related activist networks. Supported by contributions from unions, associations, and foundations, the Coalition of Contingent Academic Labor (COCAL) has developed an international community of interest and the New Faculty Majority (NFM) has become the first full-time advocate for contingent faculty outside of unions. COCAL and NFM work because they are independent vehicles that rely on and facilitate grassroots activism.

COCAL and NFM activists are both inside and outside the formal union structure.

Using this inside-outside approach, activists have, particularly since 1998, altered the landscape of academic unionism. In addition to picking up the pace of unionization, coalition work has led to more progressive policies on behalf of national unions and associations; stimulated coalitional efforts in Massachusetts, Illinois, and California, as well as in Canada; and dramatically increased public awareness and faculty consciousness. An international network of leaders has emerged, marking a crucial step forward for faculty organizing.

The coalition strategy has succeeded because it is tactically flexible and adaptive. Each local group controls its own message and activities. Local autonomy allows for the possibility of building unity without requiring uniformity.

COCAL and NFM facilitate communications, hold conferences, stimulate strategic thinking, and promote an international week of action. Called Fair Employment Week (FEW) and Semaine des Enseignants et Enseignantes à Statut Précaire (SEESP) in Canada, and Campus Equity Week (CEW) in the United States, the first time this week of action was held marked the first time all the major faculty unions and associations had come together to promote faculty activism.[24]

Among the many types of activities held during the week of action, the "Contingent Faculty Rights Hearing" best captures the coalition-building work and the community and public-interest aspects of Campus Equity Week. Based on the Workers' Rights hearing boards innovated by Jobs with Justice, contingent faculty rights hearings call on community members—tenured faculty, clergy, alumni, students, parents, legislators, and others—to serve on a "board of notables" that receives testimony from contingent faculty and students. The board of notables listens to evidence regarding the lack of professional working conditions and its consequences for education. The hearing draws media attention to the issues and brings the weight of public opinion to bear on higher education's dirty little secret.[25]

The coalition-building and community-organizing approach employed by contingent faculty is typical of contingent worker campaigns in general and the kind of strategy the labor movement must adopt to reverse its decline.

### Reorganizing the Life of the Mind

The ascendancy of corporate capitalism has given credence to the idea that the campus should model itself on business activity. Yet we must admit that the corporate recasting of higher education draws some of its power, and wins people's assent, from widely shared cultural and ideological assumptions about the contemporary economy. Faculty activists who aim to address contingency will ultimately have to undertake a long and challenging struggle for hearts and minds.

While corporatization includes a wide-ranging set of ideas, the most relevant to keeping contingent faculty in their place are the free market, merit, and scarcity. Market ideology, merit, and scarcity lead the campus community to see contingency and economic exploitation as the fitting outcome of normal economic activity.

In American popular consciousness, and in our own minds, the market still appears as the great and inexorable agent of history, distributing rewards to those who deserve them and punishing those who violate the logic of supply and demand. The morality of the market is self-interest and merit. The strong rise to the top and the weak are vanquished. Market ideology suggests that growing contingency is not an outcome of policy choices or historical developments but rather the result of the overproduction of advanced degrees with contingent faculty representing the less able.

Market ideas cannot account for the historic rise in the numbers of contingent faculty unless we are to believe that the academic labor pool is now composed of six hundred thousand more substandard faculty than it was in 1975, and that today's educational managers and academic departments simply sorted them into their appropriate tiers according to their merit.

Market ideology invites us to believe that the campus is a kind of laissez-faire utopia in which merit can be accurately assessed and appropriately rewarded. According to this view, it seems that academic jobs went begging after 1975 and were filled with less than qualified faculty who were being graduated at unprecedented levels.

What of the senior faculty who trained and placed many of these unqualified individuals? Are they guilty of unprofessional conduct or outright fraud? To follow the logic of the market argument is to indict the whole faculty, is it not?

This market and merit narrative also cannot account for the fact that demand has surged since the 1970s and will continue to rise. Are students demanding only substandard faculty (to stay with the market metaphor) or those without health care, offices, or tenure? In fact, if all the contingent jobs were converted to full-time tenured positions, there would be a job for almost every PhD produced. Supply and demand does not function in education as it should in a free market for a reason: higher education is not a free market.

The free market—the merit-driven market—does not describe higher education, nor does it describe our current economic system. No successful CEO of a major corporation would base a business plan or their personal compensation package on it. In our real, mixed economy, markets continue to operate but the public and private sectors are joined, and state and corporate actors shape markets through planning and policymaking.[26] Individual merit still matters, but it is difficult to quantify precisely and often overshadowed by misguided priorities, palace politics, and personality.[27]

Too tight a focus on merit leads one to miss the point. Our economy is political. Who has what is a manifestation primarily of power and only marginally of merit. Instead, contingency and declining budgets for higher education have resulted from policy choices and political struggles. Public actors chose to disinvest in higher education as educational managers opted to cut labor costs and shift institutional priorities away from instruction.

Quality concerns, on the other hand, do matter. As I suggest here, they must be at the forefront of our political strategy. The concerns over quality education are a byproduct of an educational system that actually institutionalized disincentives to quality and threatens to degrade the work of all faculty. The constitution of the campus—that is, its labor practices and policies, governance structures, and power relations—is its most important pedagogy, and on the face of it can compromise the quality of education. By abusing contingent faculty, administrations teach a hidden curriculum, in which learning is not worthy of commitment or recognition, and democracy is a luxury we can ill afford.

Market ideology draws its urgency from the perception of scarcity. Scarcity is morally persuasive if it results from shortfalls in natural resources or production. But, somehow, we are to believe that the richest country in the history of the world just does not have enough money for education. If we treat the hundreds of billions of dollars set aside for war and empire building, corporate welfare and subsidies, tax breaks, prisons, the truly vast inequities in wealth, and plain old-fashioned corruption as inevitable or sacrosanct, then we have internalized the politics and policies of the Reagan era as much of the political establishment has.

Since the early 1980s, socially constructed scarcity has paraded as an inevitable result of impersonal economics or individual merit. Consequently, we are more willing to accept shrinking budgets and everything that shrinkage means for education.

The idea of scarcity remains an important obstacle to organizing because it demoralizes our unions, inflames short-term conflicts of interest, and narrows our vision of the possible. By discouraging the higher education community from recognizing their common, long-term interests, scarcity inhibits us from staging the kind of grassroots political activity necessary to address budgetary problems. Scarcity politics trickles down to our contract negotiations, where its most pernicious effects are felt.

For the last thirty years, the standard administrative bargaining position has been that the budget is a zero-sum game (not counting the administrators' own salaries, of course) and that salary increases for tenure-track faculty take away what's available to contingents and vice versa. Yet, a historically informed view contradicts this zero-sum thinking. If the salaries for one tier of the faculty depend on the depressed compensation of the other tier, then we could expect that after decades of substandard pay and benefits for contingent faculty, the tenured faculty should be riding high. Instead, we see salary stagnation for tenured faculty and declining budgets for education. Scarcity politics are deployed through zero-sum arguments, and if we believe them, we have yielded to one of the primary divide-and-conquer strategies of contemporary politics.

Historical perspective is a good antidote to market ideology. Contingency is more fruitfully understood in the context of the decline of the mid-century social contract, the ascendancy of managerialism, and the creation of a new academic labor system based on multitiered personnel structures. The ongoing transformation of the faculty role is the result of political decisions and policy choices made by people that can be changed by people. The real question is: are we up to the challenge? That question is all the more urgent in the wake of the economic collapse of 2008. How well has free-market ideology and managerialism served us? Amid the pain, new opportunities abound. It is a teachable moment and time for new organizing and new initiatives.

Contingent faculty have organized unions because they are the only institutions capable of the educational and organizational work needed to achieve some measure of justice. Yet it is unlikely that conventional unionism is up to the task. To find the necessary levers of power, successful faculty activists will have to reach out to the wider community and articulate their demands as part of an ambitious social movement aimed at transforming the campus and reviving democracy. In that way the demands for proportional compensation, job security, and shared governance are not simply the demands for self-interest but part of a larger political project.

Contingent faculty organizing can be usefully understood by locating contingent faculty issues within their broader political and historical context. The problems facing contingent faculty are not unique to them alone but pose a challenge to the entire profession. The labor movement among contingent faculty is politically significant, not only because they are now the majority, but also because the mass de-tenuring of the faculty is the cutting edge of managerial authority and corporatization.

The struggle of contingent faculty to organize themselves and to achieve academic freedom, workplace democracy, and fair compensation is inextricably bound up with the changing nature of academic work, the fate of academic unions, and the future of institutions of higher learning.

## Section 3: Campus Democracy and the Political Economy of Corporatization

The ascendancy of managerial authority and modes of thinking influenced by the business world—the so-called corporatization of higher education—has led to a crisis of meaning for the contemporary university.[28] That crisis is seen most starkly in the conflicts over who shall govern higher education and to what ends. The democratic institutions of shared campus governance, including unionization, were created by academic citizenship and intellectual autonomy and encouraged said citizenship and autonomy. Will citizenship continue to be the model for participation in campus governance or will managerial authority dominate campus life? What shall be the social and political life of knowledge? Will the pursuit of knowledge for the common good be overshadowed by the imperatives of individual and corporate success?

Corporatization may be re-ordering existing professional and student roles by emphasizing the campus as a free market, education as vocational training, and individual careers as primarily competitive and entrepreneurial, but it is also ushering in opposition and alternative ways of thinking about higher education. The corporatization of higher education has restructured the campus to be more responsive to economic interests and managerial dictates but in so doing has thrown the relationship between property and democracy into flux, creating the opportunity for us to imagine new possibilities.

The academic labor movement can best resist the negative consequences of corporatization, defend the campus as a community, and seize new opportunities if it envisions itself as a movement for academic citizenship and campus democracy. The opposition to corporatization is diverse and polycentric, but at its best it aspires to defend and enlarge democratic rights and practices and create the campus as a center for democratic life. What are the rhetorical strategies, forms of identity, and political and historical consciousness most conducive to that project?

A successful movement for campus democracy could be an unexpected outcome of corporatization. For that to happen we need to reinvent academic ideals, such as those associated with the community of scholars; tap the latent power of democratic political traditions, citizenship foremost among them; and reconceive the political economy of corporatization.

### In the Beginning Was the Community of Scholars

The community of scholars describes the classic relationship between those who teach, research, and study, and is perhaps the most promising source from which to fashion alternative visions for higher education. Twinned at birth, the university and the community of scholars date to the twelfth century.

Teachers and students were the university. They made claims for dispassionate reason, objectivity, and intellectual independence, based on some measure of autonomy and isolation from the world of commerce and politics. The community of scholars was thoroughly hierarchical, with rank based on experience, demonstrated achievement, and mastery of a body of scholarship. While power over early universities was often contested, legitimate authority on scholarly matters came solely from the faculty. The primary value essential to the pursuit of knowledge was academic freedom, protected by the unique safeguards of tenure and self-government.[29]

The community of scholars pursued knowledge as a good for its own sake and was devoted to mutual respect and intellectual exchange as a way to model the well-rounded intellect and demonstrate the relationship between fields of study. The pursuit of truth defined the liberal arts tradition: a lusty desire for knowledge, disciplined by facts and evidence and instructed by reason. More a posture than a program, the liberal arts attempt "to cultivate discriminating sympathy, to combine a capacity for appreciation with the critical spirit."[30]

Although ancient versions of the community of scholars and the liberal arts had sought to produce leaders, citizens, or "gentlemen," America's founders tried to politicize education in a distinctly democratic way. They knew that citizens must be schooled in the "arts of liberty," so they envisioned an extensive education system.[31] Thomas Jefferson reasoned that the new republic could not afford to waste its human potential, or to lose its "natural aristocracy," and so he argued in favor of making education available at public expense to those who qualify "without regard to wealth, birth or other accidental condition or circumstance."[32]

Abraham Lincoln enlarged on Jefferson's democratic but meritocratic concepts by signing the Morrill Act in 1862. The Morrill Act not only established the land-grant college but also expressed the egalitarian impulse of the day by opening college admission to many, regardless of preparation or qualification, including women in a number of western states.[33] Well into the twentieth century, the desire to train good citizens continued to be one of the most prominent rationales for state legislatures and the general public to support public higher education.[34]

Democratic, searching, engaged in a critical embrace of the world, defending independence of mind and encompassing both merit and equality— the community of scholars and liberal arts tradition provided spiritual motivation for generations of scholars and continues to be an important aspect of the lived experience of teachers and students.

The problem in simply returning to our venerable traditions is that the rise of corporate culture on campus has, to some degree, delegitimized preexisting conceptions of higher education as forms of political consciousness. The community of scholars and the ideas on which it depended were wounded in the real campus culture wars and at least some of those wounds were self-inflicted.

The growing use of contingent faculty cast a majority of all faculty onto the very margins of any community at all. An unexamined faith in meritocracy invited elitism, divided the faculty, devalued teaching, and rationalized the abuse of adjuncts by too often presuming that one's standing in the academy or world really was a true and transparent reflection of merit.[35] To the degree that tenure and due process have been converted from universal professional rights into privileges reserved for special classes, or seen only as rewards for individual efforts, the political base of the community of scholars has narrowed. The women, minority, and working-class professors who now constitute a majority of junior faculty members fought for entrance into the academy, but have struggled thereafter with the male, middle-class, and European overtones of traditional campus community.[36]

Just as important, the old community-of-scholars ideal depended in large measure on the campus as enclave, separate from—even if in service to—the larger society. That service was, however, thought of as a by-product of teaching and research, not the direct application of knowledge to the marketplace or battlefield. In the United States, however, the campus has long had direct links to commerce, government, and society. The Morrill Act brought the worldly work of agriculture and engineering to campus. By the early twentieth century, social activism was a prominent feature of the college experience, as elite universities sponsored settlement movements that worked with the urban poor. Public service was foundational to the American conception of higher education.[37]

Whatever degree of separation from society characterized American universities in the past, the rapid expansion of higher education following World War II undermined the economic and social borderlines that distinguished the campus from the "real world."[38] While these changes made the campus much like the rest of society, it was the prolonged and continuing funding crisis that began in the mid-1970s that accelerated corporatization. Public disinvestment in higher education pushed administrators to adopt and promote a more business-like approach to teaching and research that sought to control labor costs, commercialize research, and emphasize the vocational aspects of undergraduate education. Corporatization required that managerial authority eclipse democracy as the ideal for campus governance. Now, thirty years hence, the corporation commends itself as the only version of the real world worth emulating.

## *The Campus as Democratic Community*

The cultural and political project now taking shape in the emerging academic labor movement will require articulating compelling alternatives to corporatization—alternatives that advance the best of our existing values and traditions in a way that does not simply hearken back to the past. We can enhance democracy on campus if we learn from current organizing efforts and political developments and from past conceptions of the university.

The polycentric academic labor movement is the most coherent force promoting campus democracy and citizenship as ideals. Graduate student unionization, contingent faculty activism, the student-labor solidarity networks, living wage initiatives, alumni activism, staff campaigns for unions and fairness, gender equity campaigns, and much of the work of governance organizations, unions, and associations strongly suggest a connection between the creation of campus democracy and the defense of the public interest in quality education. Increasingly, successful union efforts and collective bargaining campaigns are based on coalition building between faculty, staff, students, and community members. When these diverse constituencies come together over contract demands, educational forums, or fair labor codes, a new campus community is being born and it is the only one with the potential power to win.

The concept of campus democracy implies that the campus is a distinctive but integral part of the broader society, and that it should be recognized as a social institution serving the public good. If the public good is the defense and extension of our core values, then the campus should be an exemplar of freedom, democracy, equality, and justice. The meaning of those values has changed over time and the campus is an ideal incubator in which representative and participatory democracy can be engaged, practiced, and theorized. The movement has begun this work in that it struggles to extend to other constituencies, in their appropriate and corresponding areas of work, the exercise of workplace democracy that already exists for tenured faculty.[39]

While classroom instruction is important, citizenship must also be taught by example and learned in action. The constitution of the campus should be considered its most important pedagogy and the efforts to reshape that constitution our best classroom. The current constitutions of our colleges and universities, changed gradually and without debate these last three decades, should be reformed in the light of public discourse and in accordance with the public good.[40]

The scientific and technical products of the campus should not be the entitlement of the corporate sector but applied to the general welfare. The living wage movement points the way toward a gradual reclamation of the products created by educational institutions with a simple and compelling logic: corporations that receive subsidies or contracts from the public owe allegiance and compensation in return.[41]

It is clear that a regular, systemic, and ongoing relationship between enterprise and campus exists. That relationship should be one marked by adherence to community standards, including obligations to the community in forms of job security, environmental standards, and the proportional return on profits made from transferred technology rather than the token payments universities usually receive.

The teacher-student relationship is at the center of the social life of knowledge and that relationship should be the practical focus and moral center of campus activities. By refocusing our attention on teaching, we might start to restore the integrity of the teaching-research-service triad and more justly and productively balance the research-driven reward structure created by business and government.[42]

The academic labor movement reasserts the centrality of the educational mission in that it advocates for the idea that teaching and learning must be regarded as activities worthy of professional working conditions, decent compensation, and academic freedom protections. Student governments and student movements are also predisposed to revitalize the student-teacher relation. By fighting for resources for instruction, insuring access through low tuition, and promoting diverse student populations as essential learning experiences, students and faculty can reposition learning as central to the campus community.

Teaching is also one of our most effective means of promoting the connection between learning and democracy. Speaking in defense of the Supreme Court decision in *Brown v. Board of Education*, renowned educator Robert M. Hutchins claimed:

> The essence of a community is learning together. And a political community arises when the citizens are learning together how to achieve the good of the community and how to govern themselves. A democratic political community arises when all the people are citizens. A democratic community has as its constitution a charter of learning.[43]

If we are to gain campus democracy and enjoy a "charter of learning," the citizens of all campus constituencies, including students, workers, and administrators, must bear the rights and responsibilities of the community. And the first responsibility is to ensure that the campus sets an example of freedom, fairness, and engagement for all who work and study. That takes activism and service to the community.

## The New Academic Citizen

Traditionally, academic citizens participated in governance and union activities and those institutions remain the primary arenas for citizen engagement on campus. The resistance to corporatization is, however, lending renewed vigor and a broader scope to academic citizenship. The new academic citizen encompasses an array of identities emerging from the campus labor movement. Activism is transforming professional identities, with a shift away from predominantly individualistic, isolated, and depoliticized conceptions of professional work and subjectivity, which seem almost to float above the fray, toward those founded on collective action, political engagement, professional activism, collaborative work, class consciousness, and community-mindedness.[44]

The duties of academic citizenship are political ones that cannot be completely disposed of by reference to one's teaching or scholarly work. Instruction and scholarship certainly matter, but governance, union and professional activism, electoral and legislative activity, involvement in neighborhood and church groups, and participation in social movements provide the best fieldwork for citizen training and should be, like teaching, financially and morally supported by the campus reward structure.[45]

Academic citizenship should also be encouraged by the restoration of the conventional teaching-research-service triad that presumably sets the standard for faculty appointment and review. Each component should demand attention in hiring and response from the reward structure. Service should be a credited category of activity.

Corporatization and the rise of managerial authority have largely resolved the old either/or distinctions between worker and professional identity by casting both into roughly equivalent and allied positions. While the degradation of teaching and teachers has led to a resurgence of classic worker identity and activism, particularly among the leadership of graduate employees and contingent faculty, the threats against professional standards has also demanded increased activism, including union activism, from those wishing to defend professional autonomy and authority. Worker identity and professional identity are equally good paths toward academic citizenship. Many academics already see themselves as citizen-scholars working for the public interest and view their activity as an expression of ethical codes, scholarly traditions, or social movements.

The academic citizen has no quarrels with other forms of oppositional political identity. As I argue later, corporate culture has dissolved the distinction between the public political sphere and the economic sphere (formally understood as private) and so has created the historical conditions under which the real-world distinctions between the citizen, worker, or professional are no longer politically salient. The actions a person must take to be a citizen, a class-conscious worker, or an engaged and dedicated professional are now nearly identical. It is our activity that makes us who we are.

Democracy is what matters in the long run, and if we pursue it, that makes us citizens. The citizen is the cultural figure with the most intimate relationship to democratic governance. Both the figure and relationship have been constructed and reconstructed by centuries of historical experience, political struggles, and cultural expectations. The extension or transformation of citizenship rights usually occurs during upheavals like revolution and war, but great events are the culmination of longer evolutionary processes like the nascent movement toward campus democracy.

### Democracy, Property, and the Corporate Interregnum

Behind the current hollowing out of our democratic institutions is a slow historic shift in the relationship between democracy and property. In order to reimagine a future for higher education that draws on the latent power of American traditions of freedom and addresses corporate prerogatives, it is helpful to understand the peculiar relationships that existed between property and freedom in historical conceptions of citizenship.

For our purposes, the most important domestic economic underpinning of democracy was private but widely dispersed property holdings among citizens. The classic models of the citizen were the yeoman farmer and the small proprietor, whose independent state of mind qualified them as worthy citizens. Their intellectual and political integrity rested on wisdom born of self-mastery. The yeoman and proprietor enjoyed a sufficient measure of economic security, regulated their own work, and answered to no earthly lord.

Both the republican and liberal strains of the American political tradition depended on an economic component to democracy. Property was understood as a source of freedom, a guardian of political rights best left outside the realm of government control.[46] In our time, the exemption of private enterprise from the Bill of Rights has invited corporate tyranny, but in the eighteenth and nineteenth centuries the economic order was believed to act as the private foundation of public freedom.

By the early twentieth century, America's traditional structure of citizenship had been overthrown. The corporations bureaucratized and centralized property, leaving most US citizens as the property-less masses that James Madison and the other founders had so feared as undisciplined, dependent, and easily manipulated. Instead of the work-place independence and self-control experienced by generations of yeomen, small proprietors, craftsmen, and even some workers, a new ideology of "scientific management" emerged.[47] The new model claimed skill and craft knowledge (the day-to-day basis of workplace authority for workers as well as professionals) as the intellectual property of management.

Workers and farmers organized themselves into social movements, trade unions, and political parties to resist the threat to their understanding of democracy. As we know, the corporations won that conflict, due to their superior economic might, their command of a vast private army, and most importantly for our purposes, their ability to articulate a vision that promised to realize the best values of Western civilization and the best interests of America. Looking back, many historians see the last century as the fall of the house of labor and the slow retreat of civic virtue and good government.

By the dawn of the twenty-first century, however, the corporate vision showed signs of having run its course. The corporate elites cannot articulate the next chapter of the American political tradition in a way that is coherent and compelling. The evidence on the ground reveals the corrosive effect of corporate power and money on politics. The concentration of wealth and political influence in the hands of international corporations has disempowered the vast majority of people and produced an unending string of scandals, crises, and corruption, which has become the normal way that the economy works, electoral campaigns are run, government conducted, and wars fought. By supplanting corporate control over economic democracy (i.e., the right to participate in shaping one's work and workplace and widely dispersed property holdings), the corporate order has subverted democratic politics.

### Rethinking Corporatization against Itself

Campus democracy and the academic citizen must be firmly grounded, not only in the aspirations of activists but in contemporary economic life itself, or else it is but a dream we have no way of bringing into existence. To accomplish this, we should make the corporate coming-to-power open to multiple interpretations and treat it as a transition rather than the end of history. Important, if under-appreciated, economic and historical developments suggest that the corporate order created the possibility for its own transformation because it also called into being a new order of property relations that politicized property, forever fusing together formally private economic activity and the public political sphere.

The corporation became necessary in the late nineteenth century because business activity outgrew pre-existing notions of individual ownership, competition, and the free market. Business leaders demanded protection from cutthroat competition, even though it was success in that competition on which their socially legitimate ownership rested. They desperately wanted to retain control over the vast wealth piled high by industrialization and impe-rial expansion and other forces greater than that for which their individual efforts could reasonably account. The response to this crisis of legitimacy, meaning, and political control was to invent a new legal and economic form, which we know as the corporation.

The corporation instituted a novel division of labor that institutional-ized highly centralized and private but ultimately group ownership based on wide-ranging relationships. Corporations also produced all manner of con-tingency. Stockholders required no intimate knowledge with, or work in, the enterprise to rank as owners. Property was theirs for a day, or a year, or a decade, and selling their property did not require the consent or even ac-quaintance with other owners or the property itself.

Speculation was a powerful solvent that dissolved property rights as con-trol over things or objects and reconstituted them as highly volatile human relationships no one could easily predict or control.[48] Property rights became tangible only as a relationship between people because the ultimate value of property depended on the interplay of social, political, and cultural forces.[49] The attempt to control such volatility required that corporations exercise the powers of government and sovereignty. Corporations were born political actors.

The dissolution of the nineteenth-century notion of the existence of a distinct public sphere of politics and a private economic sphere has been one of the most important, if under-appreciated, developments of the twentieth century. The mixed economy, in which market forces merge with policy deci-sions (be they cash transfers to the poor, corporate welfare, military spending, investor and bank bailouts, or tax relief to the wealthy), is not some aberra-tion but the underlying truth of our economic system.[50] Despite the daily, ritual evocations of the free market, it is impossible to imagine our economy without systemic, regular, and pervasive connections between government and business.[51] The campus occupies a strategic position in this new political economy.

This fusion of the public and private spheres is the flashpoint for struggles over corporatization: it has led to both the rise of a managerial and authori-tarian governance style and a democratic opposition.

To succeed, the opposition would do well to act on the opportunity and challenge of corporatization: political democracy and economic democracy (that is, civic democracy and workplace democracy) are now intertwined, and one cannot likely exist without the other. This is the world we have inherited. So be it: it is the job of the academic labor movement to swing the door in the other direction by bringing the democratic culture of civil society to work. We can begin by making democratic claims on the workplace.

## *Alternative Forms of Property Suggest New Forms of Democracy*

I want to argue, perhaps unconventionally, that if we take a more careful and historical view of economic activity, we can ground our professional standards in current economic realities and—not without effort and struggle, of course—we can articulate and perhaps even live out an alternative view for the future of the university.

Corporations have become a powerful part of our government on every level. In order to reclaim shared governance or democracy in our political worlds, we must, then, have a say over corporate policy. Democracy, and participation in governance of the corporation and the university, depends on due process protections that are only possible if jobs are treated as our property. According to the Constitution and the economic rules that corporations must at least claim to honor, property cannot be taken from you without due process. Far from being outlandish, these concepts simply follow the way corporations and faculty and many workers already act in the world.

What historical developments of the past century might offer a way to restore the connections between economic and political democracy? Corporate capitalism left most people with no productive property and solely reliant on their mental and physical capacities to earn a living. It is then no surprise that the *job*—its character, quality, numbers, and regulation—became the major locus of workplace conflict in the twentieth century. The last century of labor and economic history established the practice and precedents for the struggle to recognize jobs as a new form of property.

Prior to the 1948 Taft-Hartley Act, so-called closed shop agreements recognized strong union power where it existed by yielding control over jobs to union administration. After 1948, unions retreated from direct control over jobs but still won contract regulations giving workers due process rights and some measure of control over shop floor activities. An elaborate system of workplace jurisprudence arose to adjudicate conflict over jobs as part of the mid-century social contract.

The profound industrial dislocations of the 1980s (the flight of capital, the increasing resort to contingent labor, the transfer of work to nonunion shops or poor nations, and the subsequent decline in union power) eroded the existing system of work rules, but the retention and control over jobs remained the preeminent struggle for labor.

During the 1980s and early 1990s, the desire to save jobs took the form of union/ management cooperation that boosted productivity by tapping worker innovation and sharing control of shop floor activities between the two parties. Both the workplace rules established by mid-century unionists and the cooperative relationships produced during the 1980s treated jobs as a type of property jointly owned by union, individual, corporation, and community. As the practice of cooperation weakened in the mid-1990s, the historic Teamsters' strike at UPS and the equally seismic autoworkers' actions at Dayton in 1996 and Flint in 1998 confirmed that the struggle over the number and quality of jobs remained a pressing concern.

At times of deepest crisis, such as the collapse of the steel industry in Pennsylvania and Ohio in the 1980s, the concept of job property rights reached the threshold of public consciousness. In Youngstown, for example, workers, community activists, and legal scholars argued that the steel industry's long association with the region satisfied the legal requirements for a transfer of property rights from corporation to community.

For the last century, workers have exerted a claim of control over their jobs that in broad political terms is theoretically indistinguishable from the forms of ownership and economic activity foundational to corporate capitalism. Both cases require that property is a social relationship and that public and private resources and responsibilities are inextricably related. The essential difference between the two is the disproportion in power relations that protects corporate ownership with volumes of law and decades of precedent and leaves job property rights the real but unarticulated object of workplace politics.[52] Were job property rights to prevail as a legal right, the workplace could be infused with the kind of democratic practices and freedoms found in the public sphere because workers could have a liberating rather than an oppressive connection to property, much as citizens of the eighteenth and nineteenth centuries enjoyed.

What, then, do job property rights have to do with campus democracy and academic citizenship? For the academic labor movement, a broader appreciation for job property rights provides a new context for the special prerogatives, rights, and duties of the professoriate, and allows us to reinterpret the meaning of contemporary campus organizing.

In the academy, our professional standards implicitly recognize that social relationships are property. After a long period of training, work, and apprenticeship, and an equally lengthy and rigorous probationary period, a candidate is awarded the right to freely practice his or her profession, protected by the kind of due process rights accorded the owner of property. This distinctly social property is not for sale, is possessed only within a certain institutional setting, and exists for the common good, but nonetheless establishes a property right. We, of course, know this job property right as "tenure." While corporate spokespersons attack tenure as some anachronism, it is technically and structurally indistinguishable from the forms of ownership modeled by corporations.

The due process protections of tenure (innocent until proven guilty, hearing by jury of peers, just cause for punitive action, punishment fits the infraction) allow the freedom and prerogatives of the public and civil sphere to be practiced in the academic workplace. We call this "academic freedom."

Academic freedom does more than guarantee that creative inquiry and teaching can proceed unfettered by authority, commercial interest, or the political passions of the day. Only under the conditions of freedom at work can citizenship thrive and participatory and representative democracy be exercised. We claim this prerogative as the right to faculty governance, including the right to collective bargaining.

The rights of tenured faculty represent the real-world benchmarks for a revitalized movement capable of contesting corporatization and creating campus democracy. We have made a modest beginning with efforts to increase the number of tenure-eligible positions and to win economic security and due process protections for contingent faculty.

The rise of corporate capitalism, with its innovative forms of property and its fusion of public and private, has opened the possibility that jobs may now play the same role that widely dispersed property ownership did for the late eighteenth and nineteenth centuries. The conceptual understanding of jobs as property represents an opportunity for both continuity with our best traditions and a transition between what is and what ought to be. Property concepts are essential to maintaining the existing order, yet if applied to jobs would significantly transform society. If widely practiced throughout our economy, job property rights would reinvigorate democratic political traditions by reestablishing a new form of the traditional economic foundation for political democracy.

I have tried to show that democracy is the best organizing principle for the social and political life of knowledge and for the academic labor movement, and that claims for democracy are based not only on tradition and the aspirations of activists but also made possible by the unintended consequences of corporatization itself. When we think about how we will live in the twenty-first century, about what we will leave for our descendants, it would be tragic indeed to suggest that our greatest national treasure, our political ideals, are an impractical legacy. Job property rights of tenure are important not only because they play a special role in university life, and are our traditional standards, but because as widely dispersed property holdings they promote economic democracy and are a living example of how the American political tradition might again become the everyday practice of the American people.

## NOTES

1.  I would like to thank Rutgers Council of AAUP-AFT Chapters for allowing me to take sabbatical leave earned at the National AAUP. Without leave from my organizing duties, this project would have never been completed. I have learned from so many activists and organizers over the past thirty-five years

it would be impossible to list them all. Since 1998 I have worked with scores of faculty activists dedicated to addressing the problems of contingent work. I have learned much from their courage, vision, and tenacity. Special thanks to Joe Berry for reading and commenting on the entire essay. I am deeply indebted to my old friend and veteran journalist Paul Gottlieb, who reworked my tangled prose, helping me better find my own voice—a talent only the most gifted editors possess.

2.  "The Status of Non-Tenure-Track Faculty." In AAUP, *Policy Documents and Reports*, 9th ed. (Washington, DC: AAUP, 2001), 77.

3.  For accounts of the mid-century social contract (also called "the labor/capital accord") see David Brody, *Workers in Industrial America: Essays on the Twentieth Century* (New York: Oxford University Press, 1980), chapters 5 and 6; Barry Bluestone and Irving Bluestone, *Negotiating the Future: A Labor Perspective on American Business* (New York: Basic Books, 1992), chapter 2; Nelson Lichtenstein and Stephen Meyer, *On the Line: Essays in the History of Auto Work* (Urbana: University of Illinois Press, 1989), 1–16; Thomas A. Kochan, Harry C. Katz, and Robert B. McKersie, *The Transformation of American Industrial Relations* (New York: Basic Books, 1986), chapter 2; and Kevin Boyle, *The UAW and the Heyday of American Liberalism, 1945–1968* (Ithaca, NY: Cornell University Press, 1995). On the decline of the social contract see Kevin Phillips, *The Politics of Rich and Poor: Wealth and the American Electorate in the Reagan Aftermath* (New York: HarperPerennial, 1990); Jeffrey Madrick, *The End of Affluence: The Causes and Consequences of America's Economic Dilemma* (New York: Random House, 1995); and Barry Bluestone and Bennett Harrison, *The Deindustrialization of America* (New York: Basic Books, 1982).

4.  Hazel R. O'Leary, "U.S. Labs: Big Welcome for Business," *New York Times*, 13 November 1994; Daniel Bell, *The Coming of Post-Industrial Society: A Venture in Social Forecasting* (New York: Basic Books, 1973), 234, 323.

5.  Ernst Benjamin, "Faculty Appointments: An Overview of the Data" (table 2, derived from USDE/NCES, Fall Staff) (background paper prepared for the Conference on the Growing Use of Part-Time and Adjunct Faculty, Washington, DC, 2–28 September 1997).

6.  Linda Bell, "More Good News, So Why the Blues?: The Annual Report on the Economic Status of the Profession," *Academe*, March-April 2000, 13.

7.  National Labor Relations Board v. Yeshiva University, 444 U.S. 672 (1980).

8.  Thomas Ferguson and Joel Rogers, *Right Turn: The Decline of the Democrats and the Future of American Politics* (New York: Hill and Wang, 1986), 83–86, 130–39; Boyle, *UAW*, 1.

9.  While precise figures vary according to different methodologies and ideological biases, the current concentration of wealth and income in the top 1 percent is the most extreme in the industrialized world and the greatest in twentieth-century American history since the levels reached on the eve of the Great Depression. This income inequality occurred prior to the 2008 crisis and before Occupy did the important work of raising popular consciousness about it. For sources on the historic shift, see Phillips, *Politics*, chapter 4; Ferguson and Rogers, *Right Turn*, 138–39; Edward N. Wolff, *Top Heavy: The Increasing Inequity of Wealth in America and What Can Be Done about It* (New York: New

Press, 1996); Denny Braun, *The Rich Get Richer: The Rise of Income Inequality in The United States and the World* (Chicago: Nelson-Hall Publishers, 1991); James D. Smith, "Recent Trends in the Distribution of Wealth in the US: Data, Research Problems, and Prospects," in *International Comparisons of the Distribution of Household Wealth*, ed. Edward N. Wolff (New York: Oxford University Press, 1987), 72–89; Richard B. Du Boff, *Accumulation and Power: An Economic History of the United States* (London: M. E. Sharpe, 1989); Keith Bradsher, "Gap in Wealth in U.S. Called Widest in West," *New York Times*, 17 April 1995, 1; Jason DeParle, "Census Report Sees Incomes in Decline and More Poverty," *New York Times*, 6 October 1995, 1.

10. John W. Curtis (primary author), "Figure 1: Trends in Instructional Staff Employment Status, 1975–2009," in Saranna Thornton et al., "It's Not Over Yet: The Annual Report on the Economic Status of the Profession, 2010-11," *Academe*, March-April 2011, 7.

11. Jack H. Schuster and Martin J. Finkelstein, *The American Faculty: The Restructuring of Academic Work and Careers* (Baltimore, MD: Johns Hopkins University Press, 2006), 8. See also Jack H. Schuster, "Reconfiguring the Professoriate: An Overview," *Academe*, January-February 1998, 49; and Courtney Leatherman, "Part-Timers Continue to Replace Full-Timers on College Faculties," *Chronicle of Higher Education*, 28 January 2000, A18.

12. Sheila Slaughter and Larry L. Leslie, *Academic Capitalism: Politics, Policies and the Entrepreneurial University* (Baltimore, MD: Johns Hopkins University Press, 1997); Gary Rhoades, *Managed Professionals: Unionized Faculty and Restructuring Academic Labor* (Albany: State University of New York Press, 1998).

13. David Foster and Edith Foster, "It's a Buyer's Market: 'Disposable Professors,' Grade Inflation and Other Problems," *Academe*, January-February 1998, 28–35.

14. "Statement from the Conference on the Growing Use of Part-Time and Adjunct Faculty," *Chronicle of Higher Education*, 26–28 September 1997.

15. Alison Schneider, "To Many Adjunct Professors, Academic Freedom Is a Myth" *Chronicle of Higher Education*, 10 December 1999: A18.

16. Clifford Geertz, *A Life of Learning* (New York: American Council of Learned Societies, 1999), *www.acls.org*.

17. The definitive work on organizing contingent faculty is Joe Berry's *Reclaiming the Ivory Tower: Organizing Adjuncts to Change Higher Education* (New York: Monthly Review Press, 2005). Also see Benjamin Johnson, Patrick Kavanagh, and Kevin Mattson, eds., *Steal This University: The Rise of the Corporate University and the Academic Labor Movement* (New York: Routledge, 2003); Deborah M. Herman and Julie M. Schmid, eds., *Cogs in the Classroom Factory: The Changing Identity of Academic Labor* (Westport, CT: Praeger, 2003); and Ellen Dannin, ed., *Symposium on Organizing Contingent Academics*, in *WorkingUSA: The Journal of Labor and Society*, 6, no. 4 (Spring 2003). A brief history is presented in Eileen E. Schell, "Toward a New Labor Movement in Higher Education: Contingent Labor and Organizing for Change," in *Tenured Bosses and Disposable Teachers: Writing Instruction in the Managed University*,

eds. Marc Bousquet, Tony Scott, and Leo Parascondola (Carbondale: Southern Illinois Press, 2004), 100–110.

18. See Barbara Gottfried and Gary Zabel, "Social Movement Unionism and Adjunct Faculty Organizing in Boston," in Johnson, Kavanagh, and Mattson, *Steal This University*, 207–20.

19. Barbara Wolf, *Degrees of Shame: Part-Time Faculty; Migrant Workers of the Information Economy* (Cincinnati: Barbara Wolf Video Work, 1997); *A Simple Matter of Justice: Contingent Faculty Organize* (Cincinnati: Barbara Wolf Video Work, 2001). For copies, contact Barbara Wolf at (513) 861-2462 or *barbara@ barbarawolf.com*.

20. Large regional institutions such as the California Faculty Association, the Professional Staff Congress, and the United University Professions overcome this problem to some degree in part because their unions are regional and conform to their labor markets to a greater degree than do most single institution unions. In 2013 the SEIU launched an aggressive metropolitan strategy in Boston and in Washington, DC.

21. Berry, *Contingent Faculty*.

22. Faculty unions at UMass-Boston, SUNY, CUNY, Western Michigan, California State University, Connecticut State, Rider, Hofstra, Curry, and a number of California community colleges demonstrate the value of combined units.

23. Joe Berry, "The Value of Forging Alliances," *Chronicle of Higher Education*, 16 June 2006.

24. While the North American Alliance for Fair Employment (NAFFE) no longer exists, this network played a crucial role in the development of the contingent worker movement. The first CEW occurred in 2001, and was followed with CEWs in 2003, 2004 (in Canada), and 2005, and in more sporadic fashion in subsequent years. For more information, see *campusequityweek.org*. The author was the first chair of CEW.

25. For an example of a hearing, see "Contingent Rights Faculty Hearing: Campus Equity Week 2005, Rutgers University," Rutgers Council of AAUP Chapters, accessed 17 May 2013, *www.rutgersaaup.org/misc/cewreport.htm*. The living wage movement also has the potential to mobilize the higher education community. The various efforts for a living wage have resulted in higher wages and 116 new laws in over 70 localities. At last count, there were twenty-nine campaigns on college and university campuses.

26. Corporate capitalism has been widely discussed. Among the more influential works are Daniel Bell, *The Coming of Post-Industrial Society: A Venture in Social Forecasting* (New York: Basic Books, 1973); Martin J. Sklar, *The Corporate Reconstruction of American Capitalism, 1890–1916: The Market, the Law, and Politics* (New York: Cambridge University Press, 1988); and Martin J. Sklar, *The United States as a Developing Country: Studies in U.S. History in the Progressive Era and the 1920s* (New York: Cambridge University Press, 1992).

27. Denise Marie Tanguay, "Inefficient Efficiency: A Critique of Merit Pay," in Johnson, Kavanagh, and Mattson, *Steal This University*, 49–60.

28. For the last half-century, the project of turning our campuses into corporate

centers of power and profit-making has made significant gains, winning the allegiance of a majority of administrators and government officials and a proportion of students, faculty, staff, and the general public. Managerial elites and other corporate actors win people's support, in part, because they posit a compelling utopian vision: a magical free market and a coming techno-utopia capable of relieving all social problems by creating technological solutions and material abundance for all. Despite its profound practical shortcomings and the ongoing critique and deconstruction of its assumptions, this modern mythology will, in the absence of a competing social vision, continue to dominate everyday thought and behavior on and off campus. It seems that earlier conceptions of higher education were better able to manage and contain diverse understanding and expressions of campus life. See Clark Kerr, *The Uses of the University* (Cambridge, MA: Harvard University Press, 1982). There is a growing body of literature on the corporatization of higher education. See the literature section at the end of this chapter.

29. Hastings Rashdall, *The Universities of Europe in the Middle Ages* (Oxford: Oxford University Press, 1936). See also Robert Nisbet, *The Degradation of the Academic Dogma: The University in America, 1945–1970* (New York: Basic Books, 1971), chapters 1–4; Robert Paul Wolf, *The Ideal of the University* (Boston: Beacon Press, 1969), chapter 1.

30. Jackson Lears, "The Radicalism of Tradition: Teaching the Liberal Arts in a Managerial Age," *Hedgehog Review* 2, no. 3 (Fall 2000): 13. See also David Damrosch, *We Scholars: Changing the Culture of the University* (Cambridge, MA: Harvard University Press, 1995).

31. Benjamin R. Barber, "The 'Engaged University' in a Disengaged Society: Realistic Goal or Bad Joke?" *Diversity Digest* (Association of American Colleges and Universities), Summer 2001, 1.

32. Quoted in A. Whitney Griswold, *In the University Tradition* (New Haven, CT: Yale University Press, 1957), 54. In the Northwest Ordinance, Article 3, Jefferson wrote, "Religion, morality, and knowledge, being necessary to good government and the happiness of mankind, schools and the means of education shall forever be encouraged" (text available at *www.ourdocuments.gov*).

33. Maurice R. Berube, *The Urban University in America* (Westport, CT: Greenwood Press, 1978), 20–21.

34. For example, see Gail Kennedy, ed., *Education for Democracy* (Boston: D. C. Heath, 1952), and Robert Maynard Hutchins, *Education for Freedom* (New York: Grove, 1963).

35. Berube, *Urban University in America*, chapter 2.

36. For the demographic data see Martin J. Finkelstein and Jack H. Schuster, "Assessing the Silent Revolution" *AAHE Bulletin*, October 2001, 3.

37. Berube, *Urban University in America*, 9.

38. The federal grant system and preparation for hot and cold wars advanced the government agenda on campus rewarding research over teaching, and placing new demands on administration. The GI Bill and the community college systems drew millions of working-class Americans to campus. The social movements of the mid-century reshaped curriculum and new fields of study

were created. Women, Latinos, and African Americans enrolled in significant numbers as students challenged in loco parentis and claimed adult social roles. The numbers of students soared and, with a growing range of social support services, entertainment venues and community activities, the campus came more to resemble a city than a sanctuary. For an account of higher education as it was being transformed see Jacques Barzun, *The American University: How It Runs, Where It Is Going* (Chicago: University of Chicago Press, 1968).

39. This is evident in the international efforts to create better conditions for contingent faculty, in the efforts for living wages and fair labor standards for staff, and in the inclusion of the growing number of academic professionals in unions and AAUP policy recommendations.

40. The "Teach CUNY" teach-in sponsored by the PSC is a good example, as are the "Future of the CSU" forums organized by the CFA and similar events sponsored by the University of New Mexico AAUP chapter.

41. See the website of House the Homeless's Universal Living Wage Campaign (*www.universallivingwage.org*) for an overview.

42. For background, see Barzun, *American University*.

43. Robert Maynard Hutchins, *Dialogues in Americanism* (Chicago: Henry Regnery, 1964).

44. Cary Nelson, "Between Crisis and Opportunity," in *Will Teach for Food: Academic Labor in Crisis*, ed. Cary Nelson (Minneapolis: University of Minnesota Press, 1997); Damrosch, *We Scholars*, chapter 3.

45. The "service learning" and citizenship programs found on scores of campuses are a gesture in this direction.

46. James W. Ely, *The Guardian of Every Other Right: A Constitutional History of Property Rights* (New York: Oxford University Press, 1992), 9, 54; Jennifer Nedelsky, *Private Property and the Limits of American Constitutionalism: The Madisonian Framework and Its Legacy* (Chicago: University of Chicago Press, 1990), 264.

47. David Montgomery, *The Fall of the House of Labor: The Workplace, the State, and America Labor Activism, 1865–1925* (New York: Cambridge University Press, 1987), page 5 and chapter 5.

48. This interpretation of corporate capitalism is derived from the work of Adolf A. Berle and Gardiner C. Means, *The Modern Corporation and Private Property* (New York: Harcourt, Brace and World, 1932); William A. Williams, *Contours of American History* (New York: World Publishing Company, 1961); Arthur J. Porter, *Job Property Rights* (New York: King's Crown Press, Columbia University, 1954); Daniel Bell, *Coming of Post-Industrial Society*; Sklar, *Corporate Reconstruction* and *United States*; and James Livingston, *Pragmatism and the Political Economy of Cultural Revolution, 1850–1940* (Chapel Hill: University of North Carolina Press, 1994).

49. Sklar, *United States*, 59; Livingston, *Pragmatism*, 194.

50. I borrow the term "public/private mix" from Sklar, *United States*. See also Daniel Bell, *The Cultural Contradictions of Capitalism* (New York: Basic Books, 1976), 224–27. This relationship between government and business is often referred to by critics as "corporate welfare." That designation implies, however, that public support of private wealth is an exceptional or aberrant aspect of

our economy rather than its true basis. For studies on corporate welfare, see
Cato Institute, *Ending Corporate Welfare as We Know It* (Washington, DC: Cato
Institute, 1996); Robert Sherill, "The Looting Decade: S&Ls, Big Banks and
Other Triumphs of Capitalism," *Nation*, 19 November 1990, 592–93; Stephen
Pizzo, Mark Fricker, and Paul Mulo, *Inside Job: The Looting of America's Savings
and Loans* (New York: HarperPerennial, 1991); Mark Zepezauer and Arthur
Naiman, *Take the Rich off Welfare* (Tucson, AZ: Odonian Press, 1996).

51. Over twenty-five years ago, Daniel Bell looked at emerging forms of corporate
ownership and pronounced their private character to be "simply a legal
fiction" (*Coming of Post-Industrial Society*, 294). Today one is hard-pressed to
name an industry not touched by public policy and funding. Agriculture is
thoroughly dependent on public resources whether it is a corporate welfare
giant like ADM or a program to assist small tobacco farmers. The oil and auto
industries would be transformed if government did not encourage them to
"externalize" pollution and accident costs, let alone if the extraordinary tax
breaks, political favors, and direct subsides they receive from the public were to
cease. We will all be paying to subsidize the financial industry for many years
to come. The savings and loan bailout of the 1980s has been dwarfed by the
immense infusion of public capital into financial markets in late 2008. The
vast wealth accumulated by the technology giants rests on an infrastructure and
technological foundation built up largely through public efforts. The global
media networks that so shape public thinking regarding the free market rarely
account for its free use of the publicly owned airwaves. Corporate sovereignty
has taken its mature form in a powerful array of institutionalized relationships.
In the same way that the Federal Reserve and corporate funding of electoral
campaigning set the domestic political and economic agenda, the World Bank,
the International Monetary Fund, and the World Trade Organization now
attempt to govern global corporate activity and dictate policy to nations.

52. Richard Moser, "Autoworkers at Lordstown: Workplace Democracy and
American Citizenship," in *The World the Sixties Made: Politics and Culture
in Recent America*, ed. Van Gosse and Richard Moser (Philadelphia: Temple
University Press, 2003), 303–8.

## Literature on the Corporatization of Higher Education

Aronowitz, Stanley. *The Knowledge Factory: Dismantling the Corporate University and
Creating True Higher Learning*. Boston: Beacon Press, 2000.
Berdahl, Robert M. "The Privatization of Public Universities," speech, Erfurt,
Germany, 23 May 2000 (available at *firgoa.usc.es/drupal/node/26315*).
Bok, Derek. *Universities in the Marketplace: The Commercialization of Higher
Education*. Princeton, NJ: Princeton University Press, 2003.
Bruneau, William, and Donald C. Savage. *Counting Out the Scholars*. Toronto:
Lorimer, 2002.

Bruyn, Severyn T. "Universities and Markets: Potential for Civil Decline." *Good Society* 10, no. 1 (2001): 35–43.

Engel, Michael. *The Struggle for the Control of Public Education: Market Ideology vs. Democratic Values.* Philadelphia: Temple University Press, 2000.

Gould, Eric. *The University in a Corporate Culture.* New Haven, CT: Yale University Press, 2003.

Herman, Deborah M., and Julie M. Schmid, eds. *Cogs in the Classroom Factory: The Changing Identity of Academic Labor.* Westport, CT: Praeger, 2003.

Johnson, Benjamin, Patrick Kavanagh, and Kevin Mattson, eds. *Steal This University: The Rise of the Corporate University and the Academic Labor Movement.* New York: Routledge, 2003.

Martin, Randy. *Chalk Lines: The Politics of Work in the Managed University.* Durham, NC: Duke University Press, 1998.

Noble, David. *Digital Diploma Mills: The Automation of Higher Education.* New York: Monthly Review Press, 2002.

Ohmann, Richard. "Historical Reflections of Accountability." *Academe*, January–February 2000.

Press, Eyal, and Jennifer Washburn. "The Kept University." *Atlantic Monthly*, March 2000, 39.

Rhoades, Gary. *Managed Professionals: Unionized Faculty and Restructuring Academic Labor.* Albany: State University of New York Press, 1998.

Schmidt, Jeff. *Disciplined Minds: A Critical Look at Salaried Professionals and the Soul-Battering System That Shapes Their Lives.* Lanham, MD: Rowman and Littlefield, 2000.

Shulman, Seth. *Owning the Future.* New York: Houghton Mifflin, 1999.

Slaughter, Sheila, and Larry L. Leslie. *Academic Capitalism: Politics, Policies and the Entrepreneurial University.* Baltimore, MD: Johns Hopkins University Press, 1997.

Soley, Lawrence C. *Leasing the Ivory Tower: The Corporate Takeover of Academia.* Boston: South End Press, 1995.

Stankiewicz, Rikard. *Academics and Entrepreneurs: Developing University-Industry Relations.* New York: St. Martin's Press, 1986.

Stein, Donald G., ed. *Buying In or Selling Out? The Commercialization of the American Research University.* New Brunswick, NJ: Rutgers University Press, 2004.

Tudiver, Neil. *Universities for Sale.* Toronto: Lorimer, 1999.

Turk, James. *The Corporate Campus: Commercialization and the Dangers to Canada's Universities and Colleges.* Toronto: Lorimer, 2000.

Washburn, Jennifer. *University Inc.: The Corporate Corruption of American Higher Education.* New York: Basic Books, 2005.

# 5

# The Academic Labor System
# of Faculty Apartheid

*Keith Hoeller*

In 2009, *Money Magazine* published a survey titled "The 50 Best Jobs in America."[1] Their reporters analyzed job data and conducted an online survey of thirty-five thousand people, taking into account such factors as salaries, flexibility, benefit to society, satisfaction, stress, job security, and growth prospects. The proverbial college professor sat high on the list at No. 3, with a median salary of $70,400 for nine months' work, top pay of $115,000, and a ten-year growth prospect of 23 percent. College teaching earned "A" grades for flexibility, benefit to society, and satisfaction, and a "B" for job stress, with 59.2 percent of surveyed professors reporting low stress.

While acknowledging that "competition for tenure-track positions at four-year institutions is intense," *Money* claimed that graduate students with only a master's degree could find a part-time teaching job: "You'll find lots of available positions at community colleges and professional programs, where you can enter the professoriate as an adjunct faculty member or non-tenure-track instructor without a doctorate degree."[2]

Similarly, the 2000 "American Faculty Poll" conducted by the academic pension giant Teachers Insurance and Annuity Association-College Retirement Equities Fund (TIAA-CREF) seemed to corroborate the high job satisfaction rate for professors. "The poll found that 90 percent of the faculty members surveyed were satisfied with their career choices and would probably make the same decisions again," reported Courtney Leatherman, in her *Chronicle of Higher Education* story about the survey.[3]

US Department of Education statistics on faculty salaries lend further credence to this portrait of the affluent college professor. In *The Condition of Education 2009*, the department stated that "in 2007-08, the average faculty salary was $71,100."[4] In addition, "the average compensation package for faculty was about $90,800, including $71,100 in salaries, and $19,800 [or 28 percent of their salaries] in benefits."[5]

The department's "Salaries of Full-Time Instructional Staff, 2008–09" indicates that "four-year public institutions reported that on average their staff earned an average salary of $76,126." While there were two years (1999–2000 and 2007–2008) when professor salaries in public colleges and universities decreased by 1 percent, salaries overall increased by 22 percent, after adjusting for inflation, in the period from 1979–2008.[6]

There is one thing wrong with this aggregate picture, however; it ignores the one million professors who now teach off the tenure track and who make up 75 percent of all college professors. Indeed, *Money*'s portrayal of the professoriate has not been a true picture for the past thirty-five years.

Throughout the country, college administrators, often with the collaboration of academic unions, have gone to great lengths to keep their increasing numbers of adjunct faculty secret from students, parents, legislators, accreditors, foundations, and the public. Since *US News and World Report* started using the number of adjuncts to calculate their rankings in *America's Best Colleges*, some colleges have not reported them to the magazine.[7] Reporter Scott Jaschik writes:

> If the factor that would-be students and their families care about is a percentage of full-time faculty, you can't count on the numbers about research universities to be correct. The two universities with the top scores in this category (both claiming 100 percent full-time faculty) have both acknowledged to *Inside Higher Ed* that they do not include adjunct faculty members in their calculations. . . . But the two with 100 percent claims are not alone in boosting their numbers by leaving adjuncts out.

In 2004, Peter Umbach and Ryan Wells did survey contingent faculty about their jobs and found they were far less satisfied than the tenure-stream faculty: Reporting the results in the *Chronicle of Higher Education*, Peter Schmidt wrote, "Adjuncts were about 7 percentage points less likely to be satisfied with their salaries, 14 percentage points less likely to be satisfied with their benefits, and 9 percentage points less likely to be satisfied with their jobs overall. Adjuncts were also 8 percentage points less likely to say yes to the question: 'If you had to do it over again, would you still choose an academic career?'"[8]

Real dissatisfaction levels may in fact be much higher. In his 1987 Carnegie Foundation report, *The Academic Life*, Burton Clark writes, "What is certain is that part-timers slip through the cracks of national statistics in ways that cause them to be underreported. Many are 'unrostered.' Unless deliberately designed to find them, faculty surveys also largely miss them."[9] Adjuncts may also see little point in filling out a survey for fear their answers may not remain anonymous.

In this essay, I will paint a picture of the disparities in salaries, benefits, and working conditions experienced by the one million professors who currently teach off the tenure track. Though I have tried to use whatever data I could locate, there have been few efforts to gather statistics on non-tenure-track faculty. I have outlined the situation based on my own experience, having taught as an adjunct professor at over a dozen colleges and universities, both public and private, since 1972. I have also relied on knowledge gained through my adjunct activism on the state and national levels, and in my conversations with leading activists around the country.

## The Wal-Martization of Academe

The surveys conducted by *Money*, TIAA-CREF, and others appear to turn a blind eye to the changes occurring in academe that Rich Moser has termed "the new academic labor system."[10] Under this system, according to Moser, "the exploitation of graduate students and the abuse and overuse of adjunct and non-tenure-track faculty is the most prominent characteristic of a new employment strategy sometimes referred to as the two or multitiered labor system."[11]

In the past thirty-eight years, the percentage of professors holding tenure-track positions has been cut nearly in half. Full-time tenure-stream professors went from 45.1 percent of America's professoriate in 1975 to only 24.1 percent in 2011, with only one in six (16.7 percent) professors now possessing tenure.[12]

In the meantime, the percentage of professors teaching off the tenure track increased from 54.8 percent in 1975 to 76 percent in 2011. In 1975, there were 268,883 full-time non-tenure-track and part-time professors, as well as 160,806 graduate teaching assistants. In 2011, there were 1,046,299 full-time non-tenure-track and part-time faculty, as well as 355,916 graduate assistants. Part-time college professors went from 24 percent of the total in 1975 to 41.3 percent in 2011, with numbers now exceeding three-quarters of a million (761,996). From 1975 to 2011, the number of tenure-track and tenured professors increased by only 35.6 percent nationwide, while the number of part-time professors increased by 305.3 percent.

Wal-Mart seems to provide an apt analogy for the economic trend that has occurred in academia. Wal-Mart has become well known for keeping its number of full-time workers to a minimum, and hiring many part-time workers, with low pay, no benefits, and no job security. "There has been a widescale transformation of the faculty work force," says Gwen Bradley, communications director for the American Association of University Professors (AAUP). "It's reflecting what's happening in the economy in general. Some call it the Wal-Martization of higher education. It's much cheaper in the short term to hire part-time faculty."[13]

While it is true that college and university revenue from state and local funds has been declining for several decades—even more so with the Great Recession of 2007–2009 and its aftermath—the academy has hardly been a distressed industry. Though the percentage of college and university revenue coming from state and local funds dropped from 35 percent in the 1975–76 academic year to 27.2 percent in 2000–2001, private grants and gifts grew from 4.8 percent to 9.1 percent, with overall revenue more than doubling from $141 billion to $293 billion (in constant 2005) dollars.[14]

Academe has certainly not cut "production" in the past thirty years. Student enrollments increased by 60 percent from 1975 to 2005. Academe may be a growth industry, but it has nevertheless adopted the same business practices as corporate giants.

Wal-Mart has been the subject of several video documentaries, including *Wal-Mart: The High Cost of Low Price* by Robert Greenwald, and David Faber's *The New Age of Wal-Mart*.[15] Independent film producer Barbara Wolf has made two documentaries on the exploitation of adjunct professors: *Degrees of Shame* (modeled after Edward R. Murrow's famous *Harvest of Shame*, about migrant farm workers) and *A Simple Matter of Justice*.[16]

Though the devastating labor upheavals caused by the new global economy have been widely noted, this new academic labor system has been imposed with hardly any notice by the public at large.

## Tenurism

Flowing directly from the decision to pay contingent faculty less than the tenure-stream faculty is the negative attitude of tenured faculty toward their nontenured colleagues. Wandering into a faculty lounge at a community college, a tenured faculty member said out loud, "If an adjunct professor were any good, he would have landed a full-time tenure-track position by now." This tenured professor, who served as the grievance chair for the faculty union, did not seem to notice—or care—that an adjunct was in the room.

Such prejudice is the natural solution to cognitive dissonance, which holds that when people's belief systems conflict with their behavior, they will sometimes modify their beliefs in order to justify their behavior. The problem posed for tenure-track faculty is this: how can they justify why they are treated so well while so many of their non-tenure-track colleagues are treated so badly?

The tenured faculty member's comment reveals ignorance of the fact that for decades there have been far more qualified applicants than there have been tenure-track jobs. But it is precisely this scarcity of full-time positions that leads those who have them to see themselves as the winners in some sort of social Darwinian landscape.

No one seems to have done a breakdown on the ages of new hires, but adjuncts nearly universally believe that the longer they are adjuncts, the less chance they have of ever attaining a tenure-track job. It is not at all unusual for tenure-track search committees, composed primarily of tenure-track professors, to ignore their own accomplished adjuncts and to hire "promising" young professors with few accomplishments.

In his book *Somebodies and Nobodies: Overcoming the Abuse of Rank*, Robert Fuller, former president of Oberlin College, has laid out the consequences of dividing people by rank. Echoing much of the feminist literature, Fuller describes "a disorder without a name": *rankism*. Calling rankism "the mother of all Isms," Fuller points out that neither differences in power or rank are in themselves the crux of the problem. Rather, "difficulties arise only when these differences are used as an excuse to abuse, humiliate, exploit, and subjugate. . . . The abuse of power vested in rank-holders takes the form of disrespect, inequity, discrimination, and exploitation. Since hierarchies are pyramids of power, rankism is a malady to which hierarchies of all types are susceptible."[17]

Fuller notes that hierarchies can be used to divide people between somebodies and nobodies: "Rankism insults the dignity of subordinates by treating them as invisible, as nobodies. Nobody is another n-word and, like the original, it is used to justify denigration and inequity. Nobodies are insulted, disrespected, exploited, ignored. In contrast, somebodies are sought after, given preference, lionized."[18]

Following Fuller, I think we can now give a name to the treatment of nontenured faculty by their tenured colleagues: *tenurism*. Like racism, which categorizes people by their race, and sexism, which categorizes people by their sex, tenurism categorizes people by their tenure status and makes the false assumption that tenure (or the lack of it) somehow defines the quality of the professor.

## Professors with No Name

No commonly accepted name is used for the various types of professors who teach off the tenure track.

"Part-time" is really a misnomer, since it implies only a reduction from full-time but not any actual qualitative differences, while many of those labeled "part-time" may work full time at one college, or else teach full time by cobbling together part-time jobs at several colleges. And some of those who teach off the tenure track actually do hold full-time positions, either as teachers or researchers.

"Adjunct" is a common term, both inside and outside the academy.[19] *Webster's* first definition, "something joined or added to another thing but not essentially a part of it," does not apply, given that adjuncts make up the majority of professors and are indisputably integral to the nation's colleges.[20] And *Wikipedia's* definition of an adjunct professor as one who "does not hold a permanent or full-time position at that particular academic institution" certainly is not reflective of adjuncts who have taught for several decades at their institutions.[21] While the *Free Dictionary* defines "adjunct" as "something attached to another in a dependent or subordinate position," this definition might suggest the false impression that only a few professors, not the majority, fall into this category.[22]

The word "contingent" is another widely used term among adjuncts themselves, having been inserted, after much debate, into the moniker of the Coalition of Contingent Academic Labor (COCAL), which has held biennial conferences in different cities since 1998. The word "contingent" does have the advantage of describing the precarious nature of all those professors who teach off the tenure track, with their unpredictable income depending on enrollment and various funding sources.[23] But one definition of "contingent" surely does not apply in many, perhaps most, cases: "not necessitated: determined by free choice."

"Lecturer" is another term for those who teach off the tenure track. Where colleges have ranks, it is usually the lowest rank. It can be applied to both full-time and part-time teachers, including graduate students.

Perhaps the most all-encompassing term is simply "non-tenure track," which makes clear the one thing that all of these professors have in common: they have been denied entry into the world of the tenure-stream professors. But it is not simply a lack of tenure that differentiates the two tracks. Virtually every aspect of employment is entirely different and unequal between them. Indeed, many of these professors, given how long they have taught, have been misclassified as "temporary" employees. While such a misclassification has hurt them, the colleges and the tenure-track faculty have benefited immensely.

## The Two-Track Labor System

When people hear the words "part-time" or "temporary," they usually assume that the worker is simply working fewer hours, for a short, definite term, perhaps to filling in until the employer can hire someone for a full-time, permanent position. But people often do not imagine that such an employee would receive much lower pay and be treated differently in every other way.

Yet the two-track system in academe does set up two entirely separate, but unequal, tiers in which the upper tier, the tenure track, is treated in a vastly superior manner to the lower tier, the non-tenure track, which is treated as inferior. Contingent faculty are often not temporary, some having worked for decades, and there is no automatic advancement to the tenure track.

In this section, I detail the many areas where the salaries, benefits, and working conditions of the contingent faculty differ widely from those of the tenure-track faculty. With a couple of exceptions (i.e., among members of the Vancouver Community College Faculty Association and the California Faculty Association), these vast disparities exist whether or not the campus is unionized.

### Salaries

In the Washington State community college system, full-time tenure-stream faculty averaged salaries of $56,334 a year in 2011–2012. If a part-time faculty member had taught a full-time load, he or she would have been paid only $34,364, or 61 percent of a full-time salary.[24] But since the average part-timer is likely to be teaching only 50 percent of a full-time load, he or she is only earning $17,182 a year, or about 15 percent above the 2012 federal poverty guidelines for a family of two ($15,130) or 10 percent below the poverty guidelines for a family of three ($19,090).

In "The Ph.D. Now Comes with Food Stamps," *Chronicle of Higher Education* reporter Stacey Patton cites estimates that 360,000 people with master's degrees and doctorates are currently receiving some sort of federal aid.[25] Dr. Melissa Bruninga-Matteau, a single mother who teaches college humanities courses in Arizona, has to rely on both food stamps and Medicaid to keep herself and her child alive. "I am not a welfare queen," she protests, adding that "I find it horrifying that someone who stands in front of college classes and teaches is on welfare."[26]

To put adjunct salaries in perspective, we can compare them to average annual earnings according to highest degree attained. According to the US National Center for Education Statistics, the median salary for workers twenty-five years old or older with less than a ninth-grade education was $17,040 a year in 2010; the median for those with some high school, but who did not graduate, is $19,370; the median for high school graduates was $28,070; the median for some college, but no degree, is $31,640; the median for those with two-year degrees was $36,390.[27]

Assuming the average adjunct who teaches halftime in the Washington State community colleges is able to earn $17,182 a year, he or she would be earning more than 10 percent less than high school dropouts. If she taught full time and earned $34,364 a year, he or she would still be earning 5 percent less than the students once they graduated from the community college.

But contingent faculty have master's and doctoral degrees, earned after putting in years of hard work, deferring income from a regular job, and graduating with tens of thousands of dollars in student loans. In 2010, workers with a bachelor's degree had a median salary of $47,970; a master's degree would earn $58,190; a doctorate $82,200; and a professional degree $91,200.

The vast majority of graduate students take on large amounts of debt in order to earn their degrees. As many find out too late, student loans must be paid back; they cannot be discharged in bankruptcy.

According to the US Department of Education's National Center for Education Statistics, in 2007–2008 graduate and professional students graduated with total debt ranging from $30,000 to $120,000, with an average of $47,503.[28] People earning master's degrees graduated with an average debt of $40,208; doctoral students graduated with an average debt of $58,967; and professional degree students graduated with an average debt of $98,711.[29]

Thus, many graduate students who decide on a teaching career face a bleak future, with little chance of landing a tenure-track job, as well as years of poverty-level employment and tens of thousands of dollars of student loan debt. Given this reality for 75 percent of college professors, how can it be that statistics still do not capture the true wages of non-tenure-track faculty?

There have been few attempts to compile data on the salaries of adjunct professors. The detailed annual AAUP salary survey, which is published by the *Chronicle of Higher Education*, continues exclusively to list the salaries of the full-time tenure-stream faculty, in large part because the Department of Education has not collected data on adjuncts.

In Washington, the State Board for Community and Technical Colleges publishes average annual salaries for the full-time tenure-track faculty, but not for the part-time faculty. Instead, the board publishes an average "annualized" salary that assumes the part-timer is working full time. But since union contracts prevent the part-timers from working full time at any one college, the figure is highly inflated and entirely fictional.

In 2000 the Coalition on the Academic Workforce, a coalition of twenty-five disciplinary associations, conducted a survey in ten social science and humanities fields. The survey found that adjuncts and grad students were teaching the bulk of the nation's introductory college courses. Further, as Ana Marie Cox reported in the *Chronicle of Higher Education*, "elite Ph.D.-granting institutions are just as likely as community colleges to use non-tenured or part-time professors in English and foreign language courses."[30]

But the results of this survey, conducted by the opinion research firm Roper Starch, may very well have overinflated adjunct salaries. In conjunction with the coalition report, the Modern Language Association (MLA) released its own salary report, which named salaries for specific colleges and universities. Many of the elite colleges (such as Brown, Harvard, Yale, and Chicago) refused to respond to the survey. The response rate was only 42 percent, when the normal rate for returns was 90 percent.

William Pannapacker, who pushed for the MLA report, noted that the colleges that did respond were "probably the best of the lot. What are the other 50 percent doing? What do they have to hide? My hunch is that unethical practices flourish in secrecy in this profession."[31]

The AAUP's annual salary report for 2004–2005, prepared primarily by John W. Curtis, director of research, was the first time the organization attempted to address the issue of contingent faculty salaries. The survey cited the work of James Monks, who used 1998 data from the US Department of Education's National Study of Postsecondary Faculty. Monks concluded that contingent faculty of all stripes are paid less than tenure-track faculty per hour, per class, and overall. In the words of the AAUP report, "Specifically, full-time non-tenure-track faculty are paid 26 percent less than comparable full-time tenure-track assistant professors, and part-time non-tenure-track faculty are paid approximately 64 percent less per hour."[32]

But there are several reasons to believe even these low wages do not fully capture the extent of the disparity. The comparison is being made to lower-paid assistant professors, rather than to the average professor's salary; Monks excluded short-term—and thus lower-paid—contingent faculty from his data; and he did not take into account the fact that while tenure-stream faculty routinely receive extra compensation in the form of health and retirement benefits, part-time faculty generally do not.

The AAUP's 2005–2006 report tried again to estimate adjunct salaries, coming up with equally dismal figures. The AAUP concluded that if a single adjunct living alone was allowed to teach a full-time load, he or she would earn between 140 and 251 percent of the federal poverty level of $9,573 in 2003, depending on the type of institution where he or she taught. "Part-time faculty members with families to support would find their incomes closer to, or even below, the poverty level, which was $12,045 for a family of two in 2003, and $14,680 for a family of three."[33]

While full-time faculty are paid a living wage that includes compensation for all of the hours they work, part-time faculty are usually only paid for the hours they spend in class. Thus, full-time, tenure-stream faculty are paid not only for their in-class hours, but also for their class preparation and their grading of exams, as well as office hours and curriculum development. Most part-time faculty also engage in these activities outside of class—but they are not paid for them. And nontenure faculty are almost never paid for the time they devote to research and professional development.

## Raises

Throughout the country, nearly all tenure-stream faculty are eligible for raises, which may be awarded for experience, professional development, or merit. Some community colleges build the raises, sometimes called "increments," into their contracts. Raises often come with promotions or tenure. Yet few adjuncts ever receive a raise, no matter how long they have taught or how excellent their teaching.

In Washington State, the two faculty unions (the American Federation of Teachers and the Washington Education Association) have collectively bargained incremental step raises for all of their full-time faculty. But twenty-one of the thirty-four community colleges have bargained no raises for their part-time faculty, and the other eleven had part-time raises so tiny I call them "dinkrements."[34]

From 1999 to 2004, 90 percent ($13,160,043) of all faculty raise money ($14,671,469) went to the full-time faculty—even though the part-timers (7,912) outnumbered the full-timers (3,697) by more than two to one. During this six-year period, the average incremental raise for each full-timer was $3,560, while the average increase for each part-timer was a paltry $191.[35]

When I and the other members of the Washington Part-Time Faculty Association tried to convince the legislature to extend an equal amount of increment money to the part-time faculty, we were met with fierce opposition from leaders of the American Federation of Teachers Washington and the Washington Education Association, even though such additional money would not have taken anything away from the full-timers.

Jack Longmate and I were successful in passing an amendment to the 2006 state budget, so that each part-timer would at least receive some increment money. As a result, the full-timers are now receiving only 62 percent of the increment money, instead of the 90 percent they had been receiving. The full-timers did not lose any money and got all of their increment funding because the budget amendment provided an extra $2.4 million to pay for part-time faculty increments. Unfortunately, the unions failed to create increment systems and instead distributed these raises across the board, defeating the purpose of step raises in the first place: to reward long-term teachers for their experience.

Raises for part-time and long-term contingent faculty are not only fair and well deserved, they help to keep the wage gap from increasing. When full-time faculty receive raises that part-timers do not, the overall disparity between their salaries increases. While in the Washington State community colleges the gap was $115 million in 1995, it had actually increased to $132 million by 2008, even though the legislature had increased adjunct salaries by $60 million during this period.

## Cost of Living Adjustments

Since inflation causes workers to lose purchasing power, employers both public and private have often agreed to cost of living adjustments (COLAs) for their employees. Securing cost of living adjustments has been a major goal for unions nationwide. These COLAs are usually applied to all employees across the board, and they are in addition to any raises for merit or promotions.

Though the 2007–2009 recession led to the suspension of cost of living adjustments for many employees, professors at public colleges especially had become accustomed to receiving these raises to help them keep up with inflation. At best, adjunct professors may receive COLA money in equal percentages to the full-timers.

While on the surface this sounds fair and neutral, it is in fact regressive. Since the full-time salaries far exceed adjunct salaries, full-timers receive much larger raises in terms of dollars, thereby increasing the dollar disparity between adjunct and full-time salaries. For example, a 3 percent COLA increase on a full-time salary of $50,000 would mean a $1,500 increase in annual salary for each professor. But a 3 percent COLA on a part-time salary of $15,000 would mean an increase of less than one-third, or only $450.

P. D. Lesko, editor and publisher of the *Adjunct Advocate*, has long criticized equal percentage raises and COLAs: "My other personal cause celebre has been 'equal percentage' pay increases for full-time and part-time faculty represented in unified locals [of full-time and part-time faculty]. Obviously, unless one is incapable of doing basic math, one realizes that a 6 percent raise for a full-time faculty member who earns $80K per year with benefits is just an ever so slightly, wafer-thin, larger raise than 6 percent paid to a part-time faculty member who earns $2,000 per course without benefits. Unified local union leaders who negotiate such 'equal percentage' raises for their members are robbing the part-timers to pay the full-timers."[36]

Yet such equal percentage raises are the norm throughout academe, not only when COLAs are bestowed, but also when unions negotiate raises for their adjunct faculty.

## Health Insurance

Nearly all full-time, tenure-stream faculty receive college-paid health insurance for themselves and their families. According to the US. Department of Education, colleges and universities spent approximately $7,635 a year on health care for the average college professor in Winter 2007.[37]

While there are no national statistics on health care for adjuncts, I believe that the majority are denied health insurance by their colleges and universities. When the *Chronicle of Higher Education* surveyed adjuncts in the Chicago area in 2009, only 14 percent said they were receiving health insurance through their college.[38]

Even where adjuncts may be eligible for health care benefits, they may not be receiving them. In Washington, state employees who worked 50 percent or more of a full-time workload were eligible for state-paid health insurance under state law. But the State Board for Community and Technical Colleges established their own separate rules for eligibility, which provided health insurance only in those academic *terms* when an adjunct was teaching 50 percent or more.

As a result, many adjuncts were denied health insurance when they were teaching less than 50 percent (or not at all). This left most adjuncts without any health insurance in the summers, when most of them did not teach because there were fewer class offerings than in other quarters.

I initiated a class-action lawsuit on this issue called *Mader v. State of Washington*, which was settled out of court in 2004 with $12 million being paid to thousands of adjuncts. Though the state denied it had done anything wrong, it did change its rules to allow adjuncts to average their workloads over the entire year. As a result, adjuncts who teach 50 percent or more over the course of a year can now receive health care benefits year-round, even during summers.[39]

### Sick Leave

Full-time tenure-stream faculty usually accrue ample sick leave to cover them in an emergency and in case of a long-term illness. Such sick leave is usually cumulative, meaning that it does not evaporate from term to term, or year to year. It is also compensable, meaning that when a professor leaves or retires from the university, he or she can receive some cash payment for any unused sick leave. In addition, many colleges now maintain "shared leave" programs, which allow professors to share their sick leave with others, so that a person with a lengthy illness who runs out of sick leave can use sick leave donated by others and avoid any loss in pay.

There are still many colleges and universities, however, where contingent faculty are not eligible to receive any sick leave at all. At these colleges, if they do get sick, they must either work while ill to collect their pay, or else miss work, and have their pay docked for those days.

Even where adjuncts are eligible for sick leave, it may not be cumulative, so that if they do not use it in a term, they may lose it. In addition, they may not be eligible to be paid for sick leave they do not use, and they may be denied participation in the shared leave program.

Prior to 2000 in Washington State, the community colleges did not have a uniform system for sick leave; instead, it was negotiated by the local unions through collective bargaining. Some colleges had none, and others had a few days, which disappeared at the end of each term. Adjuncts who were sick lost income for the days they were unable to teach. And if they were victims of a lengthy illness, their classes would be taken away from them and given to others, leaving them without any income at all.

In 1999, I drafted a bill to equalize sick leave, so that adjuncts who taught a full-time load would earn as many days of sick leave as the full-timers did. Those teaching a half-time load would earn half the sick days of a full-timer.

The sick leave would be cumulative, so that it could be used for lengthy illnesses. And if unused when the adjunct left the college or retired, he or she could receive compensation for any unused days, just like the full-timers.

In addition, the final bill allowed contingent faculty to participate in the shared leave program, either donating or receiving sick leave from other faculty members.

The bill, sponsored by Seattle state senator Jeanne Kohl-Welles, passed both the House and Senate with nearly unanimous support, in large part because the State Board for Community and Technical Colleges estimated it would not cost them anything to provide sick leave to their adjuncts. Unlike the K-12 schools, where substitute teachers are hired to fill in, most colleges simply cancel classes when professors are sick for a few days and/or give the students outside assignments.

Nevertheless, when I had an operation that left me unable to teach for one term in 2008, my college refused to let me use my months of accumulated sick leave. The administration claimed that since I was not on their payroll for that term, I could not use my sick leave. Unable to teach for one term, I lost $8,000 of income just as I faced increased medical bills. The state board made it clear that the college could have allowed me to use my sick leave if it wanted. But the college where I had taught for twenty years refused.

## Retirement

In addition to receiving poverty-level wages throughout their lifetimes, adjuncts can expect to be poor during their retirement years as well. The amount of one's monthly social security payment is based on earnings during one's lifetime. Full-time tenure-stream faculty are likely to earn the maximum social security check, while adjuncts are likely to receive significantly smaller checks due to their much lower lifetime earnings. Most adjuncts may never be enrolled in any retirement system whatsoever.

Most colleges and universities enroll their professors in accounts with TIAA-CREF and then match contributions, depending on the age of the professor. A 100 percent match by the college is not uncommon, with professors over fifty having 10 percent of their salaries taken out of their paychecks, and the colleges contributing another 10 percent.

It is common for tenured faculty to retire with hundreds of thousands of dollars in their TIAA-CREF investment accounts. Some long-term professors may even have $1 million or more to rely on in their old age.

Additionally, many tenured faculty may retire and then teach part-time at their college. Just as when they were teaching, full-time faculty can count on a steady and sufficient revenue stream during their retirement years. And some may be awarded the prestigious status of emeritus professor, which may include an office and clerical support.

Professors also have the option of opening up supplemental retirement accounts with TIAA-CREF and making additional regular contributions. As with all of TIAA-CREF, the professor can then allocate his or her assets between various categories of stock funds, bonds, money market accounts, and guaranteed interest-bearing accounts.

In contrast, contingent faculty may not be able to retire at all, let alone early. While some colleges do provide health insurance for their adjuncts, even fewer provide retirement accounts.

In 1998, I was the initiator of a class-action lawsuit concerning the denial of retirement benefits to part-time faculty in Washington State's community college system.[40] Like the other class-action lawsuit I mentioned earlier, the case was called *Mader v. State of Washington*; it alleged that part-time faculty were wrongly being denied benefits because the community colleges ignored a state threshold of 50 percent or more and refused to count all of the hours they worked outside of class.

Although the state denied any wrongdoing, the case was settled out of court for $12.5 million in 2002.[41] Thousands of contingent professors received checks for thousands of dollars. More importantly, many adjuncts were now eligible for retirement.

## Job Security

Tenured faculty possess the gold standard of job security: lifetime tenure, which can be removed only for just cause and with elaborate due process protections. Tenure-track faculty can usually expect to have their annual contracts renewed until they receive a tenure decision.

While some adjuncts have multiquarter, annual, or even multiyear contracts, the norm remains the quarterly or semester contract, which provides only limited security during its term, and none beyond the end of the contract. The fact remains that contingent faculty who are hired term by term may not be rehired for any reason or even for no reason at all. They are neither fired, nor laid off, nor even "let go." They are considered temporary employees and the college feels that it is under no obligation to bring them back. Not being rehired is usually not a basis for a grievance.

### Unemployment

Seasonal workers have come to depend on our nation's unemployment compensation system to tide them over when they are not working. Construction workers, for example, can obtain unemployment when they are out of a job.

Although colleges and universities save large amounts of money by underpaying contingent faculty and using them only when they have "sufficient" enrollments, they have not hesitated to vigorously oppose unemployment applications by adjunct faculty. In some cases, colleges have even hired outside consultants in order to avoid paying unemployment to their contingent faculty. And the colleges are often successful.

In my *Chronicle of Higher Education* article "Neither Reasonable, Nor Assuring," I pointed out that the states have been misinterpreting an eligibility requirement that was originally intended to prevent full-time K-12 and college faculty from double-dipping and collecting unemployment when they are in fact still employed by the colleges.[42] In 1977, the federal government drafted artful language saying that if a "school employee" had "reasonable assurance" of returning to work after a term or summer break, they were ineligible to collect unemployment.

This policy makes perfect sense when applied to full-time teachers, who may indeed be on regularly scheduled breaks, for which they are paid and are still receiving benefits from the college. But as I wrote, "part-time faculty members do not have annual contracts, or annual salaries, and the vast majority do not receive any benefits during the summers. When part-timers are not teaching, they are unemployed—the major criteria for collecting unemployment."[43]

The routine denial of unemployment to tens of thousands of contingent faculty has become so widespread that Joe Berry, Beverly Stewart, and Helena Worthen have published "a manual for applicants and a strategy to gain full rights to benefits" called *Access to Unemployment Insurance Benefits for Contingent Faculty*.[44] The authors write that "those who drafted the unemployment legislation never contemplated current conditions in higher education, nor did they contemplate that working conditions for the majority of higher education instructors would resemble the conditions faced by factory and service workers more than they would resemble the working conditions of independent professionals, such as doctors and lawyers, to whom college educators were most often compared."[45]

In Washington State, many of our community college part-time contracts contain the following language: "It is understood that this employment is on a temporary basis and for the limited time period set forth in the contract. The appointment is not subject to tenure. Neither this appointment nor any policy, rule, or regulation shall be construed as providing the employee with an expectancy of re-employment by the [community college] district."[46]

Yet even though the state allocates money for the colleges to pay unemployment each year, administrators still challenge adjunct unemployment applications because, if they are successful, they can divert the money to areas they deem more important.

Fortunately, the law seems to favor adjunct claimants. In the 1988 decision *Cervisi v. Unemployment Insurance Appeals Board*, the California Supreme Court ruled that "an assignment that is contingent on enrollment, funding, or program changes is not a 'reasonable assurance' of employment."[47] Unfortunately, equal protection of the law is routinely being denied to contingent faculty outside the state of California.

### Class Cancellations

Not only do adjuncts receive low pay and few benefits, their income is highly variable, depending on whether they are offered future classes, and whether the classes that have been offered to them are allowed to be taught. Colleges can, and do, cancel classes for a variety of reasons, including insufficient enrollment, as well as funding and changes in their programs. Administrators often laud their ability to quickly change directions under the broad category of "flexibility."

It is usually the college that determines the exact number of students that make up a sufficient number for a class to be held. This number, which is rarely challenged by faculty or their unions, can vary from division to division, department to department, and even from class to class. The college can sometimes cancel classes as late as ten days into the term.

When an adjunct has a class canceled, she will lose the income for that course. In some circumstances, the college may pay her for an hour or two of preparation, but rarely more.

While full-time faculty can have their classes cancelled as well, they do not lose any income. Since a tenure-stream faculty member has a contract with the college to teach a certain number of classes, he has to replace the cancelled class with another. Usually this means the full-timer will take a class from a part-timer, who will be left without compensation for the course. When this happened to me, not only was I left without pay for preparing my course, I was asked to turn the curriculum I had developed over to a full-time professor who then taught my course. Part-time faculty never have the right to bump full-timers, and I have not heard of a contract that gives part-timers with seniority the right to bump less senior adjuncts.

## Workload Limitations

At virtually every college in the country, adjunct faculty contracts limit or "cap" workloads *below* full time at any one college.[48] In addition to the low pay, this is another one of the reasons for the so-called freeway flier phenomenon, where adjuncts are forced to teach at several colleges in order to put together a sufficient income.

In the Washington State community college system, each of the thirty-four campuses has set a different adjunct cap, ranging from 50 to 90 percent of a full-time teaching load. Neither the colleges nor the union leaders who regularly negotiate faculty contracts have ever provided a rationale for limiting adjunct workloads.

Yet it seems obvious that the major reason is to prevent contingent faculty from ever qualifying for tenure. The Washington State tenure law requires three years of full-time teaching to qualify for tenure. For this reason, in some cases the adjuncts, who are doing the same work as the full-timers, have successfully claimed they deserve de facto or "backdoor" tenure. In fact, a few adjuncts have made exactly this claim, and they have received tenure as a result, though it has rarely been achieved without the involvement of an attorney.

It is worth noting that the same colleges (and unions) that limit adjunct teaching to significantly below full time allow their full-time professors to teach significantly above full time, ranging from 167 percent to 200 percent of full time. Of course, the more courses taught by full-time faculty, who often have preference over part-timers in choosing courses, the fewer the classes available for the adjuncts to teach. The colleges benefit from full-timers who teach overloads because they are usually paid at the lower part-time rate, and the college avoids paying the additional health and retirement benefits if an adjunct were to teach these courses.

Furthermore, in both Washington and California the colleges and the unions have taken money intended by legislators to raise part-time salaries and diverted it to full-time faculty who moonlight, claiming that they are part-timers too. In 2001, California passed the Part-Time Faculty Equity Pay Law, awarding $57 million to increase part-time pay in the community colleges, though only $47.6 million had been distributed by 2004.

In "A Tale of Greed and Gluttony: The California Part-Time Faculty Equity Fund Boondoggle," *Adjunct Advocate* reporters Chris Cumo and P. D. Lesko write, "Of that $47.6 million that officials did distribute to faculty, not all ended up in the paychecks of part-time faculty. Full-time faculty have pocketed millions of dollars of the equity pay the state's legislators were led to believe would go toward bolstering the pay of the state's temporary faculty."[49]

In Washington State, we have been successful in convincing the state legislature to grant nearly $60 million in equity pay "solely to increase salaries and related benefits for part-time faculty" since 1996.[50] Yet a significant, but unknown, amount of this money has gone to full-time faculty who teach overloads.

When Jack Longmate filed a "whistleblower" complaint with the state auditor over this diversion of funds, the auditor, after taking six months to investigate, wrongly concluded that the funds were *not* being used to pay full-timers and thanked the colleges, but not Longmate, for their cooperation with his investigation. Our repeated attempts to get state legislators and the governor to review the auditor's work have been unsuccessful. The colleges and the unions are still diverting part-time faculty "equity" money to full-time faculty who moonlight by falsely claiming that faculty who teach full time and have tenure are "part-timers" when they teach overtime.

### Professional Leave

Many institutions go to great lengths to support the teaching and research of their tenure-stream professors, allowing them to take several days off to attend a teaching workshop, or to give a paper at a conference in another city, or even longer to do research.

Many contingent faculty may be ineligible for such paid leave time, or if eligible, may find most of the funds going to the tenure-stream faculty. Indeed, adjuncts may be hesitant to take such leave out of fear that the college may view them as shirking their commitment to their students.

Several years ago, I received an award from a national organization for scholarly work I had done. The college published an article about my award in their newsletter. I got advance approval from my division head, and arranged for my classes to be covered in my absence.

When I returned, I found out that the college had in fact docked my pay for three days, claiming that while I was eligible to take the time off, I was not eligible to be paid for it because I was an adjunct. When I mentioned this to a powerful state senator, she complained to the head of human resources for the state community college system, and he wrote the head of personnel for the college.

Ultimately, I was paid for the days I was away from campus. But soon thereafter I began to have some unusual run-ins with the division head. One quarter, she claimed to have made a mistake and not put one of my courses into the catalog. Since she claimed that it was too late to correct it, I lost the income for that class. Soon she ceased offering me any classes at all—after fifteen years of successful teaching.

Contingent faculty, all of whom teach off the tenure track, are not eligible for tenure. So in addition to teaching summers to make ends meet, adjuncts are forced to teach year after year without ever benefiting from a sabbatical.

In addition, tenure-stream faculty may often receive grants that allow for time off from teaching to either conduct research or else improve teaching. While not impossible to receive, it is still rare for contingent faculty to be awarded grants by foundations. In many cases, the foundations require the grantee to demonstrate support from the college for their work, usually in office and clerical help, and such support is lacking for most adjuncts.

### Class Assignments

As with every other aspect of the two-track system, tenure-stream faculty are given preference in the assignment of courses. When departments prepare their term schedules, tenure-stream faculty have first choice in selecting which courses they will teach. They often choose the more advanced courses, or opt for a schedule where they have to do the least amount of preparation. They also tend to prefer the daytime classes over those held at night, so that they can have their evenings free either to conduct research or to spend with their families.

After the tenure-stream faculty have chosen their courses for the term, then classes are assigned to the contingent faculty. In practice, the contingents are often left with the lower division classes, the introductory classes, and the evening classes. Of course, adjuncts must often teach in the least desirable rooms as well.

The system that always prefers tenure-stream faculty over contingent faculty can lead to the assignment of a class to a tenure-stream faculty member who may in fact be less qualified than an adjunct to teach a particular class.

### Seniority

Throughout academe, full-time tenure stream faculty have priority over contingent faculty in virtually all aspects of employment. The presumption of the two-track system is that the tenure-track professors are better and more qualified than the adjuncts. So the tenure-track professors usually have first preference in choosing classes, even when a particular adjunct might have superior credentials.

There are a few colleges where adjuncts do have a seniority system and have the right of first refusal when courses in their field are assigned. Even where adjuncts do have seniority systems, they are often course by course, as opposed to the more normal date of hire.

But the vast majority of adjuncts teach for years without developing any seniority over other adjuncts, let alone tenure-stream faculty. This means that even long-term adjuncts can see their courses offered to newer professors with less experience.

## Office Support

While the colleges save millions of dollars by paying their contingent faculty little and denying them benefits, they also cut costs by denying them adequate offices and support. Though tenure-track faculty usually have private offices, adjuncts may be placed in separate buildings or in large rooms with dozens of others. Adjuncts often give these rooms nicknames, such as "the pit" or "the corral."

In most cases, part-time offices are converted spaces, not deliberately designed to house faculty, and can be so cramped that the faculty often avoid going there because they can never have a private conversation with a student, let alone prepare for class in a quiet setting. One small office I used contained four large desks and five chairs. Often as many as eight professors signed up to use the office; there were sometimes three or four faculty holding office hours at the same time. Because of the noise and constriction, adjuncts often met with students on a bench outside the office or left a note that they would be holding office hours somewhere else on campus.

Green River Community College in Washington recently opened two brand new buildings, with plush, private offices for each full-timer, but the center of each building was filled with cubicles to be shared by the part-timers on a first-come, first-served basis. While the older buildings had plenty of shared, but private, offices for adjuncts, these were eliminated in the new buildings.

## Invisible Faculty

Although colleges proudly list tenure-stream professors in their annual catalogs, they very rarely list professors who teach off the tenure track.[51] While quarterly college course schedules routinely list the names of tenure-track professors next to the courses they will teach, courses taught by adjunct professors often carry only the word "staff" or "TBA" (To Be Announced).

Campus phone and e-mail directories often leave out contact information for adjunct faculty, who often cannot be found on campus, either because they do not have an office, or they share an office with many other adjuncts. I have called a college campus to speak with a fellow adjunct only to be told by the confident operator that no such person works there.

## Academic Freedom

Virtually everyone agrees that all professors should be protected by academic freedom. Colleges, unions, and even accreditors all state that college professors need and deserve the right to say and think what they believe is the truth without fear of discipline, retaliation, or job loss.

In their famous 1940 "Statement of Principles on Academic Freedom and Tenure," the American Association of University Professors states that academic freedom has three parts.[52] (1) "Teachers are entitled to full freedom in research and in the publication of the results"; (2) "Teachers are entitled to freedom in the classroom in discussing their subject"; and (3) "When they speak or write as citizens, they should be free from institutional censorship or discipline."[53]

The AAUP makes clear that academic freedom applies to virtually anyone who teaches in a college or university: "Both the protection of academic freedom and the requirement of academic responsibility apply not only to the full-time probationary and the tenured teacher, but also to all others, such as part-time faculty and teaching assistants, who exercise teaching responsibility."[54]

How is academic freedom supposed to be protected? The AAUP's answer is *tenure*: "Tenure is a means to certain ends, specifically: (1) freedom of teaching and research and of extramural activities, and (2) a sufficient degree of economic security to make the profession attractive to men and women of ability. Freedom and economic security, hence, tenure, are indispensable to the success of an institution in fulfilling its obligations to its students and to society."[55]

In *The Last Professors*, Frank Donoghue has raised several important questions about the AAUP's position on tenure: "Why do only the tenured enjoy the full protection of academic freedom? What about the legion of adjuncts and the graduate teaching assistants, not to mention professors on the tenure track, but not yet tenured?"[56]

Donoghue points out that the AAUP's original "General Declaration of Principles" of 1915 was far broader and more radical than the 1940 "Statement of Principles on Academic Freedom and Tenure." Perhaps to make it more palatable to colleges, the latter document was in fact coauthored with the Association of American Colleges, which was run by the administrators of undergraduate colleges. The latter document, currently in force, narrowed both the meaning and application of academic freedom.

Prior to 1940, college professors did not have tenure per se, though "the norm throughout the country was presumptive tenure—the annual contracts at most universities were automatically renewed by custom, not rule."[57] The AAUP's original 1915 "General Declaration" argued for an autonomy for all college teachers similar to that of federal court justices. It stated that teacher-student relations should be analogous to attorney-client relations, and that classroom lectures were not meant for the public and should not be published without the express permission of the professor. It also said that speeches outside the classroom should not be limited to the teacher's field of specialization.[58]

The AAUP's 1940 "Statement of Principles" ties the role of professors to their colleges and limits their speech to their fields of specialization, both on and off campus. This famous document, currently in force, contains an unacknowledged contradiction that lies at the heart of the current two-track system: while it says that academic freedom should apply to all professors, it divides the faculty between those who must undergo a probation period of seven years on the tenure track and those who either (1) pass the review and earn tenure or else (2) fail the review and must leave the university entirely.

Donoghue notes that the 1940 statement "adds the baffling principle that 'During the probationary period a teacher should have the academic freedom that all other members of the faculty have.' If, indeed, probationary faculty have that freedom from recrimination, then what additional freedom do they gain by being tenured. What is the purpose of tenure?"[59]

The AAUP has been ineffective in defending academic freedom even in the best of times. But in the worst of times, it has been abysmal, and its defense of academic freedom for adjuncts—hampered by a lack of contractual protections, to be sure—has been rare.

For years, I have heard adjuncts allege that the AAUP routinely refuses to investigate serious and blatant complaints of academic freedom. It refused a case I brought to it in the mid-1990s. And despite my personal plea when I served on its national Committee on Contingent Faculty, it turned down two important and well-documented adjunct cases with national significance. It would not even investigate them.

On February 13, 2005, Terry Knudsen and I published "Colleges Exploiting Part-Time Professors" in the Sunday edition of the Spokane, Washington, daily newspaper, the *Spokesman-Review*.[60] While colleges are often proud to have themselves identified with professors who enter the public arena, I had tried to refrain from listing the colleges where I taught. I was concerned that because I was an adjunct criticizing the two-year college system, someone at my college might take offense and retaliate against me. But when the editor asked us to identify our colleges, we relented and the college names appeared under ours in the article.

In "Teacher Says She Lost Job for Speaking Out," reporter Shawn Vestal wrote: "Knudsen says her troubles began last February, when she and Hoeller published an op-ed in *The Spokesman-Review* saying adjuncts 'may very well be the state's most mistreated and exploited employees' and calling the community college system a 'state-run feudal system.' . . . Soon thereafter, she says, she was called into her dean's office [in actuality, her department chair's office], where she was told that her comments had offended full-time faculty members and that she'd lost support."[61]

According to Terry, the chair of her department "chilled" her by saying, "There are limits and consequences to free speech. I think you should leave

SCC [Spokane Community College]."[62] Within hours of this meeting, college administrators claimed that Terry, who had an unblemished teaching record of seventeen years and who had recently been awarded the title of "associate faculty," had violated several college policies and, in a series of steps, removed her senior status and ceased to offer her any further classes.

Terry has not taught in the Spokane Community College system since 2005. The college claims "that the decision not to hire her back had nothing to do with her political speech or activity."[63]

I referred Terry's case to Committee A of the AAUP, in the hopes that it would agree that this was a significant case of the violation of the AAUP's principles of academic freedom. Here was a long-term adjunct, who had documented every step of the case, claiming that she had been fired because of an opinion article that she had published in the local newspaper.

Yet when I called the national headquarters and talked to the staff person who was looking into her case, I found that he had gotten nearly all the facts of the case wrong. Terry told me that in her conversations with him she had gotten the distinct feeling he was looking for any excuse not to investigate any further.

I appealed directly to both Ernest Benjamin, the AAUP's executive director, and Cary Nelson, its president, to have the national AAUP conduct a full-scale investigation of her case, even resending all of the documentation myself. The AAUP refused to do so. To this day, Terry has never received any explanation as to why.

In 2009, the AAUP issued a report entitled *Conversion of Appointments to the Tenure Track*, in which it states that "the best practice for institutions of all types is to convert the status of faculty serving contingently to *eligible for tenure* with only minor changes in job description" (italics added).[64] It's important to underscore that the AAUP's official policy has not come out in favor of tenure for contingent faculty; rather, it has only come out in favor of converting some contingent faculty to tenure-track jobs. These faculty will then have to serve a lengthy probationary period, perhaps as long as seven years, with dubious protection of their academic freedom during this period, and then they may earn tenure—or they may lose their jobs, even after decades of excellent teaching.

In 2010, AAUP president Cary Nelson published an article entitled "Solidarity vs. Contingency" in which he stated:

> In its new policy paper—"Tenure and Tenure-Intensive Appointments"—
> the AAUP recommends that all long-term contingent faculty members be
> granted tenure. Since tenure can be awarded to both part-time and full-time
> faculty members—a person could have tenure at less than full-time percent-
> age appointment—the AAUP's proposal carries no necessary cost.[65]

Actually, the 2010 policy proposal from the AAUP's Committee on Contingent Faculty contains no such language. As with the 2009 proposal from the same committee, the later paper says only that long-term adjuncts should be converted to *the tenure track*, which is not the same as granting them tenure: "*The best practice for institutions of all types is to convert the status of contingent appointments to appointments eligible for tenure with only minor changes in job description*" (italics in the original).[66]

It is not clear what importance to give Nelson's views, since he appears to have been speaking only for himself and not for the AAUP. Did he mean to go beyond the AAUP's official policy? Or was he simply not careful to make a distinction between "tenure-eligible" and "tenure"?

In any event, *Chronicle* reporter Audrey June has said, "For administrators, non-tenure-track faculty members equal flexibility, a term that means that colleges can cut costs in these strained economic times by nixing the jobs of those who work outside the tenure system. It's difficult to envision a scenario in which institutions would willingly give up that arrow in their quivers."[67]

## Shared Governance

Virtually everyone in academe agrees that faculty should be active participants in "shared governance." Indeed, colleges and universities often leave many decisions in the hands of the faculty, and the faculty consult and advise in many others.

Departments develop their curriculum, and divisions produce bylaws. Faculty senates often speak for professors on a multitude of issues. And, of course, unions negotiate contracts.

Whereas tenure-stream faculty have ample opportunities to express their views in meaningful ways, adjuncts rarely do. Adjuncts are routinely left off of tenure committees, even though students may sometimes serve on them, and student evaluations are used to determine tenure decisions. And faculty senates nationwide either exclude contingent faculty or else allow only a few token slots. Even where contingents do have the right to participate, there are several major obstacles that stand in the way.

The full-time tenure-stream faculty are hired not only to teach, but also to help run the university. Consequently, their annual pay compensates them for all of their on-campus activities and rewards them accordingly. Service to the college is often one component in their tenure review.

In contrast, the vast majority of contingent faculty are hired solely to teach, as if this piecemeal approach were possible, and they are paid only for their classroom contact hours. Adjunct faculty, already paid at least 50 percent less than their tenure-track counterparts, are in fact donating their time when they participate in the life of the college community. Often this is time taken away from supplementing their meager incomes by teaching at other colleges.

Adjuncts also run the risk of losing their jobs if they engage in activities where they might take issue with the tenure-stream faculty or administrators who control every aspect of their employment, including whether or not they are rehired. While the tenure-track faculty are indeed vulnerable to retaliation for rocking the boat, they have much firmer protections than adjuncts, who may have only term-to-term contracts.

## Grievances

If for no other reason than to avoid losing lawsuits, all colleges and universities have some kind of due process rights for faculty who believe they have been treated wrongly. These grievance procedures can be found either in faculty handbooks or else in union contracts. Sometimes rules governing procedures for the awarding and denial of tenure at public colleges are written into state law. Normally, employees must show that they have exhausted all internal remedies before they can take a case to court. The rules specify which kind of actions can be grieved, the process for filing a grievance, and strict deadlines for complying with each step.

Virtually all tenure-stream faculty have access to extensive grievance procedures concerning each and every aspect of their employment, including their dismissal, which must follow strict guidelines. Though tenure-track faculty can expect to have their contracts automatically renewed during the probationary period, they can be dismissed for cause.

Tenured faculty can also be fired, but the procedures are so onerous for the college, and the publicity so negative, that it remains a rare occurrence. There are usually substantial due process rights afforded to both tenure-track and tenured faculty, and they have the right to grieve their dismissal, if they wish. If the faculty member is covered by a union contract, he or she may be represented by the union, which usually has a grievance committee with a grievance chair.

Colleges and universities, however, do insist on special clauses to cover financial emergencies and strict rules for what is often called a "reduction in force." During the current recession, some colleges have declared a "financial emergency," and laid off some tenure-stream faculty, though the nationwide number has remained relatively small.

Nearly all colleges give adjuncts access to some form of grievance procedures, although there are several major hurdles unique to adjuncts. A major obstacle is the fact that an adjunct who pursues any kind of grievance runs the risk of losing her job. Even if she were to win the battle of her particular grievance, she is likely to lose the war of ever being hired back by the college.

Finally, in many cases the grievance may be against a tenure-stream faculty member who serves as his or her supervisor and who is also a member and/or official of the same union. Many professors are under the illusion that they have a right to a grievance when in fact they do not if there is a union contract. The union has a right to a grievance, not the individual, and the union has a right to settle a grievance.

In the event the adjunct has a grievance against a tenure-stream faculty, the union, if dominated by such faculty, may simply decline to bring a grievance, or else the adjunct may be barred by law from bringing a grievance against another member of the same bargaining unit.

### Evaluations and Awards

Evaluations are to help the instructor improve and should result in a reward, such as a raise or a promotion. Awards often serve the function of highlighting excellent work and can also lead to better jobs.

But none of this applies to contingent professors. While negative evaluations can lead to the loss of a job, positive evaluations and even winning a teaching award generally do not lead to raises or promotions.

Like other treatment of contingent faculty, the overriding feature of evaluation might be ambivalence. Tenure-stream faculty generally evaluate adjuncts (but never vice versa). Rarely does the institution have specific rules as to how teaching evaluations will be used, who will perform them, or who will review them, nor does the institution provide for any kind of appeal procedure if the adjunct should disagree. All this means is that a department chair who likes an adjunct's teaching evaluations may offer continuing employment or extra courses, or may never hire the adjunct again.

One institution that considers faculty evaluations important is Vancouver Community College in British Columbia, which distinguishes between evaluations that have a bearing on an instructor's future employment and those that are for the enrichment of the instructor's teaching. The failure to make that distinction—and the presumption that all evaluations are job-bearing—underscores the perpetual probationary status of contingent faculty in US education.

In most academic disciplines, contention exists between differing schools. In philosophy, for example, analytic philosophers dominate those who take a historical or European approach to the subject. Yet there are still analytic philosophers who do not think that continental philosophers are really doing philosophy, which makes adjuncts who teach from this point of view vulnerable to prejudice when being evaluated by analytic philosophers.

In psychology, likewise, while Freudianism was once dominant, biological approaches have become the norm. Jeffrey Schaler, an opponent of biological approaches to "mental illness," published a book entitled *Addiction is a Choice*, in which he objects to dominant views about twelve-step programs.

When hired as an adjunct to teach psychology at Chestnut Hill College, a tenured faculty member objected to Schaler's views. When he went to the department chair, he was grilled about his perspective on Alcoholics Anonymous and mental illness, and after answering honestly, Schaler claims he was no longer hired to teach any more courses. The AAUP failed to pursue his complaint.[68]

While some colleges have set up separate teaching awards for adjuncts, winners are not viewed as the best teachers; they are simply the best *adjunct* teachers. When contingent and tenure-stream faculty must compete for the same awards, however, the adjuncts usually lose.

Since 1985, the Green River Foundation has run the Distinguished Faculty Awards program for Green River Community College in Auburn, Washington, with prizes of up to $1,500, giving as many as three awards a year. During the first twenty-six years of the program, virtually every longtime tenured professor won the award, but no adjunct professor had ever done so, even though by 2011 the adjuncts outnumbered the tenure-track professors by more than two to one.

Until about five years ago, adjuncts could not even vote. Astronomy adjunct Dana Rush, who has been nominated five times for the award, was not eligible to vote even when he became a finalist. It was only after the foundation was asked to change their policy that adjuncts were allowed to vote and one was placed on the committee that chose the finalists.

In June 2012, I became the first adjunct ever to win the Distinguished Faculty Award at Green River.

## The Unions' Role in Dividing the Faculty

Unions have long extolled their ability to secure higher wages, greater job security, and better working conditions for their members. This "union premium" can be as high as 28 percent in wages alone in contrast to those of unorganized workers.[69]

But for college professors, little evidence exists to support a union premium. Research is scant, and what little there is indicates that unions have little or no effect for tenured faculty, and virtually none for those off the tenure track.

Studying faculty salaries at four-year colleges from 1988 to 2004, David Hedrick, Steven Henson, John Krieg, and Charles Wassell Jr. found that higher education unions had a "weak effect" on wages and that the union wage premium was statistically insignificant.[70]

Hedrick and his colleagues reaffirmed the earlier research of Gordon Tullock (1994), who wrote: "Unions may be able to shift funds around among the faculty but . . . there is little chance of increasing total salaries." At the same time, Hedrick et al. hypothesized that "the presence of faculty unions may result in improvements in amenities, benefits, and working conditions."[71]

In 2011, *Chronicle of Higher Education* reporter Peter Schmidt analyzed the data on academic unions and came to a similar conclusion in "What Good Do Faculty Unions Do?"[72] He subtitled his article "Research Sheds Little Light on Quantifiable Benefits of Collective Bargaining" and wrote that "many faculty members work without union contracts without feeling particularly exploited." He further wrote: "The chief benefits of unionization appear to have less to do with getting faculty members more bread than in giving them some say over how it is sliced."

Hedrick et al., however, studied only the salaries of full-time faculty. The scope of their study excluded the nation's one million college professors who teach part time off the tenure track; Schmidt too concentrated on full-time faculty.

In *Unionization in the Academy*, Judith Wagner DeCew describes the only study conducted on adjuncts and unions: *Managed Professionals: Unionized Faculty and Restructuring Academic Labor* (1998), by Gary Rhoades, former general secretary of the AAUP. DeCew writes, "Despite claims by unions that they want to protect part-time faculty's procedural rights, Rhoades found they had done little to enhance working conditions for part-time faculty. He found a striking absence of provisions about process and personnel actions surrounding hiring and firing for part-timers in 80 percent of 183 contracts."[73]

Summarizing the conclusions to be drawn from Rhoades's research, DeCew writes that faculty union contracts "do not often protect, but actually further marginalize, part-time faculty. . . . Consequently, the national unions may claim to be advocating for part-time faculty, but the contracts do not show that they have made much progress."[74]

These findings align with the data presented herein, demonstrating that the two-track system divides the faculty into haves and have-nots and grants advantages to the tenure-track faculty at every turn, whether in salary, benefits, or working conditions. These inferior conditions are the rule even where the faculty have been organized into unions. If America's college campuses are sweatshops, they are in fact unionized sweatshops.

Throughout the United States, by virtually every measure of union success, collective bargaining has failed the contingent professors. Why?

## Employer-Dominated Unions

The labor movement has worked hard to abolish "employer-dominated unions" and tried to remove supervisors from the bargaining units, so as to avoid the resulting conflicts of interest. Unions that are set up and run by management are obviously sham unions, and employees are unlikely to be well represented by their own bosses. And whenever supervisors are in the same unit, employees lack the power to push for their own benefit, and face retaliation for doing so.

Per the National Labor Relations Act (NLRA) of 1935 (Section 8(2)), employers are not allowed "to dominate or interfere with the formation or administration of any labor organization or contribute financial or other support to it." Yet the US Supreme Court's *Yeshiva* decision (1980) establishes that because of their participation in "shared governance," tenured professors are "managers," and therefore not entitled to unions in private colleges and universities.[75] Public institutions are not covered by the NLRA; they fall under state public employment commissions.

Whether or not one agrees with *Yeshiva*'s characterization of tenured faculty as managers, wherever there is a two-track system—in other words, everywhere in the United States—the tenured faculty serve as de facto supervisors of the contingent workforce who often have marginal contact with college administrators. While tenure-track faculty might not be called "supervisors" by the colleges or the unions, they do in fact play an undeniable role in the managerial functions of hiring, evaluating, and rehiring the adjunct professors; in assigning classes; and in large measure determining the curriculum. Further, it is the tenure-stream faculty who generally bargain the contracts.

The benign interpretation of this state of affairs, offered up by union leaders in its defense, is that it is appropriate for the full-time tenure-track faculty to be dominant since they are on campus more often and know the college better. They also have job security, which makes it safer for them to engage in the conflicts involved in bargaining. And the adjuncts are dismissed as often being too busy and too scared to get involved. So it is customary for union leaders in mixed units to handpick a bargaining team headed by a tenured faculty member, and usually containing only one handpicked adjunct professor.

Let us take a closer look at two areas already mentioned: increments and overloads. In the Washington State community colleges, incremental step raises have been bargained by the local unions, who have made sure that all of the full-timers get regular, hefty pay raises for their longevity. At the same time, these same unions have not bargained any increments for two-thirds of the colleges, and only a few tiny steps for the others.

When it comes to "turnover" money, captured when a more expensive professor leaves or retires, all of the locals have made sure that the full-timers get to recapture and share this money, and none of the part-timers. And when part-time activists have gone to state capitals to pass legislation to cor-

rect this unfair increment system, the unions have put up vigorous opposition, even though it would not take anything away from the full-timers.

An egregious example is allowing full-time faculty the right to teach overloads, while restricting part-timers from teaching even full-time, and in so
doing deliberately preventing them from ever qualifying for tenure, which is
what Wobbly leader Bill Haywood would have called a "job trust." They are
able to restrict not only the number of tenure-track jobs, but also who gets
them.

Protecting the ability of full-time faculty to teach course overloads sheds
light on why the three faculty unions (the AAUP, the AFT, and the NEA)
have failed to bargain any meaningful job security for the contingent faculty. Job security would embolden the contingent faculty to become more
involved in their unions and to demand "fair representation" for all members,
as required by court rulings since the 1947 Taft-Hartley Act.

Unfortunately, the contingent faculty face limited choices since the
entire labor movement has been exempted from antitrust law and loathes
competition. Article 20 of the AFL-CIO Constitution forbids raiding other
AFL-CIO unions. And the AAUP and the AFT are now conducting joint organizing of faculty at research universities, and insisting that the tenure-track
and contingent faculty both be placed into the same bargaining units.

In Washington State, in 1994, the AFT and the NEA prevented Green
River Community College faculty from remaining outside the union at a
branch campus in Kent. The unions filed a complaint with the Washington Public Employment Relations Commission and won a ruling that there
could be only one faculty union at each community college.

As Seattle Community College adjunct ESL professor Douglas Collins
wrote to the *Seattle Post-Intelligencer*:

> Metaphorically, part timers are in an abusive marriage with the full timers,
> but they are not allowed to seek a divorce. For many, the only recourse is to
> keep smiling—or else lose their jobs. If part timers had a fair choice to orga-
> nize their own unions, they would get a lot more respect. Having the choice
> makes the difference. Changing state policy to allow union choice would be
> a big positive step forward.[76]

## Adjunct-Bashing and Retaliation

Wherever adjuncts have risen up, criticized unions and their leaders for their
mistreatment of the contingent faculty, and demanded change, union leaders
have uniformly responded with denial and hostility. In order to maintain the
two-track system and the privileges that come with tenure, it is important
for the unions to stifle any independent movement that might threaten the

hegemony of the tenured faculty. It is also important to make sure that no independent adjunct leaders emerge to challenge the union's power base.

Sometimes an adjunct can be discredited simply by labeling them "anti-union," or "anti-full-timer," or "anti-tenure." Because I have criticized the two-track system, union leaders across the country have long hurled such epithets at me. This process of vilifying an outspoken adjunct lets union members see the individual as a threat to the group, and to realize that if they should associate with the dissident, they may be subjected to the same hostility.

Without any job security, adjuncts who speak up run the very real risk of losing their current jobs, and not being hired for future work. They also may anger tenured faculty who evaluate their courses, provide references for future work, and serve on hiring committees.

Unions have been eager to find and promote "happy adjuncts," who will speak well of the unions and the tenured faculty who control them. If these adjuncts will also hurl darts at the independent activists, all the better.

But if a critical adjunct should sneak through, the unions have been quick to leap into action. When Doug Collins, the elected secretary of the Seattle Community College AFT, testified against a union increment bill and asked that it be amended to be fair to adjunct professors, he was subjected to an unprecedented recall vote and removed from office.[77]

When nearly ten years later, Jack Longmate, elected secretary of the Olympic College NEA, also testified against a union increment bill and asked that it be amended to provide equal increments for adjuncts, union leaders, including the president of the statewide Washington Education Association, quickly retaliated. After Jack rejected tenured faculty members' demands that he resign, he was purged from office when the full-timers ran a tenured faculty member against him.[78] With only 8 percent of the Olympic College adjuncts choosing to join the union, it was easy for the full-timers to replace him.

It is the two-track system that divides the faculty into the haves and have-nots. Unions that support it do not want solidarity among the faculty.

## How to Achieve Equality for Contingent Faculty

Given how entrenched the two-track system now is throughout the United States, can adjuncts ever expect to make any improvements, let alone gain full equality with their tenured colleagues? How can contingent faculty ever make any substantial improvements when the three faculty unions lack any kind of coherent plan to make substantial improvements and oftentimes seem to remain determined to represent the tenured faculty at the expense of their contingents?

Not surprisingly, after ignoring the adjuncts for decades, the faculty unions are now claiming to be their saviors. Union leaders and naïve observers think: If only the adjuncts will organize themselves into local chapters of the AAUP, the AFT, or the NEA, collective bargaining will take care of everything. Solidarity can thereby be achieved and the colleges will not be able to pit one group against the other.

Apart from lip service to adjuncts, there is no evidence that any of these unions or their leaders have any serious intention of abandoning the supremacy of the tenured faculty.

Indeed, it would be hard to find a more cynical solution to the adjunct faculty crisis than the one offered by the AFT: the Faculty and College Excellence (FACE) plan, which seeks to restore the tenure-stream faculty to 75 percent. While the FACE plan gives a small nod to improving adjuncts a bit, its primary goal is to obtain legislative funding to convert part-time positions to full-time ones. As noted, this means the loss of adjunct jobs; the AFT has since revised its literature to say it does not intend to do this.[79]

Yet in order to convert two half-time positions to one full-time position, at least one and possibly two current part-timers will lose their jobs. And if the new full-timer is allowed to teach overloads, one or more additional half-time teachers could lose their jobs as well. That is why one Washington adjunct called the Washington State FACE bill the "Adjunct Annihilation Act."

### Is Collective Bargaining the Only Solution?

It is not reasonable to suppose that collective bargaining alone offers an effective means to achieve adjunct equality. An adjunct union is likely to require two years to become established, and then another two years to obtain its first three-year union contract. Then in three years, the union may be able to make a couple of slight improvements. After ten years, in all likelihood, the adjuncts are still likely to have a weak contract. And this process would have to be repeated at each and every college and university in the country. Strikes are prohibited at nearly all public colleges, and higher ed unions have hardly been engaging in any strikes in recent years.

The faculty unions have only pledged themselves to vague improvements to the two-track system and none even has a plan to implement even any small changes. And if the unions have been behaving like abusive spouses, none has yet to even apologize and pledge to stop abusing the adjuncts. They are still at the stage of "blaming the victim" for the violence done to them.

Nonunion adjunct organizations have been successful in bringing about major gains not merely on a single campus, but statewide. The California Part-Time Faculty Association was a leader in obtaining the favorable *Cervisi* state Supreme Court decision, which has made collecting unemployment nearly automatic for adjuncts. It has also led the way in improving salaries for community college adjuncts. And it was instrumental in a campaign to lift the artificial caps in the community colleges from 60 percent to 67 percent of a full-time workload, thereby allowing adjuncts to teach an extra course each year.

The Washington Part-Time Faculty Association, which I founded with Terry Knudsen in 1997, has had a major impact on adjunct employment in the community colleges.[80] The legislature has appropriated nearly $60 million to improve adjunct salaries, moving them from 40 percent to 60 percent of a full-time salary for teaching a full-time workload.

Additionally, as I mentioned earlier, I initiated two successful class-action lawsuits, both called *Mader v. State of Washington*, which (a) greatly expanded the number of adjuncts who qualified for retirement and health care benefits, and (b) put $25 million into the pockets of adjuncts who had been denied such benefits in the past. I also drafted a 1999 bill that gave cumulative, compensable sick leave to all adjuncts in the state, and I arranged for them to purchase long-term disability insurance for the first time.

### Achieving Equality for Contingent Faculty

The two-track system is broken. Tenure-stream professors now find themselves adrift in a small, leaky lifeboat surrounded by an ocean brimming with contingent faculty who, prevented from climbing into the tenure boat, are forced either to tread water or else drown.

Even the American Association of University Professors has begun to speak of tenure in apocalyptic terms, announcing that "Today the tenure system has all but collapsed."[81] In 2010, the organization's president, Cary Nelson, wrote, "Now the average college teacher is no longer eligible for tenure, and the good ship humanities is already partly under water."[82]

Tenure is becoming extinct and nearly every week somebody publishes a story asking "Is College Worth It?" Still feeling the effects of the 2007–2009 recession, the answer appears increasingly to be "No!" It certainly isn't worth it for the millions of students who forgo income and incur student debt to obtain a graduate degree in the humanities, only to find that there are no tenure-track jobs, and that their only options are one-year appointments or a lifetime of part-time teaching in the academic ghetto.

### The Abolition of the Two-Track System

While there is widespread agreement that the mistreatment and exploitation of adjuncts is wrong, there is still no agreement on the source of the problem or what should be done about it. There remains a vast discrepancy between what union leaders say and what they do. The three faculty unions continue to focus on trying to protect tenure for the few and to increase their ranks. Far from demanding equality for the contingent faculty, the unions keep suggesting that quality can only be achieved on the tenure track.

The contingent faculty movement is in much the same state as the antislavery movement was during the 1820s, when the American Colonization Society was the dominant organization. While admitting that slavery was problematic, members did not feel that African Americans were equal, and said that they should be shipped to Africa. Even slaveholders joined the society, because it was especially concerned about the dangers of the growing numbers of free blacks.

Abraham Lincoln was a longtime proponent of colonization. He was favorably disposed to colonization as late as 1863, even after he issued the Emancipation Proclamation. In *The Fiery Trial: Abraham Lincoln and American Slavery*, Eric Foner documents Lincoln's slow evolution toward the idea of equality between the races. With Lincoln's knowledge and approval, in 1863 his own administration had signed a "colonization contract" with Wall Street brokers to transport five hundred blacks to a Haitian island for the purpose of growing cotton.[83]

It was only after this project ended in disastrous failure, with mutiny and dozens of deaths, that Lincoln finally abandoned the idea: "By 1864, although Lincoln still saw voluntary emigration as a kind of safety valve for individual blacks dissatisfied with their condition in the United States, he no longer envisioned large-scale colonization."[84]

While Lincoln had been slow to abandon the idea of colonization, America's abolition movement had turned against it decades earlier. In 1831, William Lloyd Garrison had begun publication of the *Liberator* and called for the immediate and unconditional abolition of slavery and complete equality for all blacks. His motto was "No Union with Slaveholders." In 1833, he had formed the American Anti-Slavery Society. Though it took over thirty years, and a bloody civil war, as well as aggressive efforts by the Radical Republicans in Congress, slavery was finally abolished with the ratification of the Thirteenth Amendment in 1865.

While all three faculty unions have issued policy statements deploring the plight of the contingent faculty, none has acknowledged its own role in creating and perpetuating the two-track system of faculty apartheid. None has called for the abandonment of the two-track system and complete equality between contingents and tenured faculty on such issues as salary, benefits, and job security, much less developed a coherent plan to bring about those provisions that are undeniably central to workplace rights.

All three are hoping to preserve the two-track system by reforming it with slow incremental steps. The AFT's FACE plan aims to restore the tenured faculty to what their leaders see as their rightful majority, since the easiest path to "excellence" is to get more people on the tenure track, where the advantages have already been secured. The AFT wants to convert more part-time positions to full-time *positions*; it has shown no interest in promoting existing part-timers to full-timers.

While the AAUP's Contingent Faculty Committee has at least called for converting existing contingent faculty to tenure-eligible positions, former president Cary Nelson has gone further, saying that he is in favor of tenure for all long-term adjuncts. This would of course leave them with significantly lower salaries, but Nelson says it will "give them the job security they need to advocate for better working conditions without fear of reprisal, and it eliminates the sometimes crippling stress accompanying at-will employment."[85]

And, of course, his proposal would do nothing for the short-term contingent faculty. Since the AAUP usually requires seven years until a tenure decision is made, this could still leave hundreds of thousands of adjuncts in the academic ghetto, or without any job at all if current prejudice toward adjuncts continues unabated.

In *The Invisible Faculty*, Judith Gappa and David Leslie said, "It is time for institutions of higher education that hire and use part-time faculty to end the current bifurcated system."[86] They quickly pointed out, however, that there would be resistance, not simply from college administrators but from the tenured faculty: "The major advocates of the status quo are many of the tenured faculty members who are its beneficiaries."[87]

The tenured faculty—and the unions and union leaders who represent them—all have a vested interest in maintaining the status quo of the two-track system. The tenured faculty benefit from it financially; the unions work for their benefit to control access to the tenure track.

The nineteenth-century ex-slave and abolitionist Frederick Douglass wrote:

> If there is no struggle there is no progress. . . . Power concedes nothing without a demand. It never did and it never will. Find out just what any people will quietly submit to and you have found the exact measure of injustice and wrong which will be imposed on them, and these will continue till they are resisted by either words or blows or with both. The limits of tyrants are prescribed by the endurance of those whom they oppress.[88]

Much like Garrison's American Anti-Slavery Society, we need an *American Anti-Contingency Association*, which will be dedicated to the *abolition* of the two-track system in academe and complete equality for all professors, whose teaching should be judged on its merit, not on the tenure status held by the individual. There should be a single salary scale for all professors at a college, a single scale for raises, and a single set of procedures for job security and for grievances. Whether a professor teaches part- or full-time should be at his or her discretion, and pay and nonteaching duties should be prorated according to 100 percent of a teaching load.

All college professors should have meaningful job security, and their academic freedom should be protected. America cannot be a democracy with a higher education system based on inequality. Colleges can no longer hold out the promise of opportunity and a better life to their students while denying these same opportunities to the professors who make all of this possible. Students and parents should no longer be willing to patronize academic sweatshops; they should begin to demand change or else boycott those institutions that will not change.

The contingent faculty movement is a civil and human rights movement. The time has come for direct action. Higher education is not simply another commodity produced by American factories; it is the building block of our culture and our democracy.

## NOTES

1. Donna Rosato, with Beth Braverman and Alexis Jeffries, "The 50 Best Jobs in America," *Money*, November 2009, 88–96.
2. Ibid., 91.
3. Courtney Leatherman, "Despite Their Gripes, Professors Are Generally Pleased with Careers, Poll Finds," *Chronicle of Higher Education*, 3 March 2000.
4. National Center for Education Statistics (NCES), *The Condition of Education 2009* (Washington, DC: NCES, 2009), *nces.ed.gov*. The NCES is part of the US Department of Education.
5. NCES, "Fringe Benefits of Full-Time Instructional Faculty at Title IV Degree-Granting Institutions, by Contract Length and Control of Institution: United States, Academic Year 2007-08," in *IPEDS Winter 2007 Compendium Tables*, table 42, *nces.ed.gov*.
6. NCES, *Condition of Education 2009*, 104.
7. Scott Jaschik, "Calculation That Doesn't Add Up," *Inside Higher Ed*, 14 September 2009, *insidehighered.com*.
8. Peter Schmidt, "2-Year Colleges Can Win Over Adjuncts with Benefits, Study Suggests," *Chronicle of Higher Education*, 23 April 2009.
9. Burton R. Clark, *The Academic Life: Small Worlds, Different Worlds* (Princeton, NJ: Carnegie Foundation for the Advancement of Teaching, 1987), 205.
10. There have been several attempts to apply the Wal-Mart model to academe, including Oronte Churm, "The Wal-Martization of Higher Education," *Adjunct Advocate*, November-December 2006; Michael Johnson, "The Wal-Martization of Higher Education: A Very Good Idea—or a Very Bad One?" *Coeur d'Alene Press*, 26 March 2008.

11. Richard Moser, *The New Academic Labor System* (Washington, DC: AAUP, 2001), *aaup.org*.

12. John W. Curtis, "Figure 1: Trends in Instructional Staff Employment Status, 1975–2009," in Saranna Thornton et al., *It's Not Over Yet: The Annual Report on the Economic Status of the Profession, 2010-11* (Washington, DC: AAUP, 2011). I am grateful to Curtis, director of research for the American Association of University Professors, for providing me with these and other statistics, which were the latest available when I wrote this essay. See "List of Table and Figures," *www.aaup.org/list-tables-and-figures-4*. Curtis has since sent me updated statistics through 2011. These tables are included in the Appendix of this book, "Trends in Instructional Staff Employment Status."

13. Quoted in Lorraine Ash, "Number of Part-Time Professors Increases," *East Brunswick* (NJ) *Home News Tribune*, 27 August 2007, *mycentraljersey.com*.

14. Keith Hoeller, "The Future of the Contingent Faculty Movement," *Inside Higher Ed*, 13 November 2007, *insidehighered.com*.

15. Robert Greenwald, *Wal-Mart: The High Cost of Low Price* (Culver City, CA: Brave New Films, 2005); David Faber *The New Age of Wal-Mart* (Englewood Cliffs, NJ: CNBC Original, 2010).

16. Barbara Wolf, *Degrees of Shame: Part-Time Faculty; Migrant Workers of the Information Economy* (Cincinnati: Barbara Wolf Video Work, 1997); *A Simple Matter of Justice: Contingent Faculty Organize* (Cincinnati: Barbara Wolf Video Work, 2001).

17. Robert W. Fuller, *Somebodies and Nobodies: Overcoming the Abuse of Rank* (Gabriola Island, BC: New Society Publishers), 4.

18. Ibid., 5.

19. For a complete inventory of names, please see "List of Terms Used for Contingent Faculty," in Joe Berry, *Reclaiming the Ivory Tower: Organizing Adjuncts to Change Higher Education* (New York: Monthly Review Press, 2005), xi.

20. *Webster's Eleventh New Collegiate Dictionary*, s.v. "adjunct."

21. *Wikipedia*, s.v. "Adjunct Professor," accessed 12 June 2013, *en.wikipedia.org/wiki/Adjunct_professor#Adjunct_Professor*.

22. *Free Dictionary*, s.v. "adjunct," accessed 12 June 2013, *www.thefreedictionary.com*.

23. *Webster's Eleventh New Collegiate Dictionary*, s.v. "contingent."

24. John Boesenberg (Director of Human Resources, Washington State Board for Community and Technical Colleges), letter to the author, 7 January 2010. See also State Board for Community and Technical Colleges (SBCTC), *2011–12 Academic Year Report* (Olympia, WA: SBCTC, 2012), *www.sbctc.edu*.

25. Stacey Patton, "The Ph.D. Now Comes with Food Stamps," *Chronicle of Higher Education*, 6 May 2012, *chronicle.com*.

26. Quoted in Patton, "Ph.D."

27. "Table 396. Distribution of Earnings and Median Earnings of Persons Twenty-Five Years Old and Over, by Highest Level of Educational Attainment and Sex: 2010," in *Digest of Education Statistics: 2011* (Washington, DC: NCES, 2011), chapter 5, *nces.ed.gov*.

28. Data cited in "Student Loans," *FinAid*, accessed 12 November 2012, *www. finaid.org/loans*.

29. Ibid.

30. Ana Marie Cox, "Study Shows Colleges' Dependence on Their Part-Time Instructors," *Chronicle of Higher Education*, 1 December 2000.

31. Quoted in Scott Smallwood, "MLA Survey Reveals Wide Discrepancy in Part-Time Faculty Members' Earnings," *Chronicle of Higher Education*, 5 January 2001.

32. John W. Curtis et al., *Inequities Persist for Women and Non-Tenure-Track Faculty: The Annual Report on the Economic Status of the Profession, 2004–05* (Washington, DC: AAUP, 2005), 26.

33. Saranna Thornton et al., *The Devaluing of Higher Education: The Annual Report of the Economic Status of the Profession, 2005–06* (Washington, DC: AAUP, 2006), 33.

34. Keith Hoeller, "Equal Pay Means Equal Raises, Too," *Chronicle of Higher Education*, 16 August 2005.

35. Keith Hoeller, "Faculty Increments, 1999–2004" (unpublished document), January 2006. Compiled from data supplied by the Washington State Board for Community and Technical Colleges.

36. P. D. Lesko, "Am I Dreaming?" *Part-Time Thoughts* (blog), 27 March 2009, *www.adjunctnation.com*.

37. NCES, "Fringe Benefits."

38. "Chronicle Survey: All Questions and Answers," *Chronicle of Higher Education*, 19 October 2009.

39. Erik Lords, "Part-Time Faculty Sue for Better Pay and Benefits," *Chronicle of Higher Education*, 15 October 1999.

40. This case was also called *Mader v. State of Washington*.

41. Ruth Schubert, "Part-Time Instructors Sue for Retirement Benefits: The $40 Million Question," *Seattle Post-Intelligencer*, 29 October 1998.

42. Keith Hoeller, "Neither Reasonable, Nor Assuring," *Chronicle of Higher Education*, 23 September 2004.

43. Ibid.

44. Joe Berry, Beverly Stewart, and Helen Worthen, *Access to Unemployment Insurance Benefits for Contingent Faculty: A Manual for Applicants and a Strategy to Gain Full Rights to Benefits* (Chicago: Chicago Coalition on Contingent Academic Labor, 2008), *chicagococal.org*.

45. Ibid., 11.

46. Hoeller, "Neither Reasonable, Nor Assuring."

47. Ibid., 42.

48. Jack Longmate, "Adjunct Faculty Bear Brunt of Higher Ed Cuts," *Tacoma* (WA) *News Tribune*, 31 December 2010, *www.thenewstribune.com*.

49. Chris Cumo and P. D. Lesko, "A Tale of Greed and Gluttony: The California Part-Time Faculty Equity Fund Boondoggle," *Adjunct Advocate*, May-June 2004.

50. The quoted language ("solely to increase . . .") appears in various Washington State budget bills over several years, including Washington State Legislature, ESSB [Engrossed Substitute Senate Bill] 6090, "Certification of Enrollment,"

2005 Regular Session, *leap.leg.wa.gov/leap/Budget/Detail/2005/00507bi110423.pdf*, page 152.

51. John W. Curtis and Monica F. Jacobe, *AAUP Contingent Faculty Index 2006* (Washington, DC: AAUP, 2006). This AAUP report does a good job of counting the actual number of contingent faculty at each campus in the United States. The introduction by Curtis and Jacobe, "Consequences: An Increasingly Contingent Faculty," gives a good description of the kinds of contingent faculty found throughout America, as well as a brief summary of their disparate working conditions.

52. AAUP, *Policy Documents and Reports* (the "Redbook"), 9th ed. (Washington, DC: AAUP, 2001), 3–10.

53. Ibid., 3–4.

54. Ibid., 6.

55. Ibid., 3.

56. Frank Donoghue, *The Last Professors: The Corporate University and the Fate of the Humanities* (New York: Fordham University Press, 2008), 74.

57. Ibid., 75.

58. Ibid., 75–76.

59. Ibid., 77.

60. Teresa Knudsen and Keith Hoeller, "Colleges Exploiting Part-Time Professors," *Spokane* (WA) *Spokesman-Review*, 13 February 2005.

61. Shawn Vestal, "Teacher Says She Lost Job for Speaking Out," *Spokane* (WA) *Spokesman-Review*, 21 February 2006.

62. Ibid.

63. Ibid.

64. AAUP, *Conversion of Appointments to the Tenure Track* (Washington, DC: AAUP, 2009), *aaup.org*.

65. Cary Nelson, "Solidarity vs. Contingency," *Inside Higher Ed*, 7 September 2010, *insidehighered.com*.

66. AAUP, *Tenure and Teaching-Intensive Appointments* (Washington, DC: AAUP, 2010), *aaup.org*.

67. Audrey Williams June, "News Analysis: Converting Adjuncts to the Tenure Track Is More Easily Discussed Than Done," *Chronicle of Higher Education*, 8 November 2009.

68. Alison Schneider, "To Many Adjunct Professors, Academic Freedom Is a Myth," *Chronicle of Higher Education*, 10 December 1999.

69. "Collective Bargaining Raises Wages—Especially for Women and People of Color," AFL-CIO, accessed 6 January 2013, *www.aflcio.org*.

70. David W. Hedrick, Steven E. Henson, John M. Krieg, and Charles S. Wassell Jr., "Is There Really a Faculty Union Salary Premium?" *ILR Review* 64, no. 3 (April 2011), *digitalcommons.ilr.cornell.edu*.

71. Gordon Tullock, "The Effect of Unionization on Faculty Salaries and Compensation," *Journal of Labor Research* 15, no. 2 (1994): 199–200.

72. Peter Schmidt, "What Good Do Faculty Unions Do? Research Sheds Little Light on Quantifiable Benefits of Collective Bargaining," *Chronicle of Higher Education*, 1 May 2011.

73. Judith DeCew, *Unionization in the Academy: Visions and Realities* (Lanham, MD: Rowman and Littlefield, 2003), 84.
74. Ibid., 85.
75. National Labor Relations Board v. Yeshiva University, 444 U.S. 672 (1980).
76. Douglas Collins, letter to the editor, *Seattle Post-Intelligencer*, 16 February 2008, *www.seattlepi.com.*
77. Keith Hoeller, "Throwing Darts at Adjunct Activists," *Adjunct Advocate*, January-February 2008.
78. Dan Berrett, "A Shop Divided," *Inside Higher Ed*, 10 February 2011, *insidehighered.com.*
79. Keith Hoeller, "Equal Rights Legislation for Adjunct Professors," *Adjunct Advocate*, January-February 2007.
80. See Eddy A. Ruiz, "The Stone That Struck Goliath: The Part-Time Faculty Association, Washington State Community Colleges, and Class-Action Lawsuits," in *The Current Landscape and Changing Perspectives of Part-Time Faculty*, special issue of *New Directions for Community Colleges*, 2007 (issue 140): 49–54; and Dan Jacoby, "Is Washington State an Unlikely Leader? Progress on Addressing Contingent Work Issues in Academia," *Education Policy Analysis Archives* 9, no. 41 (8 October 2001), *epaa.asu.edu.*
81. AAUP, *Tenure and Teaching-Intensive Appointments.*
82. Cary Nelson, "Playing Mozart on the Titanic," *Inside Higher Ed*, 4 January 2010, *insidehighered.com.*
83. Eric Foner, *The Fiery Trial: Abraham Lincoln and American Slavery* (New York: Norton, 2010), 259.
84. Ibid., 260.
85. Nelson, "Solidarity vs. Contingency."
86. Judith M. Gappa and David W. Leslie, *The Invisible Faculty: Improving the Status of Part-Timers in Higher Education* (San Francisco: Jossey-Bass, 1993), 3.
87. Ibid.
88. Frederick Douglass, "West India Emancipation," 3 August 1857, in *Frederick Douglass: Selected Speeches and Writings*, ed. Philip S. Foner and Yuval Taylor (Chicago: Lawrence Hill Books, 1999), 367.

# 6

## The Question of Academic Unions

### Community (or Conflict) of Interest?

*Jack Longmate*

A union is a fraternity of workers seeking to benefit one and all. Members are presumed to share a "community of interests."[1] This was assumed by an Olympic College (Bremerton, WA) financial officer who, when explaining why the administration would be reluctant to question the union's prerogative on distributing funds for faculty, responded by asking, "Why would a union not act in the best interests of its members?"

A union may not act in the best interests of its members when its members have diverse or competing interests, and it would seem that our country's 1.8 million higher education faculty are hardly homogeneous. According to the American Federation of Teachers, the US professoriate is 27 percent tenured faculty, 21 percent graduate assistants, 15 percent full-time nontenured faculty, and—the largest group—37 percent part-time adjuncts.[2]

Do tenured full-time instructors and nontenured part-time or adjunct faculty have substantial mutual interests that warrant being in the same bargaining unit, as they are in the thirty-four colleges of Washington's Community and Technical College (CTC) system? Or are such two-tiered workplaces more aptly categorized as "conflicts of interests"?

In Washington State colleges, the part-time faculty outnumber the tenured, roughly nine thousand to three thousand, but union membership is dominated by the tenured. At Olympic College, where I have been an adjunct instructor since 1992, roughly 82 percent of the tenured faculty are union members, compared to only 8 percent of the nontenured. (When I became a union member in the late 1990s, I was one of two adjunct members at the time.)

Such differences in union membership raise the question of why more nontenured faculty are not union members, especially when, being more numerous, they could conceivably dominate the union's agenda? Possible reasons include the following:

Some fear joining a union could interfere with their aspiration for a tenured position or their chances of being offered future classes. Others, given the meager improvements in workplace conditions over the years, have become fatalistic and complacent about the possibility for change and consider union involvement a waste of time. Some hold their unions partially responsible for the lack of job security, unequal pay, limited workload, and spotty benefits. There's also expense: for those at or below the poverty line, even a discounted membership fee may seem excessive.[3]

The following ten items are key in the "community of interests" the members of a common bargaining unit are to share. After considering each, I present a brief profile of the faculty unions of British Columbia for comparison, and offer some thoughts on remedies.

1. Wages or compensation
2. Hours of work
3. Employment benefits
4. Supervision
5. Qualifications
6. Training and skills
7. Job functions
8. Contact with other employees
9. Integration of work functions with other employees
10. History of collective bargaining[4]

## 1. Wages or Compensation

Tenured full-time and part-time faculty have separate, nonproportional pay scales. In Washington State, part-time faculty earn roughly 62 percent of full-timers when performing the same work. This fact certainly suggests differing, if not conflicting, interests.

Whereas in industry, full-time workers oftentimes urge prorated pay for their part-time colleagues, fearing that if part-timers were cheaper, they could threaten the workload of full-timers. There is no such impetus in the case of full-time faculty, who, as tenured faculty, are assured of a full-time workload. This difference may impact the collective bargaining dynamics.

Most Washington State part-time faculty wages can be described as "poverty" wages. Two factors contribute to this: the 62 percent discounted adjunct rate of pay and the fact that part-time faculty face a workload cap that restricts them from teaching more than roughly 85 percent (the percent

| PPMS 002 | DETACH AND RETAIN THIS STATEMENT OF EARNINGS AND DEDUCTIONS FOR YOUR RECORDS | | | | | | | |
|---|---|---|---|---|---|---|---|---|
| EMPLOYEE | CHECK DATE | CHECK NO. | LEAVE AS OF 12/15/09 | BEGINNING | TAKEN | EARNED | BALANCE |
| ************* 12/24/09 | 03153698 | | | | | | |
| JOHN W. LONGMATE | | | VACATION | | | | |
| OLYMPIC COLLEGE | | M 01 | SICK-COMP 427.9 | | | 427.90 | |
| PDL: P50 GROSS PAY | TOTAL DEDUCTIONS | NET PAY | SICK-NCOMP | | | | |
| CURRENT 1,038.63 | 214.96 | 823.67 | PERS HOLIDAY | | | | |
| YEAR TO DATE: GROSS PAY 18,706.52 | TAX DEFERRED 3,778.66 | TAXABLE GROSS 14,927.86 | | | | | |
| TYPE OF PAY HOURS | AMOUNT | EMPLOYEE DEDUCTION/REDUCTION | CURRENT | YEAR-TO-DATE | | | |
| P/T FA CON 16.67 | 1,038.63 | TIAA/CREF BAS R | 103.86 | Y | 1,870.66 | | |
| **TOTAL GROSS** | 1,038.63 | OASI DED | 64.40 | Y | 1,041.51 | | |
| | | FED W/H TAX | 12.67 | Y | 313.87 | | |
| | | MEDICARE INS D | 15.06 | Y | 243.58 | | |
| | | LTD DED | 7.18 | Y | 35.88 | | |
| | | MEDAID&SUP PEN | 1.40 | Y | 25.20 | | |
| | | WEA % AMT P/T | 10.39 | Y | 187.04 | | |
| | | AETNA PUB EM RED | | Y | 1,908.00 | | |
| | | TOTAL DED/RED | 214.96 | | | | |
| EMPLOYER CONTRIBUTIONS | AMOUNT | | | | | | |
| TIAA/CREF CON | 103.86 | | | | | | |
| OASI CONTRIB | 64.40 | | | | | | |
| MEDICARE INS C | 15.06 | | | | | | |
| UNIFORM DENTAL C | 745.00 | | | | | | |
| IND INS CONT | 1.76 | | | | | | |
| MEDAID&SUP PEN | 1.40 | | | | | | |

Paystub showing annual earnings for an Olympic College adjunct faculty

varies depending on the college) of a full-time load at a college. As a testament to this fact is my 2009 year-end pay stub, which shows my annual gross income for teaching at 66 percent of a full-time load as $18,706. If this were an instructor's sole income, he or she would qualify as "extremely low income."[5]

## 2. Hours of Work

Hours of work for tenured and nontenured faculty are a clear conflict of interest. While tenured faculty are assured of teaching a specified number of classes to fulfill the expectation of their full-time teaching load, they are also allowed the option to teach additional courses beyond their full-time load, which are called "overloads"; teaching overloads is also called "moonlighting." According to the Washington State Board for Community and Technical Colleges, the state's 3,455 full-time instructors taught the equivalent of 434 additional full-time loads as course overloads, which means roughly 12 percent of all classes delivered by tenured faculty are overloads.[6]

Also in 2008, the equivalent of 2,965 full-time teaching loads were taught by nontenured part-time faculty, which means that between 6,000 and 9,000 individuals were employed as part-time instructors. (The number of individuals must necessarily be much higher since part-time faculty members cannot teach full time, their workload being limited as it is by the cap.)

The option to teach course overloads is a significant dimension of full-time faculty workload and salary structure. The reasons are obvious: overloads provide tenured faculty with the means to earn income in addition to their regular salary with minimum extra effort without having to travel to a different workplace. Though the income earned is oftentimes on the discounted part-time faculty salary rate, it is an option that some full-time faculty consider their privilege to accept. Yet when full-time faculty elect to teach course overloads, they are taking work that would otherwise be apportioned to part-time faculty, which amounts to a direct conflict of interest between full-time and part-time faculty. Unlike a dispute between longshoremen and teamsters over work, this is between members of the same union.

One faculty union leader has condoned overloads, arguing that it inherently encourages tenured faculty support for improvements in the part-time salary schedule, since improvements to the part-time salary schedule amount to pay raises for some full-time faculty. But that "advantage" is more than offset when tenured faculty displace part-time faculty in teaching assignments.

A past president of the Olympic College faculty union appealed to his fellow tenured faculty members to resist the temptation to teach course overloads.[7] In December 2009, Olympic College ratified a new collective bargaining agreement that, for the first time, imposed a limit on the practice of tenured full-time faculty teaching course overloads, though the limits can hardly be considered severe. Appendix B, Section 13-3, of the agreement reads: "Full-time members of the faculty may not work for more than 167% of their quarterly annualized load."[8] Exceptions to the "167% limit" exist, along with a gratuitous proviso that "full-time faculty may not exceed 167% by 'bumping' adjunct faculty." (Since full-time faculty are barred from teaching above 167 percent, they would be barred from bumping part-time faculty in any case, as if bumping part-time faculty when teaching between 100 and 166 percent amounts to no problem.) This provision was to curtail abuse by some full-time members rumored to have taught as much as 300 percent of a full-time load. In contrast, part-time faculty members at Olympic College may teach no more than 85 percent of a full-time load.[9]

A telling example of conflict of interest over full-time and part-time hours of work has been in the legislative realm. Since 2005 in Washington State, there have been legislative attempts to promulgate a job security/job protection bill for part-time adjunct faculty, inspired in principle by the system in place in British Columbia colleges. In the proposed legislation (HB 2080/SB 5907 of 2005 and HB 1452/SB 5019 of 2007 and SB 6888 of 2008), nontenured instructors who have taught at half time for at least three years (nine quarters) would be granted annual renewable contracts that would continue from year to year and could be terminated for cause, along with "the right to a hearing and standard grievance procedures afforded to full-time faculty by contract."[10]

The Washington State chapters of the AFT and the NEA have opposed these bills. One unstated motivation behind this opposition is to avoid inter-ference with the largely unfettered ability of tenured full-time faculty to teach course overloads, which, as noted earlier, some full-time faculty consider their privilege to teach. Here is the transcribed testimony of a higher education union representative on HB 1452 on January 29, 2007:

> Part-time job security is incredibly important, but I'm not sure that this bill will do it in the way it ought to. The concerns that we have are, as already mentioned, there's no evaluative process in this. What it means is the criteria are cumulative, chronological, and retroactive. If you've been teaching one course for nine quarters, if this bill passed, you would immediately have this status. As written and without other part-time faculty circumstances significantly revised and improved, this bill could create a permanent middle tier of underpaid faculty, and we don't want to see that happen. Over the long term this status could potentially be the Trojan horse that could be used against the tenure system itself. Some college administrations will balk at the lack of robust evaluative process to determine the suitability of taking on a nine-quarter part-time teacher candidate for lifelong employment. And what I fear is that administra-tions will start terminating part-time people at eight quarters because they don't want to go through this. The collective bargaining part of this bill seems to be gratuitous in a sense because I'm not sure what's left to bargain. It is very prescriptive.[11]

The testimony identified four of the union's objections to HB 1452:

1. "No evaluative process": By employing this phrase, the rep suggests that it would be inertia (a "cumulative, chronological, and retroactive" effect) rather than a teaching excellence certified by evaluation that would contribute to part-time job protection. But if unqualified faculty are currently being hired with their incompetence going undetected term after term because no evaluation process is in place, surely it is those responsible for hiring—the college administrations—who are negligent; as such, this objection amounts to blaming part-time faculty for the incompetence of administrators. But irrespective of competence or negligence, for a union to oppose a measure that would bring job security to its members certainly suggests that the union is an extension of management and not an agent to defend the interests of nontenured faculty.
2. "Permanent middle tier of underpaid faculty": The union invokes this scenario as if the two-tier status quo, with no job protection for the

bottom tier, is preferable to the creation of a middle tier with some job protection. Categorically, all workers would prefer some job security to none at all.

3. "Lifelong employment": Such a characterization is a rather transparent scare tactic, aimed at alarming legislators by equating this "middle tier" with tenure. HB 1452 does call on college administrations to be accountable for discontinuing the employment of the newly created class of "associate faculty," as is customary in professional employment settings.

4. "Administrations will start terminating part-time people": This argument likewise would seem to be a scare tactic, but underscores the need for legislation like HB 1452. If administrators can capriciously terminate nontenured part-time people at will, those part-timers who have been hired and rehired for three years or more deserve protection from such capriciousness.

One frequently raised objection to job security bills is that job security belongs under the domain of local collective bargaining, not state legislation. But there is hypocrisy when Washington tenured faculty cite that argument in opposing job security legislation, since job security for tenured faculty is established through state statute.[12] Further, the two faculty unions have failed to bargain any meaningful job security for part-time faculty.

During the 2008 legislative session, a similar part-time faculty job security bill, SB 6888, was scheduled for a hearing in the Senate Higher Education Committee on February 4, 2008. At the moment in the hearing when SB 6888 was to be discussed, rather than testifying against the measure, all the officers and advocates of both faculty unions made a preorchestrated exit (walkout) as a show of overt nonsupport for the proposed legislation.

If bills like HB 1452 or SB 6888 would not create job security for part-time faculty "the way [they] ought to," what alternative to the perpetual probationary status do the unions favor? Union support in Washington State has been for the AFT's Faculty And College Excellence (FACE) initiative. Selected provisions of HB 1875, for example, include "new full-time tenure-track appointments" and the granting of "priority consideration" to current part-time faculty for those new jobs, with calls for each college to strive to avoid "eliminating positions" (which would be nonetheless inevitable in converting several part-time positions into a full-time one).[13] While a provision of this sort should be applauded by part-time faculty, it does offer a false promise: since part-time faculty vastly outnumber full-time faculty, even if every one of the full-time tenured faculty were to resign, those resignations would not create enough full-time openings to accommodate all current part-time faculty. Many part-timers have lost courses as a result of the creation of new full-time positions.

FACE also has called on each institution to "determine a salary standard for adjunct faculty members [that] constitutes a pro rata salary compared to the salaries of full-time tenured faculty . . . doing comparable work."[14] Again, while improvements in part-time faculty pay should be encouraged, disquieting is the likelihood of inviting each of Washington's thirty-four colleges to develop its own salary standard, as there are those within the college establishment, including some tenured faculty, who now argue that current statewide part-time faculty pay rate of 62 percent is, in fact, an appropriate prorated salary, on the grounds that full-time faculty are contracted for more duties than part-time faculty. Washington's 2005 *Best Employment Practices For Part-Time Faculty* report, commissioned by the legislature, points out that the cost of upgrading all faculty salaries to the full-time rate (similar to British Columbia's) would amount to an additional expenditure of $115.5 million per biennium.[15] This is a sad reflection of how severely underpaid current part-time faculty are in Washington State.

In short, the approach favored by the unions is to reward a few part-time faculty with full-time positions and encourage each college to establish a pro rata salary. The former would not benefit those part-time faculty who are not converted to full time, who would remain the majority. Prorated salaries are unlikely, given the state's current budget deficit problems. However, extending job security to part-time faculty in the form proposed by HB 1452 would have only a nominal budgetary impact. The failure of the unions to embrace HB 1452, or even to incorporate job security provisions for existing part-time faculty into FACE legislation, could reflect a conflict of interest: full-time faculty interests do not wish to see part-time faculty job protection because it could interfere with their ability to teach course overloads at will.

## 3. Employment Benefits

While tenured faculty receive full benefits upon hire, nontenured adjuncts in Washington qualify for health care and retirement when they teach at 50 percent of a full-time teaching load for two consecutive terms. Part-time faculty benefits are contingent on workload, which intensifies the importance of job protection for part-time faculty. Some colleges in Washington State have been known to employ a money-saving hiring practice known as "gapping," where the employee's workload is deliberately structured to prevent eligibility for benefits (e.g., hiring an adjunct to teach 60 percent of full-time in one term, 30 percent in the next, and then 60 percent, thereby precluding him or her from ever satisfying the qualifying criteria of two consecutive terms at 50 percent).

Because nontenured adjuncts who qualify for benefits constitute an additional expense for colleges, colleges may gravitate toward full-time faculty overloads since no additional benefit expense is incurred. Thus, with regard to benefits, the needs of part-time faculty are pitted against full-time jobs.

Unemployment insurance (UI) stands out as a benefit where full-time and part-time faculty do not share a community of interest. UI is of little concern for tenured faculty but it is of vital interest for contingent faculty who, at the end of every term, are no longer employed and are thus eligible to file for unemployment benefits. While there has been increased awareness of this issue within Washington State NEA-affiliated locals, several in faculty union leadership positions have been unaware that part-timers could or should apply for unemployment between quarters, which is a further indication of the absence of a community of workplace interests. Since most if not all colleges in Washington State contract with private firms that are in the business of minimizing unemployment expenditures by regularly challenging unemployment claims filed by adjuncts and staffed by individuals trained in unnerving or intimidating unemployment claimants, it is incumbent on unions to provide guidance and support for adjuncts when they file.

## 4. Supervision

If a formal organizational chart were developed for community college faculty, it would likely show an administrator, such as a dean, as the official supervisor to whom faculty members would report. However, tenured faculty oftentimes are active participants in executing supervisory and job-assignment functions over adjuncts. A tenured instructor from an English department of an Illinois college discloses the supervisory role over adjuncts:

> Fortunately, I am not responsible for all of the hiring, management, and evaluation procedures. A full-time faculty member serves as coordinator of adjunct faculty. The coordinator is released from teaching one class to do the job, and so far, each has chosen to serve for just one academic year. These coordinators have played important roles in developing procedures, preparing forms, and providing day-to-day supervision and evaluation of part-time faculty.[16]

In some Washington colleges, tenured faculty members serve as division chairs who perform direct supervisory functions over adjunct faculty.

Since those tenured faculty and the adjuncts they supervise are in the same bargaining unit, there is a clear conflict of interest and a violation of the union principle made explicit by a University of California publication: "Bargaining units may not include supervisors, managers or confidential employees."[17]

An example of this conflict was evident during a workplace dispute at a community college that had launched a new program. Two existing part-time faculty members were hired to teach and two tenured full-time faculty were assigned supervisory duties. But one of the part-time instructors was terminated mid-term, allegedly on the grounds that her teaching style was incompatible with the program's needs. The laid-off instructor, who was profoundly offended by the action, disputed the disparaging opinion of her teaching style, charged that the layoff was unprofessional and unwarranted, and defended herself by saying that she had been given no prior indication of deficiencies in her teaching and no chance to correct them. Moreover, not once had either of the two tenured faculty or any other representative from the institution observed her classroom teaching.

When the laid-off instructor complained to the union about her termination, the issue was awkward since the two tenured full-time instructors who had recommended laying off the instructor were union members. The faculty union was caught between defending the interests of the two tenured faculty and the laid-off adjunct faculty. On the basis of social relationships alone, adjuncts caught in such positions are at a disadvantage.

Here is another observation about supervision. I hold a non-teaching job for a Department of Defense contractor, and my company has a policy of periodic performance reviews of employees with their supervisors. While perfunctory, these evaluations are reassuring and can be helpful in disclosing areas where one might need to improve or areas for training. They also sometimes provide insights on how to better compete for job advancements, and they tend to affirm the company's appreciation for the employee's service. But in my twenty years of adjunct teaching, I have received only one formal performance review, and that was delivered by a tenured faculty member who evaluated a single class. At Olympic College, I have never had any discussion about recommended training or my career path. Even though I've been treated graciously by the institution and continue to be offered teaching opportunities most (but not all) terms, I believe that this seemingly cavalier attitude toward adjunct instructional staff is distinct from the treatment received by tenure-track staff, who are supported by a tenure review committee whose members take an interest in the employee's professional development and performance.

## 5. Qualifications

On initial hire, full-time and part-time faculty are expected to satisfy the same qualification requirements. However, once they are employed, full-time faculty have a decided advantage in maintaining and upgrading their qualifications. They are generally supported by an annual professional development stipend and a salary structure that rewards both teaching longevity and professional development credit. By contrast, part-time faculty are provided neither a regularized professional development stipend nor salary incentive to maintain currency in their teaching field. Since they often hold multiple jobs, there is little motivation on their part to devote personal time toward maintaining currency in their teaching field.

Part-time faculty may compete with full-time faculty for professional development grants, but are at a distinct disadvantage when doing so, being less well-known and less prominent personalities on campus. Also, reviewing committees are reluctant to expend precious grant funds on nontenured faculty, who are temporary employees, fearing accusations of irresponsible stewardship. As such, this would seem to be yet another conflict of interest.

At Olympic College, per its collective bargaining agreement, a yearly allotment of $5,000 has been set aside for professional enrichment grants to the 380 adjuncts. However, in 2009, the union president reported that the $5,000 allocation for adjunct professional development had not been spent, and that the administration had asked him if that amount could be transferred to the next year's professional development account. (For what it's worth, at least one application for funding during the 2008–2009 academic year had come from an adjunct; it was not approved.)

## 6. Training and Skills

With the advent of new teaching technology, there is an ongoing need for faculty to acquire new skills, apart from maintaining their qualifications in their teaching discipline. When training is made available, however, nontenured faculty are often unable to take advantage of it. Being contracted for classroom teaching only, they must generally use their personal time to receive such training, but limited compensation requires many adjuncts to hold multiple jobs, so they may not have the disposable time for acquiring additional skills, even when they have the desire to do so.

Poorly paid, nonpermanent employees may see little point in making personal sacrifices to acquire new skills for jobs that they aren't sure they'll keep.

## 7. Job Functions

Full-time faculty are assigned a wider range of job functions than part-time faculty; that fact is commonly used to argue—wrongly, in my opinion—that part-time faculty do not deserve equal pay since they are not assigned equal work. Full-time faculty functions include the following:

- Advising students
- Holding office hours
- Developing curriculum
- Serving on campus governance or departmental committees
- Executing administrative duties
- Pursuing professional development
- Participating in nonteaching days

Adjuncts are not expected to perform these functions but to "just teach," which is how the discount in adjunct pay is often justified; since adjuncts don't do the same work as full-time faculty, they don't deserve the same pay.

But many part-time faculty perform many of these functions as responsible educators; it just so happens that they are not compensated for executing them.

Additionally, when it comes to the core functions of teaching, there is no difference between tenured full-time instructors and nontenured part-time instructors. The same tuition is charged for their classes, and the grades and credits awarded carry the same value, whether they are conferred by tenured full-time instructors or nontenured part-time instructors.

## 8. Contact with Other Employees

Full-time and part-time faculty differ sharply with respect to their contact with fellow employees.

With their offices co-located with their peers, full-time faculty are immersed in the affairs of the campus and with fellow employees. Part-time faculty, by contrast, have an "out of sight, out of mind" status as implied by "Those Unfamiliar Names and Faces," the title of the article by the tenured supervisor I quoted earlier. Aside from contact with their students, part-time faculty have little presence on campus, not having personal offices, and after teaching their classes they may scramble away, often to other jobs. One Olympic College adjunct taught for several years before he met his first tenured faculty member. But even amid concentrations of full-time faculty, part-timers are not necessarily prone to meet or interact with tenured faculty on a routine basis. Not only are part-time faculty isolated from full-time faculty; they are, perhaps even more significantly, isolated from each other.

One distinct difference in contact with other employees surrounds the hiring process. Full-time faculty are commonly recruited through a nationally advertised job search, reviewed by a hiring committee and the college president, and, once hired, scrutinized by a tenure review committee. When they are granted tenure, that accomplishment is publicly heralded as a significant professional milestone and announced to the community. Their names are inducted into the college catalog.

Part-time faculty, by contrast, are hired in a far more casual manner, with no public fanfare; they may or may not undergo a performance evaluation, and generally are not issued a contract that extends beyond the current term. Their names are rarely included in the college catalog, and in class schedules, oftentimes in lieu of their names are "Staff" or "TBA."

Full-time faculty, proud of their professional accomplishments, may tend to see part-time faculty, who have not undergone the rigors of the tenure review process, as lesser faculty and may respond to adjunct calls for "equal pay for equal work" with offense, as if the adjuncts are asking for a reward that is not deserved.

Further, because full-time faculty have a permanent presence on the campus, with private offices, computers, nameplates, and the like, they may perceive the campus as their domain, and when it comes to decisions affecting the campus, they may see part-time faculty as intruders onto their turf rather than fellow professionals who happen to be employed on a part-time basis. Such social dynamics work to contribute to a conflict rather than a community of interest among faculty.

## 9. Integration of Work Functions with Other Employees

Lacking regular contact with co-workers affects the integration of work functions, as does the lack of job security. Karen Thompson of Rutgers explains this:

> The working condition I want to emphasize . . . is job security. It is a condition from which other working conditions emerge: "no need for an office if we don't know if you're staying," "why provide health or pension benefits if you're not going to be around long," "salary concerns are irrelevant if you're leaving soon." Part-time and adjunct faculty don't just have poor working conditions; for the most part, they have no working conditions. If every-

thing you do professionally is colored by a context of wondering if you'll be teaching again next term, then the ultimate working condition becomes knowing whether you have a job or not.

The literature already abounds with detailed stories of freeway flyers piecing multiple jobs together into a livelihood; of award-winning teachers worrying from semester to semester whether they are employed; of conscientious, highly credentialed instructors losing their positions overnight. What is the impact of thousands of postsecondary educators . . . functioning in these circumstances? It means we are vulnerable and insecure. It means we are teaching without academic freedom, unless you're counting on First Amendment Rights being enforced. And even if institutions or associations claim all teachers do have academic freedom, we know that anyone worried about whether they'll be back in the fall is watching what they say, stepping to the proper beat, or just plain anxious to please. They are less likely to complain about improprieties, to object to mistreatment, and especially less likely to form unions. Educationally, this means innovation, experimentation, and certainly open inquiry will inevitably be compromised.[18]

Thompson emphasizes how the lack of job security stifles academic freedom and undermines the integrity of the educational system by inducing compliance and compromise. Grade inflation, as a means to minimize student complaints and thus bolster the likelihood of rehire, is a predictable outcome.

But apart from effects on the integrity of higher education itself, the uncertain job security and subordinate status of part-time faculty impact the psychology of the individual. While it is admittedly farfetched to draw a parallel with the finding of the Milgram experiment—the "extreme willingness of adults to go to almost any lengths" on the command of an authority figure—the sobering reality is that adjunct faculty may see their relationships with tenured faculty as crucial to their continuing employment, and thus may be induced to "almost any lengths" to compromise or comply, which could even mean acting against their own best interest as workers.[19]

Barbara Ehrenreich's 2001 *Nickel and Dimed—On (Not) Getting By in America* was written with entry-level workers rather than contingent faculty in mind, but it may have implications here: "If you are constantly reminded of your lowly position in the social hierarchy, whether by individual managers of by a plethora of impersonal rules, you begin to accept that unfortunate status."[20]

If the psychological impact on the individual induces part-time faculty into being less inclined to defend their own interests and more inclined to seek compliance, that behavior also undermines the community of interests that is predicated on trust and solidarity.

## 10. History of Collective Bargaining

While some argue that neither full-time nor part-time faculty have prospered under collective bargaining in recent decades, the fact that part-time faculty compensation is at the poverty level, with no job security, decidedly inferior workplace conditions, and dismal prospects of improvement, would seem to indict the collective bargaining process as particularly ineffective from the standpoint of part-time faculty.

A union needs solidarity, trust, and fraternity to be an effective force. As an example of the lack of these things, here is a personal anecdote: In the fall of 1999, I proposed to the Olympic College Board of Trustees that the subject of adjunct faculty be discussed. While I can't say with confidence that my request was the catalyst, the board of trustees convened a special study session on the topic on March 28, 2000. The union president and several tenured faculty union members of the negotiating team attended the session and made a presentation. While I was a union member and had some stature as a part-time faculty advocate at the time, neither I nor any other part-time faculty were invited to attend or even to provide input or review, even though a resolution I had authored was presented to the trustees as the union's own. I learned of the study session *after* it had taken place, with the union president sheepishly apologizing to me, saying that he hadn't contacted me since he didn't know if I were around. While I may or may not have reason to feel personally slighted at not being invited, the more significant observation is that the full-time faculty leadership presumed they had the right to assume the voice of the part-time faculty and speak on its behalf. Naturally, this incident did not engender trust and confidence and respect for my fellow faculty.

## Comparison with British Columbia

The bifurcation between tenured and nontenured faculty that is universal in US higher education is often not present in the colleges of British Columbia, Canada. The lack of bifurcation is epitomized by the province's largest two-year institution, Vancouver Community College.[21] There, standard working conditions promote a community of interests. The structural conditions make this clear. All faculty, whether full-time or part-time, whether probationary or regular, are paid according to the same eleven-step salary scale.

After teaching for a specific period of time at a minimum of 50 percent of a full-time load with satisfactory evaluations, probationary faculty are awarded regular status, which is the functional equivalent of tenure. Thus, regular faculty do not compete with probationary term faculty in the distribution of funds; at US institutions, where tenured and nontenured faculty have significantly different pay scales, the structural conditions create conflict.

Workload is assigned at the department level, and the primary determinant in that assignment is seniority, not full-time or part-time status. Seniority is accrued by all faculty according to a well-defined and transparent system: Term faculty accrue seniority on a prorated basis; teaching at 50 percent of full-time yields 50 percent of seniority accrual. For regular faculty, whether full-time or part-time, seniority is accrued as if full-time, irrespective of teaching load, which thereby ensures that a given faculty member, once regularized, will maintain his or her seniority ranking, even if he or she does not teach as many courses as other colleagues. The seniority rankings, furthermore, are publicly posted for all to review. Since seniority accrual is accessible to all faculty, there is little ground for conflicts of interests among faculty. Indeed, the common system engenders a "we're all in this together" culture. The strike is an active tool in the defense of faculty rights and working conditions.

## Conclusion

Whenever a social system establishes itself, people become accustomed to that system and, before long, come to think of it as the natural and normal order. Many come to believe that it is correct and proper for tenured faculty to receive significantly higher wages than nontenured faculty, to be granted professional development funds annually, to be provided offices and other benefits, and to have the right to teach course overloads (overtime) at will, or, for that matter, for an adjunct to earn 62 percent of what a full-time faculty would earn for teaching the same courseload, and for adjuncts to be temporary workers on a perpetual probationary status, sometimes for decades.

The two-tier workplace of tenured and nontenured faculty, with differences in compensation, workload, and job security, among other factors, would seem to cast doubt on the "community of interests" of a single bargaining unit for both. A solution may involve a culture change, which may not be immediate. Still, two solutions come to mind.

For Washington State community and technical college faculty, one solution would be the creation of separate bargaining units for nontenured faculty. Some adjunct unions exist with some success (e.g., AFT Local 6100, the Madison Area Technical Colleges union, in Wisconsin). It is possible that these new unions could have a transformative effect and inspire guarded, frustrated, and disenfranchised contingents into activism, which would be key to bringing about reform. Of course, it is also possible that, just as contingent faculty rarely join full-time faculty unions now, their reluctance may carry over to the new union. Also, workers at the poverty level may not have expendable income for dues, and the dues collected from low-income workers may be a problematic funding source for union activity.

Another solution would be, through collective bargaining and legislation, to remove the discriminatory features of the two-tier system, thereby creating the framework for a single faculty. A primary move would be to provide job security for nontenured faculty. Being no longer temporary and probationary but on an employment path that could lead to full-time employment would erode the lion's share of conflicts now inherent in the two-tier system.

Arguing for the later approach are the colleges like Vancouver Community College in British Columbia, Canada, which are models of the "community of interests." The absence of a pay differential between full- and part-time faculty removes the cost incentive for hiring armies of part-timers, as is typical in the United States. It could very well be, however, that a more important strategy is cultivating a unionist mentality that earnestly sees equity for all faculty as the goal and takes seriously the union's role of representing *all* its members, especially those who are the most vulnerable.

But investing in adjuncts by making them regular employees, as opposed to temporary, probationary employees on a perpetual basis, could be done legislatively by conferring job security for those who have worked at 50 percent of a full-time load for nine quarters. The qualifying criteria would be the college's own hiring record. Such a change would not make even a nominal impact on the state budget and would grant adjuncts a sense of membership in the college community and the collective bargaining process.

As noted earlier, a social system, once established, becomes seen as the natural and normal order. Nontenured faculty in Washington State and elsewhere may lack a vision of equity or of equal pay for equal work, and feel undeserving of equal status. However, if they were granted job security, the change in culture could transform their vision.

## NOTES

1.  "Teacher's Unions/Collective Bargaining," in *Encyclopedia of Everyday Law*, ed. Shirelle Phelps (Farmington Hills, MI: Gale Cengage, 2003), *enotes.com*.
2.  American Federation of Teachers (AFT), *The State of the Higher Education Workforce, 1997–2007* (Washington, DC: AFT, 2009), *aft.org*.
3.  Jack Longmate, "Recruiting Contingent Faculty," *NEA Higher Education Advocate*, October 2009, 12, *www.nea.org*.
4.  "Teacher's Unions/Collective Bargaining."

5.  "Income Guidelines for Kitsap County (Annual Salary by Family Size)," Kitsap County (WA) government website, 2008, *www.kitsapgov.com*.

6.  Washington State Board for Community and Technical Colleges (SBCTC), *Academic Year Report, 2011–2012* (Olympia, WA: SBCTC, 2012), 58, *www.sbctc.ctc.edu/college/d_acad.aspx*.

7.  I mention Nat Hong's appeal (made during a union meeting at which I was present) in "Cutting Colleges' Adjunct Instructors Not a Wise Move," *Tacoma News Tribune*, 27 January 2009, *www.thenewstribune.com*.

8.  Olympic College, *Collective Bargaining Agreement between Olympic College Board of Trustees and the Olympic College Association for Higher Education, 2009–2013* (Bremerton, WA: Olympic College, 2009), *www.olympic.edu*.

9.  As this new policy was being implemented in Spring 2010, at least one full-time faculty member complained about no longer being able to teach more than a 167 percent overload limit in addition to her full-time wage.

10.  Washington State Legislature, SB 6888, "An Act Relating to Higher Education," 2008 Regular Session, *apps.leg.wa.gov*.

11.  Nathaniel Hong, House Higher Education Committee, "WEA Union Testimony on HB 1452," 29 January 2007, from approximately 3:18 to 3:20 p.m. (from the 1:49:40 mark to the 1:51:55 mark on the recording); accessed 9 February 2007 at *www.tvw.org*.

12.  Revised Code of Washington (RCW), chapters 28B.50.850 through 28B.50.870.

13.  Washington State Legislature, HB 1875, "Employment Opportunities at Institutions of Higher Education," 2007 Regular Session, *www.leg.wa.gov*.

14.  Ibid.

15.  SBCTC, *2005 Best Employment Practices For Part-Time Faculty* (Olympia, WA: SBCTC, 2005), 3, *www.sbctc.edu*.

16.  Marlys M. Styne, "Those Unfamiliar Names and Faces: The Hiring, Management, and Evaluation of Part-Time Faculty," *Teaching English in the Two-Year College* 24, no. 1 (February 1997): 50–54.

17.  University of California, Berkeley, "Information for Directors, Managers, and Supervisors about Collective Bargaining at the University of California, Berkeley," Human Resources at UC Berkeley, accessed 3 April 2013, *hrweb.berkeley.edu*.

18.  Karen Thompson, "The Ultimate Working Condition: Knowing Whether You Have a Job or Not," *Forum: Newsletter of the Non-Tenure-Track Faculty Special Interest Group, Conference on College Composition and Communication*, Winter 1998, A19–24.

19.  Quoted in Howard Zinn, *Declarations of Independence: Cross-Examining American Ideology* (New York: Perennial, 1991), 38.

20.  Barbara Ehrenreich, *Nickel and Dimed—On (Not) Getting By in America* (New York: Metropolitan Books, 2001), 210.

21.  See Cosco's essay in this volume.

# 7

# Do College Teachers Have to Be Scholars?

*Frank Donoghue*

A fascinating op-ed piece from the March 6, 2009, issue of the *Chronicle of Higher Education* prompted me to ask my title question: do college teachers have to be scholars? The editorial, by Douglas Texter, is brashly titled, "No Tenure? No Problem: How to Make $100,000 a Year as an Adjunct English Instructor." To the question "Do college teachers have to be scholars?" Texter emphatically answers "no." He maps out a job description—his own—in which he renounces any professional identity as a scholar. A PhD in English from the University of Minnesota, he reasons that there are virtually no tenure-track jobs at research universities (where scholarship is prized most highly and thus rewarded), yet there is an abundance of adjunct positions. So rather than feel demoralized by taking on a low-level, likely part-time position while continuing to aspire to the life of a tenured scholar, he embraces the life of the adjunct, committing himself to excellence in teaching and teaching as much as he can—enough, he asserts, to make $100,000 a year.

Texter describes, in the most radical terms, the main guidelines for making the emotional and psychological adjustments required to change professional goals. First, he says, "Stop thinking of yourself as an intellectual. You're not Henry Giroux or Russell Jacoby or Judith Butler. . . . If you must write scholarship . . . consider it a hobby. Frame the cover. Show your mother." Instead, he insists that you "conceive of yourself as a self-employed professional seeking to provide the best possible services to the greatest number of clients." Second, he says, "Change your associates." Texter characterizes his fellow English graduate students at the University of Minnesota as "pretentious sheep" and maintains that by his last year of graduate school he was "teaching in another department; working at a community college; writing for an ad agency; pumping out fiction, satire, and scholarship"; and making $60,000. As a PhD student, these freelance work habits inclined him not only to stop thinking of himself as an intellectual, but to stop socializing with people who clung to that self-definition. Third, Texter advises, "Change what you read. Stop reading scholarship . . . and start cracking goal-setting, time-management, and

Originally published in *The Hedgehog Review, Volume 14.1* (Spring 2012): 29–42.
Reprinted with permission.

financial self-help books."[1] He makes several other suggestions in his article, but these suffice to convey his central thesis and tone.

Texter paints, from my perspective, too rosy a picture of his working conditions, conveniently eliding consideration of health and retirement benefits and the tax ramifications of his many freelance jobs. He does, though, present himself unapologetically as a new kind of academic: he earned a traditional PhD, then abandoned any pretense to reading scholarship, let alone doing scholarship. His decision and his defense of it represent a profound move, and here I explore some of the implications by asking a series of questions that seek to pull apart connections between teaching and scholarship, which so much of the academy has uncritically yoked together for years. Ultimately we need to ask why Texter's position is so likely to strike an audience of postsecondary teachers—graduate student TAs, his fellow adjuncts, and professors alike—as shocking, even horrifying. He states that he's changing careers, a familiar story in PhD student circles in the humanities. But Texter's story has an unfamiliar twist: he's staying in the academy as a college teacher. He's changing jobs by redefining his postsecondary teaching position in a way that both suits his practical ambitions and reflects the realities of postsecondary teaching in today's world.

Barring heroic and successful unionization efforts, the number of adjuncts is certain to continue to grow exponentially. Let's not forget, too, that unionization efforts are, more often than not, aimed at improving the working conditions and job security of adjuncts rather than at converting adjunct positions into tenured positions. The key factor in the surge of adjunct hires has been the expansion of community colleges in the United States. Their numbers continue to grow, and they now enroll 43 percent of the country's twenty-million postsecondary students.[2]

Community colleges are thus increasingly where the jobs are, but they are rarely tenure-track jobs. Here the numbers get very confusing: 82.5 percent of the faculty at two-year colleges are not eligible for tenure, although in 2008, 43 percent of all new hires at community colleges were tenure-track, suggesting that community colleges, as a collective, may be in the process of realizing that maintaining a stable teaching workforce is in fact cheaper than scrambling to staff courses at the last minute every academic term. At the same time, adjunct hiring nationwide at all types of institutions has, since 2003 at least, been outpacing tenure-track hiring by a rate of more than three to one.[3]

We also have to acknowledge, like it or not, that for-profit colleges and universities now constitute a significant sector of the higher education system. They educate 11 percent of the students currently enrolled in college. The for-profits operate on a very different model than most of their traditional counterparts, one that simply does not recognize or reward scholarship as part of a faculty member's job. Indeed, the traditional college faculty standard, the PhD, is not part of the equation. The minimum qualification for teaching at for-profit Strayer University, for example, is "eighteen hours at the graduate level—or six classes—not even a master's degree."[4]

So, as professors become increasingly outnumbered—until at some point they will become an insignificant part of the higher-education workforce—adjuncts of one kind or another will become the typical and numerically preponderant postsecondary educators, and they will not be rewarded or given time off for doing scholarship. A key question is, will the adjuncts of the future adopt Texter's attitude? Will they, in other words, reject intellectual life, embrace the principles of business self-help philosophy, and opt out of belonging to any community of scholars (the better to avoid "pretentious sheep")? My guess is that they will not, but I reach that conclusion with mixed feelings: Texter's hostility toward the entirety of the academic culture in which I was nourished horrifies me. At the same time, though, I'm worried that the typical academic attitudes toward work—the very attitudes that Texter repudiates—will make the adjuncts of the future extremely vulnerable to exploitation.

As many have documented, the use of adjunct labor, especially in the humanities, is one of academia's most notorious scandals.[5] Professors who are tenured or eligible for tenure now make up only 32 percent of the college teaching workforce. They would likely be shocked by the working conditions of the adjuncts who make up the remaining 68 percent, not to mention the teaching assistants, who are technically counted as students. Professors know that adjuncts are not eligible for tenure and have heard them euphemistically, even romantically, described as "freeway fliers" or "scholar gypsies," but do not, I suspect, know many details beyond that.

Not only are adjuncts ineligible for tenure, but 85 percent of them are hired on contracts of a year or less in duration, meaning their work schedules can vary significantly from one academic term to the next. They are usually employed on a part-time basis, which means that they are also ineligible for benefits such as health insurance and retirement plans. They are typically paid either by the course or by the hour and earn as little as $1,500 per class taught. Their part-time status often forces them to work simultaneously at more than one university and to commute between jobs. Twelve percent of them work at least three jobs.[6] They rarely have a voice in departmental meetings, especially the important deliberations about hiring, tenure, and salaries. In fact, they rarely have adequate office space, if they have any at all: according to a recent Department of Education survey, 37 percent did not have a computer in their office, and 33 percent had no office space at all. Taking into account the job-to-job commute, one adjunct calculated her salary in 2001 as an hourly wage of $2.12, without benefits.[7] Material conditions have not improved much in the last decade.

Martin Scott's account of his experiences teaching in some of Houston's community colleges focuses on the micromanaged working conditions that many adjuncts face. His workload is representative of adjuncts everywhere—"five classes a semester . . . at widely spaced campuses"—but his description of his day-to-day experiences reveals the role of management to be far more forceful than tenured professors might ever suspect.[8] Barraged by regular warnings about such matters as "not turning in some form on time or not giving out our home numbers to students," Scott concludes that "judging by the faculty meetings, one would think that education had no place in a community college."[9] His eeriest image is of a learning space literally transformed into a factory. He recalls teaching in a building where the back walls of all the classrooms were made of glass. An administrator would circulate through the building "making sure none of us released our class five minutes early."[10]

In the world of part-time academic labor, we constantly find teachers overpowered by the hard realities of their wage labor and the micromanagement of working conditions. Adjuncts cannot help being preoccupied with the huge financial strain caused by the low pay of the intellectual piecework they do. They note the irony that they cannot afford to participate in the very education system they themselves help run: they are unable to repay student loans and cannot foresee being able to send their children to college. Because they are often employed simultaneously by more than one university in an often random series of term appointments, they struggle to see themselves as part of a profession that they can rationally hope to negotiate.

How did this happen? Why are the details of adjunct working conditions so widely unacknowledged, familiar only to those who specifically study the subject of academic labor? There are several key explanations. First, the abundant use of part-time, adjunct labor is a fairly recent phenomenon. In 1975, 43 percent of college faculty were ineligible for tenure. That is, colleges actually *were* mainly populated by professors and students not too long ago, so it's not surprising that so many assume that they still are today. Only relatively recent graduates have experienced a university environment in which a steadily growing percentage of the teachers are adjuncts.[11]

One can't point to a systematic, gradualist administrative strategy to replace tenured faculty with adjuncts. Hiring adjuncts in times of budget shortfalls simply became a widespread practice, and adjuncts, introduced as stopgap personnel, then became a permanent underclass. The logic is easy to understand. As Judith Gappa and David Leslie summarize it: "once part-timers are employed to absorb new enrollment without commensurate budget increments it becomes difficult in future budget cycles to recoup the lost funding."[12] As a result, an adjunct workforce, however imperceptible its origins and insidious its expansion, has now mushroomed into a significant fact of academic life, and it continues to gather momentum.

Second, adjunct instructors are distributed very unevenly across America's universities in a way that defies easy generalization, as peer institutions have widely disparate ratios. For example, at Stanford, 6.4 percent of full-time faculty members are off the tenure track, while at Harvard the figure is 45.4 percent.[13] One pattern, though, is indisputable: those sectors of higher education that are currently expanding at the fastest pace—community colleges and for-profit institutions—are most resistant to the idea of a tenured faculty. Nationwide, 65 percent of the faculty at two-year institutions are part-timers, and 80 percent are not on the tenure track.[14] At some two-year colleges, the entire faculty may consist of instructors paid by the course. This distribution becomes more firmly entrenched over time because students are increasingly likely to enter the postsecondary hierarchy at the bottom—community colleges—rather than at the top. Moreover, the community college boom has been accompanied by the rapid growth of for-profit universities, where none of the faculty has tenure and 90 percent of instructors work part time. Time and time again, nostalgic memories combine with an idealized sense of the uniformity of American colleges and universities to obscure the real profile of the people who teach there today.

Many attribute the personnel shift in the higher education workforce to "late capitalism" or our "post-Fordist" production economy. Stefano Harney and Frederick Moten, for example, state matter-of-factly that higher education teachers, including professors, are "part of the service sector proletariat."[15] More creatively, Marc Bousquet argues that PhDs are actually the waste product of graduate education—if they fail to find tenure-track jobs, they find themselves overqualified to work as adjuncts and thus fall into an employment limbo. The real product of graduate education, according to Bousquet, is the vast contingent of ABDs who make up higher education's on-demand labor force.[16] Unquestionably, this is how the system functions, and it seems to do so without anyone's explicit approval.

Adjuncts, along with graduate students, are currently organizing more aggressively than any other sector of the teaching workforce, though that remains an extremely difficult challenge. Yet the aims of adjunct activism are deeply ambivalent, leading each of the major higher education union organizations—the American Association of University Professors (AAUP), the American Federation of Teachers (AFT), and the National Education Association (NEA)—to approach the subject differently. The philosophical divide is as follows: the AAUP and the AFT seek to convert as much of the higher education teaching workforce as possible to tenured and tenure-track status, virtually eliminating the category of "adjunct" altogether. Younger PhDs currently working as adjuncts view these positions as way stations on the path to tenure-track jobs. They look favorably on the AAUP and AFT plan because it would ideally lead to the creation of more tenure-track jobs. Older adjuncts, those who have been teaching for a decade or more and have thus been unable to keep up a scholarly profile, worry that they would never be considered for these newly created tenure-track positions, but would simply be terminated as universities phase out adjunct labor.

The NEA's plan seeks instead to improve the working conditions of adjuncts, guaranteeing them improvements in pay, benefits, and job security. This plan, were it to gain widespread backing, would offer immediate relief to the vast majority of the adjunct workforce, but would institutionalize it as well. For some, this is too high a price to pay for improved working conditions, for it would grant official status to what they consider an academic underclass and thus promote the further erosion of tenured and tenure-track positions. Neither of these plans, nor the assumptions that underlie them, have slowed the steady progress toward more and more adjunct hiring.

Such is the demographic and organizational backdrop against which Texter's revision of the job description of adjunct instructor must be read. In order to capture the contrarian spirit of his argument, and to begin to answer my title question, though, we must look at the expectations and professional fantasies that animate people both at the top (tenured professors at research universities) of the academic labor pool and the bottom (the growing corps of adjuncts). In no other workforce is there such a wide disparity, both in income and in day-to-day life, between groups of people whose jobs are, in part at least, so similar. We need, in other words, to figure out what holds adjuncts in their places for minimum wage.

A step toward an answer, I believe, is to question whether the laws of supply and demand affect professionals differently than other working people because professions don't prepare their members to deal with layoffs, chronic unemployment, or underemployment. Such phenomena, long routine in the world of manual production, crept into the professional domain, including academia, in the 1970s and have become increasingly common ever since. Exploitative working conditions are equally painful for everyone, but professionals—and adjuncts get the same professional training as those who end up with tenure—are socialized to view success or failure in personal terms.

No profession more fervently believes in the myth of meritocracy than academics. The conviction that somehow one's talent alone ultimately determines one's place in the hierarchy of academic labor gives rise to a constellation of fantasies: my charisma as a teacher will be properly valued; my completed dissertation or published monograph will confirm my rare intelligence. In short, someone will discover me and celebrate my intellectual powers. Since these epiphanies almost never happen, meritocracies have the effect of making everyone feel insufficiently appreciated. For adjuncts, the academic meritocracy creates a state of mind in which giving up hope signifies something far worse psychologically than a sensible change of careers, and finding a foothold on the first rung of the ladder seems impossible as well.

In response to this intense pressure, adjuncts have evolved success narratives that give purpose to their professional lives. They need to retrieve a measure of dignity from low-paying, overmanaged jobs made all the more difficult because adjuncts often perform those jobs side by side with far more generously compensated professors. Adjuncts cast themselves as self-sacrificing artists, and they seek to benefit from the aura of prestige that universities strenuously try to project. These myths connect adjuncts in complex ways to the icon of the professor. The first hint of this link is that, amid all their material complaints, adjuncts also say a lot of things one might expect to hear from a tenured professor. Among the sentiments expressed in Michael Dubson's collection of reflections by adjuncts, *Ghosts in the Classroom*, are the following: "I love the work. I love my field. I love the students." "For as long as I can remember I have loved all aspects of English." "It's the most rewarding job I've ever had or will ever have."[17] Many specifically state that a few magic moments in the classroom are rewarding enough to offset the constant material deprivation. Their accounts are remarkably similar to one another, and every tenured professor can certainly relate to them:

> I love the energy of the classroom and those special moments when I can do something good, when I see their eyes glowing and their faces shining, knowing that I am reaching them, I am doing something worthwhile.[18]

> The rewards of teaching may be intermittent and transparent, but they are there lurking in the ether of the classroom. . . . It takes only one serious inquiry, one student who genuinely wants to know why a certain painting looks the way it does . . . a single pair of shining eyes in your dim classroom that cancels out all the dulled ones. . . . Those brief flames in your teaching week are a kind of fuel. They are enough to sustain you from class to class.[19]

> There are moments when . . . you feel that you're not speaking into the void the way you thought, that you are having an effect on how people think about life and reading.[20]

In each of these cases, job satisfaction is something one gets *instead of* rather than in addition to a decent salary.

Andrew Ross makes sense of this sad artifice by explaining that academics of all ranks, along with artists and musicians, are notably willing to tolerate exploitation in the workplace. Ross claims that scholars' readiness to accept a discounted wage out of "love for their subject" has helped not only to sustain the cheap labor supply but also to magnify its strength and volume. Like artists and performers, academics are inclined by training to sacrifice earnings for the opportunity to exercise their craft.[21] The adjuncts' willingness to accept this tradeoff illustrates in extreme form "the mental labor problem" that Ross describes, since the sacrifices they make differ so much in degree from any that professors might have to consider.

Some elite universities compound the problem by adding the lure of prestige to the craftsman's ethic on which adjuncts already lean so heavily. Micki McGee argues that "prestige has played an important factor in the de-professionalization of college teaching." From the perspective of the general public, all college teachers, from tenured professors to part-timers, benefit equally from their association with their institution. "What adjunct faculty member earning minimum wage or scarcely more," McGee asks, "has not had the experience of being asked what they do and then seeing the eyes of their interlocutor light up after they've revealed that they teach at such-and-such prestigious university?" The university eagerly reinforces this reaction, as it has "a vested interest in maintaining that its faculty, whether full- or part-time, are the experts, the bearers of excellence, the best that money can buy (even if paid at a bargain basement rate)."[22]

While the traffic in prestige is not a factor in the lives of adjuncts at two-year colleges, it is crucial to the workings of research universities. These are the very places where professors and adjuncts teach in parallel situations but are compensated at vastly different rates; thus, they are also the places where the dynamics of prestige are most important and potentially most divisive.

Indeed, in McGee's experience, adjunct faculty are actually instructed by administrators "not to share the conditions of their employment with their students, the consumers, or others," but instead to "be upbeat."[23] Strayer contractually obliges its faculty (all adjuncts) never to criticize the mission of the university.[24] Institutions of higher learning are, in other words, unwilling to admit how they are changing. Under financial pressure since the 1970s, universities across the country have regularly cut corners by phasing in a cheaper, less credentialed instructional workforce, but they have not shared the extent of that personnel shift with the public or even with their own students. Their silence serves a public relations interest by presenting the education they deliver as undiminished and undiluted. Left ignorant about the status of the people who are teaching them, students are usually able to identify graduate teaching assistants by their relative youth, but discern little else. They have no way of distinguishing tenured professors from adjuncts and have no sense of the very different working conditions that those two positions entail.

Students, moreover, aren't the only ones who are ignorant. Gary Rhoades concludes that most tenured and tenure-track professors are "oblivious" to "the scope and significance of the restructuring that is ongoing in higher education."[25] Others claim that professors rationalize these ongoing changes in ways that are worse than obliviousness. Professors tend to naturalize the role of management, accepting the erosion of their working conditions as an unpleasant fact of life. As such, they deal with hardships such as "responsibility based" budgeting and administratively determined decisions to hire more and more adjuncts by assuming that such concessions themselves are inevitable. Rhoades describes what is at stake for professors who underestimate this seemingly inexorable drift toward casualization by noting that professors, like any professional group, establish "closure" by controlling entry into, and the definition and practice of, a domain of work. The growing number of part-time faculty is a challenge to the academic profession's closure. It is a challenge most plainly to the professor's definition of faculty positions as full time and as careers—not mere jobs—with a secure future. It is a challenge to tenure as the professional structure defining faculty's terms of employment, for part-time faculty have no chance to gain tenure.[26]

Instead, almost everyone contributes to an illusion born of incomplete awareness or outright denial of the situation of academic labor. Adjuncts stay on the job because they are transfixed by the ideal of the starving artist whose sacrifices are part of a dedication to craft. They currently have neither the time, the resources, nor the means of access that would allow them to present the realities of their work lives even to an audience of academics. They are invisible.[27] The university recognizes that its public image depends on a uniform faculty profile, on the impression that everyone who teaches has undergone the same rigorous screening and is compensated on the same salary scale. Accordingly, it produces advertising copy showcasing this message to attract students. Students are uninformed because, either through edict or by custom, their teachers do not divulge the details of their working conditions. Tenured and tenure-track professors are largely unaware of the accelerating rate at which their teaching tasks are being outsourced. As we have seen, they are rewarded for published scholarship and socialized to recognize only that less time spent teaching means more time for research; they are not accustomed to worry about who will teach in their places.

What if, in light of these broad rationales—the mental labor problem and the problem of prestige through professional affiliation—that explain how easy it is for universities to exploit adjuncts, we return to Texter's recommendations and take them seriously? His central recommendations hinge on the relationship between scholarship and college teaching. Texter simply asserts that there need not be any relationship between the two. Attempting to demonstrate that he is wrong proves to be a daunting and perhaps even impossible challenge. And the fact that his argument may prove irrefutable should cause us to rethink the entire research model.

Texter's first bubble-bursting recommendation—"stop thinking of yourself as an intellectual"—strikes at the heart of hopes and ambitions of academics at every rank. Yet it is in fact quite reasonable. The three figures Texter mentions—Judith Butler, Henry Giroux, Russell Jacoby—represent a very rare breed. They are academics who originally worked in the humanities and who are now recognized as public intellectuals. There are others—Noam Chomsky, Henry Louis Gates, the late Edward Said, even Camille Paglia—but it is a very short list. Any academic aspiring to that stratum is likely delusional, though I suspect many do secretly harbor that very aspiration—that is why Texter's admonition is so stinging. Curiously enough, though, he shares his position with no less a public intellectual than Stanley Fish. Fish distinguishes academics from intellectuals in the following terms:

> It is not impossible for someone to be an academic and a public intellectual. . . . It is just that the academic who goes public successfully will have done so not by extending his professional literary skills, but by learning the skills of another profession. If "public intellectual" is anything, it is a job description, and, as I have already said, it is not a job for which academics, as academics, are particularly qualified.[28]

What they lack, he argues is "any awareness of the routes and networks that would have to be in place before academic views, however packaged and however translated (and they would have to be), could even have a chance of being heard in extra-academic precincts."[29] Fish elaborates:

> A public intellectual is not someone who takes as his or her subject matters of public concern—every law professor does that; a public intellectual is someone who . . . has the public's attention. Since one cannot gain that attention from the stage of the academy (except by some happy contingency), academics, by definition, are not candidates for the role of public intellectual. Whatever the answer to the question "How does one get to be a public intellectual?" we know the answer won't be "by joining the academy."[30]

Over the past two generations, the tendency of professors to extend their "professional literary skills," as measured in scholarly publication, has mushroomed, but this has, if anything, validated Fish's claim that academics aren't particularly qualified to be public intellectuals. Published scholarship is counted rather than read. A survey cited by Deborah C. Rhode in her book *In Pursuit of Knowledge* confirms her claim that "the vast majority of scholarship vanishes without apparent influence": 98 percent of all publications (articles and monographs alike) in the arts and humanities are never cited.[31]

Mark Bauerlein comes to similar conclusions in his article "The Research Bust." He offers the following hypothetical example:

> If a professor who makes $75,000 a year spends five years on a book on Charles Dickens (which sold 43 copies to individuals and 250 copies to libraries, the library copies averaging only two checkouts in the six years after its publication), the university paid $125,000 for its production. Certainly that money could have gone toward a more effective appreciation of that professor's expertise and talent.[32]

If the preponderance of scholarship goes unread, we need to question its legitimacy and its relationship to the teaching that we do. That is, of course, if we continue, for the most part, to conceive of scholarship in the traditional forms of publication—articles and monographs—that are then cited in other scholarly publications (or not).

But this definition is far too narrow. Two examples from my own professional life, neither of them unique by any means, confirm the fact that published citations simply cannot be equated with influence. The first move I make when I prepare to teach a new literary text is to skim the published scholarship on that text. Some pieces I read cursorily, but others substantively influence my teaching approach. And this review of scholarship usually doesn't involve checking books out of the library. Research databases such as JSTOR make downloading PDFs of recent articles effortless. I also belong to several reading groups in which a dozen or so professors and graduate students meet once a term or so to discuss some recent piece of published scholarship. No citations come out of either of these near universal professional practices, but considerable intellectual influence and shared knowledge does.

The situation is, however, complicated by the fact that, in the eyes of administrators, published scholarship and published citations count as important credentials; reading groups and teaching preparation do not (though teaching evaluations sometimes do). Professors coming up for tenure and promotion at many institutions are required to publish a preestablished quantity of scholarship and to list the number of published citations that their scholarship draws. That's a dangerous reward system, since, I believe, it produces an institutional incentive for graduate students and professors to publish too much, leading to the embarrassing imbalances that Rhode and Bauerlein expose. Yet the current research model, deeply flawed, and maybe altogether broken, must be followed by PhD students who wish to get tenure-track jobs and by assistant professors who wish to get tenure.

If we were to do away with that model altogether, however, we might actually create de-intellectualized universities in which Texter's harsh rejection of the life of the mind would make perfect sense. That is, if all postsecondary instructors were relieved of the burden of doing scholarship, and were thus "fully deployed to teach," we would end up with universities in which new knowledge is neither created nor distributed.[33] Given the bizarre economy of scholarly publication, even tenured professors are dangerously close to that fate now, for if so much of our published scholarship goes unread, we cannot justify all of the free time we are given to write it. We somehow need to convince the public that teaching deserves the same degree of legitimacy as scholarship—that, as Ernest Boyer put it in his book *Scholarship Reconsidered*, pedagogy is scholarship.[34]

By "we" I mean tenured professors, those who can call for fundamental reforms without risk. PhD students and untenured professors have no choice but to play by the existing rules: to scramble for time out of the classroom so that they can publish monographs and articles (even though it's impossible to know who reads them). In short, they need to project the very image of the intellectual that Texter has abandoned and scorns. Tenured professors have an opportunity——indeed, I would say, an obligation—to reimagine our professional identities.

We need somehow to react to the realities of our working conditions. Not only do adjuncts teach the vast majority of college and university courses, but the latest evidence confirms that they teach—in large numbers—not only introductory courses such as English composition, but upper-level undergraduate courses as well.[35] We know they are not publishing scholars—and thus not scholars in the eyes of administrators, and hence not rewarded for being scholars. Meanwhile, tenured and tenure-track professors, the only postsecondary teachers who formally qualify as scholars, produce new knowledge in the form of monographs and articles, but they do so in part because they are required to, while no one is required to consume that knowledge. Sooner or later, this arcane arrangement and division of labor is going to collapse.

So, *do* college teachers need to be scholars? Texter's decision to remain a college teacher while brashly rejecting scholarship implicitly poses that question in the most uncomfortable terms. I think that the answer is yes, but only in an ideal world in which we broaden the definition of scholarship in the way that Boyer first outlined in 1997. The problem with Boyer's profound redefinition of pedagogy as scholarship is that no major universities have ever adopted it as policy: college and university administrators cling to the narrow conception of scholarship expressed exclusively as publication, and that is what they reward.

Let me describe a utopian situation that I don't believe could ever become a reality, simply because universities, like most complex institutions, change from the top down rather than vice versa. What if pedagogy—class preparation and reading groups—were recognized as scholarship by administrators? Presumably, some professors, and adjuncts, would continue doing conventional scholarship, publishing articles and monographs, motivated by a mix of intellectual curiosity and professional ambition. There would thus still be an abundance of scholarship for teachers to read as they prepared for class and for faculty and graduate students to discuss in reading groups. The tradition of published scholarship would not die out; it would simply be brought into balance because it would no longer be measured as a credential, but rather as some other more idealistic aspect of our intellectual life. And the people making use of that scholarship would be recognized as scholars themselves, as they should be.

But how could we ever make that case? Administrators and professors have been at loggerheads over the conception of scholarship (in English, at least, and other disciplines in the humanities, I suspect) ever since the collapse of the job market in the early 1970s, at which point administrators and department chairs chose publications and the promise of publishable articles and monographs as the metric by which they determined who was hirable and who was not. It was a decisive and unfortunate turning point in the way that the work of PhD students and assistant professors came to be assessed, but it is very hard to see how that metric of assessment could be reversed. Those of us in English departments would somehow need to convince administrators that teachers of composition don't need to be scholars in the traditional sense. They need to be good writers and skilled in the techniques of teaching writing—two different talents, but talents that tend to coalesce during a graduate career that entails many opportunities to teach first-year writing. Teachers of lower-division literature courses don't have to be scholars in the conventional sense either—they just have to be fine close readers, since that's the chief skill at which sophomore readers of literature most need to improve. As we move to upper-level literature courses and graduate courses, then teachers certainly need to be scholars—they need to be familiar with the critical conversation about the texts that they teach—but they don't necessarily have to participate in that conversation by publishing themselves. It's a natural and even easy argument for professors to make, but if you're a dean, who wants to say: "Come teach at my university: you won't have to publish"? No easy solutions here.

## NOTES

1. Douglas W. Texter, "No Tenure? No Problem," *Chronicle of Higher Education*, 6 March 2009, *chronicle.com*.
2. Abby Rogers, "A Record 43% of US College Students Are Enrolled

in Community College," *Business Insider*, 8 November 2011, *articles. businessinsider.com.*

3. 2007 ADE Ad Hoc Committee on Staffing, *Education in the Balance: A Report on the Academic Workforce in English* (New York: Modern Language Association and Association of Departments of English, 2008), *www.mla.org.*

4. Brenna Ryan, "Telling the Tale: Strayer University's Complicity in a Contemporary Middle Passage" (unpublished essay, 2011), 3.

5. The first to do so was Paul Lauter in the collection of essays that became *Canons and Contexts* (New York: Oxford University Press, 1991).

6. I obtained these details from various National Study of Postsecondary Faculty publications and products, which are listed at the National Center for Education Statistics website: *nces.ed.gov.* Useful digests of this information can be found in *NEA Higher Education Resource Center* 7 (2001): 1–8; and John Lee and Sue Clery, "Key Trends in Higher Education," *American Academic* 1 (2004): 30–33.

7. Michael Dubson, ed., *Ghosts in the Classroom: Stories of College Adjunct Faculty—and the Price We All Pay* (Boston: Camel's Back, 2001), 36.

8. Martin Scott, "Pagers, Nikes and Wordsworth: Teaching College English in a Shopping Mall," *Profession*, 2001: 93.

9. Ibid.

10. Ibid., 93–94.

11. Roger G. Baldwin and Jay L. Chronister, "What Happened to the Tenure Track," in *The Question of Tenure*, ed. Richard Chait (Cambridge, MA: Harvard University Press, 2002), 129. See also Scott Jaschik, "The Job Security Rankings," *Inside Higher Ed*, 11 December 2006, *insidehighered.com.*

12. Judith M. Gappa and David W. Leslie, *The Invisible Faculty: Improving the Status of Part-Timers in Higher Education* (San Francisco: Jossey-Bass, 1993), 105.

13. John W. Curtis and Monica F. Jacobe, *AAUP Contingent Faculty Index 2006* (Washington, DC: AAUP, 2006). See also Jaschik, "Job Security Rankings."

14. Gary Rhoades, *Managed Professionals: Unionized Faculty and Restructuring Academic Labor* (Albany: State University of New York Press, 1998), 136.

15. Stefano Harney and Frederick Moten, "Doing Academic Work," in *Chalk Lines: The Politics of Work in the Managed University*, ed. Randy Martin (Durham, NC: Duke University Press, 1998), 155.

16. Marc Bousquet, "The Waste Product of Graduate Education: Toward a Dictatorship of the Flexible," *Social Text* 20, no. 1 (2001): 81–104.

17. Dubson, *Ghosts*, 10, 16, 38.

18. Ibid., 10.

19. Ibid., 29.

20. Scott, "Pagers," 96.

21. Andrew Ross, "The Mental Labor Problem," *Social Text* 18, no. 2 (Summer 2000): 1–31.

22. Micki McGee, "Hooked on Higher Education and Other Tales from Adjunct Faculty Organizing," *Social Text* 20, no. 1 (Spring 2002): 64, 65.

23. McGee, "Hooked," 67, quoting New York University's adjunct faculty handbook.

24. Ryan, "Telling the Tale," 12.

25. Rhoades, *Managed Professionals*, 4.

26. Ibid.,134.

27. In addition to *The Invisible Faculty* and *Ghosts in the Classroom*, already mentioned, a popular blog titled *The Invisible Adjunct* ran from 2003 to 2004 at *www.invisibleadjunct.com*; its posts remain available via the Internet Archive (*archive.org*; accessed 4 April 2013).

28. Stanley Fish, *Professional Correctness: Literary Studies and Political Change* (Oxford: Clarendon, 1995), 125.

29. Ibid., 123.

30. Ibid., 118.

31. Deborah L. Rhode, *In Pursuit of Knowledge: Scholars, Status, and Academic Culture* (Stanford, CA: Stanford University Press, 2006), 84.

32. Mark Bauerlein, "The Research Bust," *Chronicle of Higher Education*, 4 December 2011, *chronicle.com*.

33. The phrase is from Richard S. Ruch, *Higher Ed, Inc.: The Rise of the For-Profit University* (Baltimore, MD: Johns Hopkins University Press, 2001), 17.

34. See Ernest L. Boyer, *Scholarship Reconsidered: Priorities of the Professoriate* (New York: Jossey-Bass, 1997).

35. See 2007 ADE Ad Hoc Committee on Staffing, *Education in the Balance*.

# PART III

## Roadmaps for Achieving Equality

# 8

# The New Abolition Movement

*Lantz Simpson*

The major crisis festering in American higher education today, in terms of both academic freedom and teaching conditions, is that about 75 percent of the almost 1.8 million higher education faculty in the United States teach on contingent employment contracts. This means that most of these faculty have little or no institutional support and often have only part-time assignments. This two-tiered employment system—largely unknown and hidden to parents and the public—deprives both students and institutions of having a fully professional faculty. In other words, if one believes that a large cadre of full-time tenured faculty with strong institutional support is the preferred model for American higher education, then the current system falls far short of realizing the full potential of American higher education.

What follows in this essay is a brief overview of the problem, followed by a proposal whose aim is largely to abolish the contingent faculty system in the United States. My proposal is simply this: the current two-tiered system, mired in contingency, should be replaced with the systematic regularization of faculty—that is, contingent faculty routinely moving onto the tenure track and thereby achieving full-time tenured status throughout the country.

Over the past forty years John Dewey's original purpose in founding the American Association of University Professors (AAUP) in 1915—to protect academic freedom—has been dramatically undermined by the effort of American higher education administrations to erode, and possibly eventually eradicate, tenure by using the contingent strategy.

Since the Nixon administration, the use of contingent faculty in the United States has exploded and continues to expand. In 1975 about 43 percent of faculty nationwide were contingent. Today it is about 75 percent. Growing college enrollments, fueled by the growing population and the rapid development of advanced technology, have mostly led to the hiring of the needed new faculty on a contingent basis. Conventional wisdom states that the contingent system exists for budgetary reasons. It has been assumed for decades that the use of large numbers of contingent faculty saves money. To my knowledge, however, no serious cost-benefit analysis of using contingent faculty has ever been done. Compare 75 percent contingency in higher education with K-12 public schools, where there is virtually no contingency. Why two-tiered salary structures, as part of a two-tiered employment system, are good for higher education and its faculty but not good for the public schools and their teachers is a case that has never been made.

In addition, retiring tenured faculty are being replaced by more and more contingent faculty. Why tenure was good for now retiring full-time faculty but not good for newly hired contingent faculty is another case that has never been made. Most arguments against tenure are based on fallacious "one bad apple" and "straw man" arguments, along with the assumption that almost all college and university faculty are tenured. In reality, it is well known within higher education that competition is intense in most disciplines for full-time tenured positions because of the numerous overqualified applicants, which makes it very difficult for incompetents to be granted tenure. If some current tenured faculty are truly incompetent, the golden handshake is a better option than abolition or restriction of tenure itself.

Available data posted on the AAUP website confirms these observations. Since the 1990s, the majority of full-time faculty hires in four-year institutions have been off the tenure track. These faculty are usually called "lecturers." In contrast, only 3.3 percent of full-time hires in 1969 were off the tenure track. Non-tenure-track positions of all types now account for about 75 percent of all faculty appointments in American higher education. One result of this policy is that a person can be employed as faculty by a college or university for five, ten, fifteen, twenty years or more, and still be classified as contingent and therefore "temporary," which is an absurd legal fiction.

This historical examination of the development of the contingent system reveals that it came about like a thief in the night. There was no overt policy movement arguing for the steady creation of larger and larger numbers of contingents. It just seemed to happen. Ironically, no one now defends the current employment system on educational, legal, or moral grounds. Instead, administrators who oversee this increasing contingent expansion usually defend their growing use of contingent faculty on two grounds: budget difficulties and the need for "flexibility." Their complaints about the lack of flexibility in current law and budgeting procedures usually sway regents, trustees, and state legislators so that the contingent system continues to expand. As Marc Bousquet, a tenured professor at Santa Clara University, points out in his powerful book *How the University Works*, management solidarity is much greater than faculty solidarity.[1] It is this management solidarity that has led to the successful assaults on full-time faculty positions and tenure. Faculty have failed to offer successful big-picture alternative political strategies, partly because of the lack of faculty solidarity in policy development and implementation.

Over the past decade faculty advocacy organizations, joined by some existing teacher unions, have led reform efforts in a few states so that incremental reforms aimed at contingent faculty have been achieved. Since I have lived in California and worked in the community college system for over twenty-five years, I will use California as an example. In California, under several different governors, the legislature passed the Educational Employment Relations Act (also called the EERA, the collective bargaining law governing the state's teachers), AB 1725 (a community college reform bill), and proposals concerning State Teachers Retirement System (STRS) service credit (helping part-time faculty get a better retirement), contingent faculty health benefits, and contingent office hour pay, which were all good. These state-level reforms were the result of strong and effective advocacy by faculty organizations, including the California Federation of Teachers (CFT) and the Faculty Association of California Community Colleges (FACCC). On the local level, collective bargaining wins on pro rata pay, contingent health benefits, office hour pay, hiring preferences, and seniority were all good. All of these gains, however, were incremental. Incrementalism can be good. Incremental reforms can prepare the way for final and complete reform.

In another important example from California, the California Part-Time Faculty Association (CPFA), formed in 1998, had by 2000 successfully lobbied the community college system stakeholders and the legislature for a limited amount of funds dedicated to the goal of parity pay for contingent faculty (called "temporary part-time" in California). Looking at other states, gains have also been made in Washington State (increased pay, retirement and health care reform, sick leave), New Jersey, and New York (better salaries and employment rights). Yet, the primary problem lives on because the various supports of the contingent faculty system in laws, regulations, and contracts remain untouched in a complicated, complex, and fragmented world.

Indeed, an additional and difficult obstacle to universal employment reform in American higher education is its fragmentation. There are three basic kinds of fragmentation in American higher education. The first kind of fragmentation is the existence of the tenure system alongside the contingency system. The second kind is the division between public vs. private institutions. The third kind is the three tiers of public higher education: research universities, teachers colleges, and community colleges. As one can see, each of these three kinds of fragmentation creates a three-dimensional matrix of fragmentation, which in turn leads to almost countless sub-fragmentations. Indeed, each of the fragmented elements has its own unique set of laws, regulations, and contracts, often at odds with other fragmented elements.

To examine some of the sub-fragmentations, one might examine collective bargaining systems and agreements. Again, take California as an example. California has the classic three tiers, or sets, of public higher education: the

University of California system, the California State University system, and the California community college system. Each one of these systems has its own collective bargaining subsets.

At the University of California (UC), which has ten campuses, the full-time tenured faculty as a group decided not to organize in order to bargain collectively because they feared that unionization would level out some of the very high salaries a few professors are making. Instead, each faculty person has an individual employment contract with the university (along with a different salary). However, the non-tenure-track UC faculty organized with the American Federation of Teachers (AFT) and those faculty now have a collective bargaining contract with the university. Ironically, despite achieving better salaries and benefits through collective bargaining, the non-tenure-track UC faculty are locked out of winning through bargaining what they really want the most, tenure.

In the California State University (CSU) system, with its twenty-three campuses, the tenured faculty and the contingent faculty are organized together by the California Faculty Association (CFA) into one large all-inclusive ("wall-to-wall") bargaining unit. This unit represents all faculty at all CSUs, who are thus covered by one comprehensive collective bargaining agreement that applies across the entire CSU system.

By contrast, the California community college system divides itself into 72 districts with a total of 103 colleges. Therefore, some districts have more than one college. For example, the Los Angeles district has nine colleges. Districts are governed by locally elected trustees but receive 75 percent of their funding from the state. Collective bargaining for community college faculty is therefore organized district by district. This results in what is called "local bargaining." Therefore, the faculty in each district are represented by a different bargaining organization in each separate district, which results in a separate collective bargaining agreement in each district. As a result, all faculty at all of the colleges in the Los Angeles district work under one contract, negotiated by the AFT. In the neighboring district of Santa Monica, the faculty are represented by an independent bargaining unit, the Santa Monica College Faculty Association (SMCFA), which is not affiliated with either the AFT or its rival, the California Teachers Association (CTA), which is affiliated with the National Education Association (NEA). Go but a few miles northeast, and one crosses into the Rio Hondo community college district in Whittier, where the CTA represents faculty.

Most of the community college locals in California are wall-to-wall bargaining units, but a few are split. For example, the faculty in the Long Beach community college district are divided into a full-time tenured faculty bargaining unit and a part-time contingent faculty unit. Both are represented by CTA. Meanwhile, in the Mira Costa district in northern San Diego County, the full-time faculty does not have a bargaining unit but the part-time faculty has a unit represented by CTA. There are several other odd combinations throughout California, including a part-time faculty unit represented by the Communications Workers of America (CWA) in the Butte community college district.

The AFT community college locals have a state-level organization, the Community College Council (CCC) of the CFT. In turn, the CTA locals have their statewide group, the Community College Association (CCA) of the CTA. There have been talks about merger talks between the CFT and CTA in California, but so far nothing has developed. Even the independent locals somewhat oxymoronically have their own statewide organization, the California Community College Independents (CCCI).

Given this sort of organizational fragmentation, it is no wonder that the faculty lack solidarity. This fragmentation repeats itself in every state, each state in a different way. No wonder there are so many different attempts and ways and strategies to try to improve the salaries, working conditions, and employment rights of contingent faculty. One must ask how any universal employment reform is even possible.

Yet it remains that the current contingent faculty system has been repeatedly criticized for depriving students of full access to their professors, for depriving institutions of full-service faculty, and for depriving contingent faculty themselves of full professional participation and professional compensation. It is obvious to fair-minded and pragmatic individuals that the current contingent faculty system should be abolished. But how is this to be accomplished?

To abolish mass contingency, three problems must be overcome: first, the administrative demand for flexibility, protected and reinforced by the ideology and fact of management solidarity; second, the necessity of increased funding to pay for a nationwide, fully professional faculty, despite the lack of support from administrations and the painful fact of the now crumbling US economy; and finally, the actual abolition of contingency throughout the fragmented system.

Administrative resistance must be met head on and aggressively by a strong faculty movement that includes right-minded and determined full-time faculty. To borrow from William Lloyd Garrison's abolitionist movement of the nineteenth century, faculty should describe themselves as "immediatists"—because they want the contingency system abolished immediately without any foot dragging and incrementalism. Faculty who support the abolition of contingency must openly proclaim themselves as abolitionists and must carry the abolitionist cause at all levels of authority, but particularly in state legislatures who control the laws and the budgets that fund higher education.

Faculty abolitionists must argue that the contingency system is bad for administrators because the cost of administrating contingency is in reality a drag on administrative efficiency. In California, a 75 percent contingency rate means that administrators spend far too much of their costly time monitoring compliance of the 67 percent law, conferring with lawyers and trustees when alleged violations of the 67 percent law occur, budgeting for part-time faculty hires, administering the paperwork and reviewing the evaluations of part-time faculty rehires, approving department chair recommendations for new part-time hires, maintaining part-time hiring pools and equal opportunity guidelines, terminating unwanted or unneeded part-time faculty, developing strategies to avoid grievances, lawsuits, and discrimination filings from terminated part-time faculty, implementing complex benefits and teacher's retirement rules for part-time faculty and then troubleshooting errors made in payroll and benefits, planning ways to evade paying unemployment to part-time faculty during semester breaks and paying private consulting companies to do the same, devising ways to finance more parking spaces for more and more part-time faculty, and spending many hours on preparation for negotiating collective bargaining issues specific to part-time faculty issues. If administrators could imagine a world without these administrative headaches and their endless, absurd, and time-consuming administrative details, then administrators would form in solidarity around the abolition of contingency also.

In addition, faculty abolitionists must offer counterarguments to the current doctrine of flexibility. These arguments must be made repeatedly and forcefully. The counterarguments to the flexibility mantra include first, that the degree of flexibility truly needed by colleges is far less than the exaggerated claims by their administrations. Enrollments go up and down at every college from term to term, but not by 75 percent—the current level of contingency throughout the country. Even a 10 percent enrollment increase or decrease from one semester to the next is considered extreme at most colleges. Therefore, the rational basis for the true necessary number of contingent faculty should be around 10 percent, not 75 percent.

Second, current flexibility patterns should be ridiculed and described as whimsical and not reflecting any true rational use of flexibility. Absent any assignment system of seniority, merit, or rotation, the truth is that contingent faculty are assigned their teaching sections for the most part on administrative whim. Perhaps flexibility should be renamed "whimsicalibility."

Finally, a new kind of flexibility, in what should be called "infinite flexibility," should replace the current whimsy. As new class sections at individual colleges are added or as tenured faculty retire, contingent and partial assignment faculty would be rolled over into regular (tenured) assignments, and new faculty would be added from a hiring pool as needed, who in turn would work their way through the regularization process. This process is termed "infinite flexibility" because there is no limitation to the rollover process.

Infinite flexibility would also lead to the regularization (placing on the tenure track) of contingent faculty. Should a true budget crisis lead to the temporary need for layoffs, reduction-in-force (RIFs) plans can be built into the process. This regularization process already exists throughout British Columbia and works very well. However, regularization was very hard won. Abolitionists should remember that the regularization process was achieved in British Columbia by faculty through a strike action.

How would regularization reform work its way through the system's fragmentation? Initially, faculty advocacy organizations must unite their policies and resources to support mass regularization in the public sector. This can be achieved throughout the country on a statewide basis in law, on a local basis through college regulations, or through both state and local collective bargaining. (Sometimes a fragmentary system calls for a fragmentary solution.) As regularization gains momentum, a critical turning point would be reached, resistance would greatly diminish, and private higher education would also be reformed either through voluntary compliance or legislation.

Let me again use the California community colleges as an example, and explicitly state the various steps that need to be taken to abolish the provisions for contingency that are currently established in the California Education Code. The following list of legislative actions is taken from a proposal I developed in 1999, which was endorsed by the independent California Part-Time Faculty Association.[2] These actions would accomplish the goals of the immediate abolition of contingency and establish a new employment system of regularization. These actions would also end the practice of whimsicalibility and create real, infinite flexibility.

1. Repeal of Sec. 87421 et seq. and all other statutes relating to the definition and existence of the temporary part-time faculty as a legal category, leaving temporary faculty to be used only as day-to-day substitutes.
2. Repeal of Sec. 87482.5, the 67% law. This law currently prohibits temporary part-time faculty from having more than 67% of a full-time assignment. Hence the 67% law (recently upped from 60%) only exacerbates the phenomenon known as freeway flyers, contingent faculty who must teach in multiple districts in order to scrape out a living.
3a. Repeal of Sec. 87804, the law permitting two-tiered salary schedules for community college faculty.
3b. Passage of an Education Code provision that requires uniformity of salary schedules for employees with the same employment classification, similar to Sec. 45028, which relates to public school employees.

4. Passage of an Education Code provision that establishes two kinds of faculty: regular assignment and partial assignment, both of which would fall under current Education Code definitions for contract and regular faculty (Sections 87400 et seq.), and both of which would retain all other faculty rights, including tenure rights.

5. Passage of an Education Code provision that allows districts to employ partial assignment faculty to teach no more than 10% of a district's Weekly Faculty Contact Hours. Districts would be given full mandated funding and allowed three years to reach this goal.

6. Passage of an Education Code provision that requires districts to establish faculty hiring eligibility lists, similar to the kinds of eligibility lists now used in classified merit systems, to rank the order in which new faculty are hired as enrollment growth dictates. There would be three types of lists: regular assignment only, partial assignment only, and partial assignment rolling over into regular assignment. These employment lists would not in any way conflict with any other hiring procedures established by AB 1725.

These are the legislative steps necessary in California. In other words, should the California state legislature pass a regularization bill, how would regularization work as a practical matter? Let me explain as follows.

Assignment and load as well as RIFs (Reductions in Force) are already included within the scope of bargaining under existing California bargaining laws, and all faculty who have a union contract at a public college or university should have such provisions in their collective bargaining contracts. Under RIF agreements, administrators already have the flexibility they need should a real budget crisis hit, while faculty would be protected by an orderly RIF procedure.

The new laws would establish the structure of regularization while the procedure for making faculty assignments under a new regularization law would be collectively bargained. Infinite flexibility should be the preferred model and the goal of bargaining. It is not only possible but also necessary to bargain that some faculty with a part-time assignment may self-select to remain on such an assignment indefinitely. In other words, tenure and full-time assignments should not be conflated.

With such collective bargaining agreements in place, administrators would thus be freed from all of their current labor spent on the administration of part-time faculty, and be granted the infinite flexibility needed in rolling over new faculty assignments.

Infinite flexibility would work like this: as class sections are added, some partial assignment faculty would be rolled over into regular assignments, and new partial assignment faculty would be added from the hiring list as needed.

Administrators, freed from monitoring the 67 percent law, would no longer in times of enrollment growth be held hostage to the necessity of hiring large numbers of new part-time faculty at the last minute every semester.

Through political action, solidarity, and strength, advocacy groups and abolitionists must press Congress and state legislatures for the necessary funding. The politics of higher education funding is the subject for another article, but history has shown that critical mass can be reached and improvements in funding achieved. For example, the concept of federal aid to education was ridiculed when it was first proposed, but such federal aid has endured since enacted because it is an effective supplement to local funds and has been the right thing to do.

The problem of mass contingency in a fragmented and often under-funded system can be remedied with successful political effort built around a rational and pragmatic campaign plan. Thus, contingency can be abolished through the process of regularization by infinite flexibility when coupled with adequate funding.

## NOTES

1. Marc Bousquet, *How the University Works: Higher Education and the Low-Wage Nation* (New York: New York University Press, 2008).
2. "Lantz Simpson's Legislative Proposal," Santa Monica College Faculty Association, 17 March 1999, *www.smcfa.org/index.php/documents/18-position-papers/35-lantz-simpsons-legislative.*

# 9

# The Vancouver Model of Equality for College Faculty Employment

*Frank Cosco*

In most North American advocacy forums concerned with the rights of post-secondary faculty, the disparate categories of part-time and full-time are set in solid stone with a next to impassable chasm between them. Those on the part-time side of the chasm are often not deemed to be real employees, while the full-timers are. Countless blog posts, papers, e-mail exchanges, presentations, and discussions rail against inequitable conditions regarding pay, workload, and benefits that North American part-time faculty endure.

The approach for unionized faculty at Vancouver Community College (VCC) has been to build and strengthen a single career path for all faculty that minimizes the part-time/full-time distinction.

With a significant measure of success, the Vancouver Community College Faculty Association (VCCFA) has established, as codified in the VCC-VCCFA Collective Agreement, a place of greater equity where the part-time/full-time distinction has diminished in importance.[1] Being part-time, at least at the half-time or above level, can be a career choice that brings with it most of what a full-timer has. By diminishing the importance of the full-time/part-time distinction, a workplace where faculty are treated much more equally has been established.

In the Vancouver model, the part-time or full-time distinction is not the crucial one. Nor is rank the crucial distinction—there is only one rank, instructor, and all instructors are on the same eleven-step salary scale. Pay equity is absolute: 30 percent and 60 percent instructors respectively make exactly 30 percent and 60 percent of a full-time salary at the same salary step over the same period of time. The most important distinction between instructors is between term and regular status; that is, between probationary, time-limited employment and nonprobationary, continuing employment.

Given that there is work available, and given a successful evaluation process, the Vancouver model provides a fair, transparent career path that most often leads from probationary part-time work to regular full-time work, but only if one wishes to be full-time. There is nothing second class or contingent about remaining at half, two-thirds, or three-quarters time-status.

In what follows, I describe key details of the Vancouver model and provide some statistics. I outline the development of this model over the past two decades. I further comment on how the system might handle research, tenure, and academic freedom. I touch on the relationship between the VCCFA and shared governance at VCC. I conclude with thirteen goals the VCCFA would hypothetically set for itself if it found itself transposed to a nearby American community college with typically inequitable working conditions.

These comments are those of the author, and are not attributable to VCC, to the VCCFA, or any organization to which the VCCFA belongs. They are not to be construed as representing the situation anywhere in British Columbia (BC) outside of the VCC workplace. Nor are they to be construed as representing the VCC workplace as a place that has achieved a steady state of satisfactory equity for all; indeed, there remains much to be done.

## Section 1: Description of the VCCFA and VCC

The faculty union at what has become VCC was first certified as a trade union in 1951. It has undergone many transformations from its start as the union for vocational instructors at a provincial vocational institute. It remains an independently certified union with the bargaining and grievance rights for almost all instructors at VCC. There remains a group of instructors in Continuing Studies who are not covered by the VCCFA certification. The VCCFA joined the Federation of Post-Secondary Educators (FPSE) of British Columbia in 1990. FPSE acts as an empowering resource to independently certified faculty unions at six regional and special purpose universities, and almost all the colleges and institutes in BC. It also includes faculty unions at five private colleges. The VCCFA is a member of the Vancouver and District Labour Council. Through FPSE, it belongs to the provincial and national labor federations: the BC Federation of Labour and the Canadian Labour Congress.

VCC has over forty different departments, including four-year degree programs; academic university-transfer; health, office, and hospitality careers; applied vocational and apprenticeship training; developmental adult basic education; English as a Second Language; Adult Special Education; music; and design instruction. It uses several funding models, ranging from full-cost recovery and various levels of tuition fees to tuition-free. Its 2012–2013 budget is close to 107 million in Canadian dollars, with approximately $72 million covered by government grants; about $21 million by student tuition; and the rest a mixture of instructional contract income and ancillary income. The rights and benefits of the over eight hundred VCCFA members are not affected by which program or funding model they happen to be working within. The payroll of VCCFA's members in 2012–2013 will be approximately $35 million. It should also be noted that there is no distinction made between librarians, counselors, or instructors, with respect to their collective agreement rights. All are VCCFA members and all comments herein relating to terms of employment apply equally.

## Section 2: Faculty Classifications

There are three types of faculty appointments that fall under the terms of the collective agreement.

### 1. Auxiliary Faculty

The auxiliary instructor is analogous to an on-call, relief instructor (Article 2.2). In most cases, VCC programming is available all year long. Absences caused by illness are regular occurrences. VCC does not generally cancel classes when instructors are ill; therefore, it requires auxiliary instructors to be ready to fill in at very short notice. The length of an auxiliary engagement is indeterminate. Both the college and the union agree that they are intended to be short, limited to a maximum of one month. The collective agreement states, "Auxiliary employment shall not normally exceed 19 consecutive duty days" (ibid.). The union monitors these engagements to ensure compliance.

Auxiliaries are not subject to evaluation and do not accrue seniority until they have, or have had, an initial term appointment. They are protected by the grievance and rights clauses of the collective agreement. An auxiliary's pay is prorated to that of a full-time regular on the same salary step (Article 5.4 and Appendix I). The corresponding annual amount for a full-time instructor is simply divided by 1,010 to derive an "hourly" rate for the auxiliary. That number, 1,010, is the annual number of hours every full-timer is accountable for: 5 hours a day for 202 days a year.

### 2. Term Faculty

Term faculty are hired for a particular period with a start and end date (Article 2.20). The college is under no obligation to reemploy an instructor if there is no work available. The appointment is considered probationary. The instructor is subject to summative evaluation as set out in the collective agreement (Article 16 and Appendix VII). The time status of a term may vary from a very small fraction to full time and the length of appointment may vary from a few days to a whole year (202 days; approximately ten months). Term faculty are eligible for Canadian unemployment insurance (renamed "employment insurance" by the federal government) after the completion of an appointment, as long as they reach the length of work required by the federal regulations.

## BENEFITS

The time status of a high proportion of term faculty is half time or more. Term faculty working half time or more become eligible for additional benefits when certain accrual periods are reached (Article 7.1.2 and Appendix III-A). This gives term faculty access to sick leave, basic medical coverage, extended medical coverage, short- and long-term disability, group life insurance, and dental coverage. All plan premiums, except short-term disability, are paid for by the college.

College faculty pension coverage (additional to the Old Age Security pension all Canadians receive and to the Canada Pension Plan most Canadian workers receive) is handled by a provincially legislated plan that includes all faculty at all institutions and all administrators as well.[2] An instructor, no matter what his or her classification may be, is automatically enrolled once his or her annual salary reaches a level determined by federal regulation; currently this amount is approximately $25,000. For term instructors, this requirement would be met by working at 48 percent of full time for a year at the bottom step of the salary scale. An employee may join voluntarily from their first day of work.

## ENTITLEMENTS

While term instructors are not eligible for paid leaves, they can qualify for up to a month (twenty days) of paid professional development (PD) time and PD funds if the required accrual of assigned duty within a fiscal year is met (Article 6.6 and Appendix V). For twenty days of PD time, instructors must have accrued eight months of assigned duty at half time or more. If they have accrued only seven months, they qualify for fifteen days. There is no PD entitlement for shorter accruals of duty time. Those days are paid out at the average level of accrued workload during the best months of the qualifying period.

Seniority is accrued at fully prorated amounts to that of full-time instructors. If a leave is granted, there is no loss of seniority accrual (Article 10 and Appendix IV).

## PAY AND WORKLOAD

A term instructor's pay—whether it is thought of as an annual, monthly, semi-monthly, or hourly amount—is completely prorated to that of full-time regular faculty at the same salary step. The term instructor is not usually on contract for the full twelve-month year. However, they earn the equivalent of an annual salary at their step and time-status after ten months of appointments. The prorating of salary has the salary for the two months of paid vacation of a regular instructor built in.

The workload of all instructors, regular and term, is set departmentally through approved workload profiles (Article 6). These profiles are prorated for full- and part-timers. If an instructor's department calls for 16 hours of instruction and 9 hours of other duties for a full-time regular, as a full-time term the instructor would have the same workload; as a half-time term, the instructor would have 8 hours of instruction and 4.5 hours of other duties.

## HUMAN RIGHTS AND PROTECTION FROM HARASSMENT

All faculty are protected from the discrimination and abuse caused by violations of their human rights or by workplace bullying, or through personal or sexual harassment.[3] Clear, transparent procedures have been created to ensure that whenever necessary, qualified outside investigators can be brought in at employer expense to make recommendations on how such issues can be addressed. Violations have led to dismissals, including the dismissal of a senior full-time regular instructor in a case involving a junior term instructor.

### 3. Regular Faculty

A regular instructor is nonprobationary and expected to continue working until retirement. He or she can be half time, any higher fraction up to full time, or full time. If one is hired directly into a regular position, which does occur but is not a common practice, the first year of appointment is probationary, and one must achieve a successful evaluation to maintain regular status.

A regular has all the rights and benefits of a term, plus most importantly:

- the right to notice of layoff, transfer rights, recall rights if laid off, and severance pay if final severance is necessary (Article 11)
- the right to take paid and unpaid leaves without losing seniority (Article 8)

A part-time regular accrues seniority at an equivalent rate to a full-time regular whether on leave or at work. The part-timer's accrual is not prorated, so his or her relative status vis-à-vis their colleagues is always maintained (Article 10.1.3). Every fiscal year, as a full-time regular accrues another year of seniority (measured as 261 days), a half-time or more regular accrues the same additional year of seniority (261 days).

## REGULAR STATUS AND TENURE

In the British Columbian community college system, the term "tenure" is not generally used. At all colleges, regular status is tenure-like in that regulars normally maintain their appointments till voluntary retirement. For a college to remove a regular, it must show just cause and is then subject to very rigorous due process requirements. Any such dismissal is covered by labor standards and would almost always be grieved by the VCCFA.

Layoff without cause may only occur within identified areas because of organizational change, a lack of funds, or decreased enrollment. Before any layoff, the union would intervene and hold the college to account for pursuing a suite of options designed to ultimately reduce the need for actual layoff.[4] The layoff of a regular instructor triggers a bundle of seniority, notice, transfer, severance, and recall rights. There is a sequence to layoffs; so, within a designated department or area, term instructors are usually affected first, then more junior regulars. For regular instructors facing layoff, part-time or full-time status is not determinative; rather, it is seniority that is paramount.

Indeed, because it not unusual for part-time regulars to have more seniority than full-time colleagues, if there were a layoff in an area, a junior full-timer would be given notice before a senior part-timer.

## Section 3: What's Different in the Vancouver Model?

The main features described in the previous section—the classification of descriptions and rights, with variations in terminology and scope of application—are probably found at many North American postsecondary institutions. There are, however, two key differences: equity and conversion.

### 1. Equity

The first key difference is that the discrepancies between the three categories of faculty have been consciously minimized. While it's true that regulars have more entitlements than terms, in many key areas (such as salary or weekly workload) the three categories are not determinate. Neither is part-time or full-time status, especially at the half-time or above level. Terms or regulars can be part time.

## PAY EQUITY

All salaries are derived directly from the annual salaries of full-time instructors on the single eleven-step salary scale (Articles 5.1 through 5.4 and Appendix I). The annual salary is divided by 12 to derive the monthly salary, by 24 for the semi-monthly salary, by 202 for the daily salary, and by 1,010 for the hourly salary. Upon their first appointment, everyone is placed on the single eleven-step salary scale according to experience and training and can move up the scale once a full-time equivalent year is completed (Article 5.6). There is no prohibition preventing a part-time term instructor from being placed on a higher salary step than a full-time regular.

## PRO RATA WORKLOAD

With over forty widely varied departments and approaches, no one weekly workload profile fits all departments. The VCCFA developed a flexible, template approach wherein departments democratically determine their own workload profiles, which then go to management for approval (Articles 6.1 through 6.3). Within a maximum twenty-five hours of assigned duty, departments choose how much of that time should go for instruction, office hours, preparation, and meetings or other duties. Management can refuse to approve a proposal if it does not meet the training needs of students. Management cannot, however, impose a profile on a department. Once approved, that profile becomes the profile for all faculty in the department. If one is part-time, regular, or term, one works a pro rata version of the same workload profile.

## ACCESS TO MEDICAL AND DENTAL BENEFITS

At half-time or more, all term and regular faculty have access to sick leave; basic medical, extended health, short-term and long-term disability, and group life insurance; and dental benefits. There are varying qualifying periods ranging from one month to ten months. All premiums are college-paid except short-term disability.

## ACCESS TO PROFESSIONAL DEVELOPMENT TIME AND FUNDS

All term and regular faculty with the time status of half time or more qualify for twenty duty days of PD and to PD funds. PD time and funds are prorated to one's time status if one is between half time and full time.

## SENIORITY ACCRUAL

There is only one collegewide seniority number for each faculty. All regulars, whether part time or full time, earn the same amount of seniority each fiscal year. This maintains their ranking relative to their regular colleagues. When a part-time regular has become regular prior to a full-time regular colleague, he or she will usually have a higher seniority accrual and will continue to maintain the higher ranking for the rest of his or her career.

Seniority accrual for term faculty is prorated from the annual accruals for regulars. It is appointment-based, so that the more a term instructor works during a fiscal year, the more seniority is accrued. After the first term appointment, auxiliary instructors also accrue seniority on same basis as terms. Terms retain their seniority for two years following their last appointment.

## FULL DEPARTMENTAL AND UNION MEMBERSHIP

Provisions in the collective agreement ensure the right of term instructors to be part of departmental meetings and democratic processes, such as the election of a new department head. In fact, term instructors can and do run for department head or coordinator, and if elected immediately become full-time regular faculty, a status that remains after their time as department head or coordinator is over (Article 13).

Union bylaws make as few distinctions as possible between types of faculty.[5] Part-time and full-time regulars are voting members until retirement. Terms retain their voting member status from their first appointment until two years after their last appointment. Auxiliaries are voting members for each calendar month during which they work. During job actions, picket pay is distributed based on one's time spent picketing, not on one's time status at work.

All members are eligible to run for any union election and to volunteer for any union committee. While the VCCFA has an advisory committee on "nonregular" issues, it has not found it necessary to designate union executive spots for a nonregular member.

## 2. Automatic Conversion of Type of Appointment: From Nonregular to Regular

The second key difference in the VCCFA agreement is one's ability to change appointment status within a reasonable time frame (Articles 4.7 through 4.9). In fact, the college's human resources department monitors an instructor's regularization accrual and simply informs the instructor by letter that his or her status has changed. Pay is already pro rata so there's no change in pay.

From the VCCFA's point of view, when faculty members are first hired at VCC, they are, should they wish to maintain it, on a career path that should normally be expected to continue to retirement. There is one hiring procedure, which instructors go through only when first hired.

The following outlines the key points of typical career paths at VCC, starting from the hiring process.

## HIRING

For the purposes of hiring, "areas" have been set out and listed in the collective agreement (Articles 2.1 and Appendix II). "Area" in this regard is a flexible concept; a department may only have one area, or there may be several within a department, or several departments may fall into one area. The hiring criteria for training, experience, and credentials are set by the Area Hiring Recommendation Committee (AHRC) (Articles 4.1 through 4.4). Should a layoff or subsequent transfer be necessary, it is administered by area, not necessarily by department.

The AHRC sets up a rigorous hiring process that is meant to be essentially the same for all types of positions, whether auxiliary, term, or regular. One is deemed to have been hired to the area even if the only work available is on-call, auxiliary work. Later, a term appointment may become available to an auxiliary instructor, and later still, if that term becomes a regular, there are no new or additional interview procedures.

## RIGHT OF FIRST REFUSAL FOR SUBSEQUENT TERM WORK

A department head can be confident that all auxiliaries have successfully completed the interview process. Thus, secure in that knowledge, they have a measure of choice over which auxiliary gets recommended for an initial term appointment. Term appointments may vary in length from a few days to a full year but normally last for all or most of a semester period. Once the instructor has six cumulative months of appointments, he or she automatically has a right to reappointment to available work governed by seniority (Article 4.8).

## SUMMATIVE EVALUATION

It is expected that the department head will conduct two summative evaluation processes for a term instructor, normally at a pace of one per year. The detailed procedures for evaluation are set out in the collective agreement and therefore are subject to the grievance procedure (Article 16 and Appendix VII). Almost all evaluations include department head observation and student survey modes.

## AUTOMATIC REGULARIZATION OF THE PERSON

This is the key transition in a VCC faculty member's career. The collective agreement sets out the conditions: if instructors do not receive an unsuccessful evaluation within any two-year period (i.e., of twenty-four consecutive months), which may commence and end at any point in a calendar year, and if they have maintained half-time status for 380 assigned days (approximately 19 months), then on the first day of the following month, they become regular and are no longer probationary (Article 4.9).

This is automatic; it does not matter if the program funding disappears, if no students have registered, if a senior faculty member is returning from leave, or if the class is cancelled for some other reason. Neither can the college argue that it has not finished its evaluation processes; the onus is on the college to complete evaluations in a timely way. The regularization does not apply to a position. It is regularization of the person.

In fact, on a few occasions, an instructor received their regularization and a notice of potential layoff on the same day. The VCCFA agreement made an important difference for the instructors concerned. Instead of being simply told as term instructors that their contracts could not be renewed, they were given four months' notice, as required for new regular instructors. This not only allowed them four more months of work, but also included the right to transfer to other areas where qualified. Furthermore, if they were eventually laid off, they maintained the right to be recalled as regulars for two years after the layoff.

## TOP-UP ACCRUAL FOR PART-TIME REGULARS

If a faculty member has been regularized at less than full-time status (i.e., at half time or more), he or she may maintain that status or increase that status (Article 4.8). It would be his or her choice to make, and instructors can renew their top-up rights at a later date if they waived their right. When they indicate that they wish to increase their time status, then as term work becomes available, it must be offered to them in seniority order before it can go to other terms or new instructors. Part-time regulars doing top-up appointments are simultaneously part-time regulars and part-time terms but with all the rights of regulars. If they maintain any additional fractional term status for 380 days out of any 24-month period, their part-time regular status then is automatically increased—for example, from half to three-quarters, or from three-quarters to full time.

## APPOINTMENT SEQUENCE

The collective agreement sets out for the college how available work is to be offered at the beginning of each semester or class intake (Article 4.8). In each area, after regular instructors have their time-status assignments, then further available work goes to:

- any regulars in seniority order who have been laid off and are waiting for recall
- part-time regulars in seniority order who wish to top up their appointments
- term instructors in seniority order who have had six months of appointments

- other term instructors with fewer than six months of appointments, or instructors in the auxiliary pool, or never-before-appointed faculty who have gone through the hiring process, as recommended by the department head

## NO OVERTIME
For this system to work fairly, there is no overtime or overload permitted for regulars or terms once full-time time status is reached (Article 6.3.1). This prohibition is comprehensive; there is no distinction between summer, weekend, or evening work. Very rarely, the college may approach the union for permission to waive this prohibition for organizational reasons. Examples of such waivers have been when the government has insisted on more than twenty-five hours a week in the classroom for certain programs. The union and the college have concluded letters of agreement that allow the overload but then lengthen break or leave periods to compensate so that the yearly total of hours is consistent with other programs.

## IMPORTANCE OF COMPREHENSIVENESS
The VCCFA has found it vitally important to have all these features of status change linked together. Without each of them doing their part, it would be easier for one's career progression to be blocked. Here are three examples:

Without automatic regularization of the person, a term instructor could progress through the qualifying period, 380 days of work within 24 months, only to find that the college has decided to post a regular position for the same work—a competition that could see the work going to someone else for reasons that do not have to be disclosed.

Without the right of first refusal to additional work, term instructors could see their access to work go to others with less seniority or even to new hires. This could block their accrual of 380 days of work within 24 months, thus blocking their regularization.

Without an overtime ban, the regular full-timers in an area could deny work and a career path to a potential term instructor.

## Section 4: Statistical Profile of VCCFA Instructors

The following table contains the numerical count of instructors as individuals, not in full-time equivalents. The totals come from VCCFA seniority lists issued pursuant to the collective agreement on March 31, 2001; March 31, 2008; and March 31, 2012.[6]

The VCCFA does not have exact numbers on the proportion of full-time

## Numerical Count of Instructors

|  | 2001 | % | 2008 | % | 2012 | % |
|---|---|---|---|---|---|---|
| FT Regular | 402 | 56 | 373 | 44 | 352 | 42 |
| HT+ Regular | 48 | 7 | 47 | 6 | 39 | 5 |
| HT Regular | 66 | 9 | 57 | 7 | 57 | 7 |
| *All Regulars* | *516* | *72* | *477* | *57* | *448* | *54* |
| Term ≥ 80 days | 129 | 18 | 188 | 22 | 234 | 28 |
| Term < 80 days | 70 | 10 | 174 | 21 | 154 | 18 |
| *All Terms* | *199* | *28* | *362* | *43* | *388* | *46* |
| **Total** | **715** |  | **839** |  | **836** |  |

FT= full-time; HT+ = above half-time (but less than full-time);
HT = half-time
The 80 days are 80 full-time equivalent (FTE) days and refer to 80 days of FTE seniority. It is the equivalent of being employed full-time for four months (approximately one semester).

equivalent (FTE) work done by each category. In March 2012, VCC estimated that the total active workload of VCC faculty requires 485 FTE faculty per year. Using that estimate, we can calculate the proportion done by regulars as full-timers plus half-timers plus those part-time regulars working more than half time. We first configure the individual totals above as FTE amounts. In 2012, that is 352 plus 28.5 plus 30 (the average workload of the 39 individuals in the HT+ category is 77 percent). That gives us a rounded total of 411 FTE faculty. That is 85 percent of the 485 estimated total. However, because some regulars are on leave or long-term disability that estimate should be reduced to say that at least 75 percent of faculty work at VCC is done by regular instructors.

The reduction in the overall number of regulars from 2001 to 2012 reflects two rounds of restructuring through layoffs in the last decade that the college board and administration initiated for financial and capital shortage reasons. Those cuts resulted in close to one hundred FTE regulars either retiring early with an incentive or being laid off. Many, many term positions were lost as well.

In the normal course of events, the Vancouver model results in a steady state where a relatively constant proportion of term probationary faculty move up to regular status through the regularization process. There is a minority who, if their workloads stay below half time, do not share that opportunity, but as long as they have worked for six months, they do have the right of first refusal on available work and are always paid on a completely pro rata basis.

## Section 5: What about Tenure, Academic Freedom, Research, and College Governance?

Although appointed college boards have statutory control of community colleges in British Columbia, in reality funding and policy decisions of provincial governments can and often do trump local decision making. Community colleges do not enjoy the autonomy of universities; nevertheless, they are relatively stable. Constituent groups, including college managements and boards, are quick to attribute significant reductions in courses or numbers of faculty to shortfalls in government funding. Layoffs driven by financial necessity are possible, but usually come at a significant political cost to the provincial party in power.

Unless there are student shortages, governments and administrations have a hard time justifying layoffs because there is an enduring societal consensus that affordable access to a wide variety of postsecondary education options throughout the province is vital to the social, cultural, and economic health of the province. It is a consensus that drives political parties of all stripes to do what they can to prioritize adequate funding.

### 1. Tenure
The term "tenure," meaning the heightened job security granted to a faculty minority wherein an institution must prove financial exigency or redundancy to a third party before being able to lay off those professors, is not generally used in BC community colleges. "Regular" status as described herein is the norm. In the VCCFA agreement, regular status is "tenure-like" in that it is difficult to lay someone off without cause. A laid-off instructor can receive severance of up to almost $70,000 upon termination (Article 11.6.2). If there is cause because of substandard teaching or misbehavior, then suspension or dismissal will ensue. The union is obligated by law to give serious consideration to grieving and disputing a dismissal.

Before pursuing "tenure," the VCCFA would ask many questions about what it would mean in a community college. If tenure created a diminution of the equity and rights achieved for the nonregulars, then it would certainly be undesirable. The possible introduction of the concept of tenure would require the consideration of many issues:

If tenure is meant to bring academic or intellectual freedom, then should not all faculty have such freedom? Why would such freedom be limited to full-timers? To the extent that service is required of a full-timer with tenure, then should not a part-timer be expected to provide a pro rata amount of service? Why would tenure be connected to salary? Should not the status and extra job security be their own reward? How much more job security above what had already been achieved would tenure bring? Why should part-timers above a certain time status not have job-security tenure? What level of job security would be adequate or appropriate for community college faculty?

The answers to these questions may reduce the desirability of introducing a tenure system. However, if tenure was a sign of great respect, meant to ensure that certain faculty would have an extra layer of job security beyond what the VCCFA agreement already provided; if it provided faculty, perhaps through reduced teaching loads, the time to pursue their research and service interests for the benefit of the institution; and if those faculty were to be chosen by their peers for that status, then establishing such collective agreement provisions would certainly be desirable.

Why, though, should those achieving such an honor be paid much more than their colleagues? Perhaps a stipend of $500 a month would suffice? Perhaps sharing access to a support-staff person? Perhaps a better office should be provided? Would not such provisions be enough? One would think so, especially in community colleges founded upon an ethos of egalitarianism.[7]

## 2. Academic Freedom

Through many rounds of bargaining, the VCCFA had unsuccessfully tried to include a strong provision for academic freedom in its collective agreement. A number of BC colleges and universities have had such provisions for some time. Recently, upon completion of the VCC-VCCFA collective agreement for 2012–2014, the union succeeded in bargaining the following new contract provision:

> Society benefits from the search for knowledge and its free exposition. Academic freedom is essential to both these purposes in the teaching function of the College as well as in its scholarship and research. Every faculty employee is entitled to exercise academic freedom in the performance of their duties. Academic freedom is the freedom to examine, question, teach and learn and it involves the right to investigate, speculate, and comment without regard to prescribed doctrine. Academic freedom ensures the following:
>
> 1. Freedom in the conduct of teaching;
> 2. Freedom in undertaking research and making public the results thereof;
> 3. Freedom from institutional censorship.

Academic freedom carries with it the duty to use that freedom in a responsible way, respecting the rights and dignity of others, and in a manner consistent with the scholarly obligation to base teaching and research in an honest search for knowledge and the obligation to follow the curriculum requirements of the instructional assignment.

This provision now applies to every VCCFA member from their first day of work. The VCCFA will investigate any alleged contravention that does not respect these rights and when necessary, seek redress and remedy through the grievance/arbitration system that would restore them.

### 3. Research
The VCCFA is currently discussing with its fellow unions in the FPSE the importance and recognition of a broad definition of scholarly activity through collective agreement workload language. Such activity would include the scholarships of inquiry. Since VCC is an institution where most faculty view their main activity as teaching, the implementation of scholarly activity would be a gradual voluntary activity, necessarily restricted by the college's primary obligations to teaching and its limited budget flexibility.

In an approach that would echo how standardized PD time was achieved, we would probably set a quota of funding for research, which would over time become available to a higher and higher proportion of faculty as they self-selected for it. In time, it could become part of their workload profile.

### 4. College Governance
In the 1990s, the provincial government made important statutory amendments to the College and Institute Act, which enshrined shared governance for BC colleges.

As a consciously designed parallel to university senates, the act created education councils at all the colleges.[8] Education councils have designated advisory and decision-making powers on education and academic policy and curriculum matters wherein elected members from constituent groups form the majority, with faculty having half the seats. The VCCFA is participating in the process of creating and revising the constituencies for the ten faculty seats at VCC, which are currently a mixture of at-large and school-based groupings. The elected chair of the council has always been a faculty member.

The act also established elected constituency spots on the Vancouver Community College Board for one faculty, one support staff, and two students.[9] The chair of the education council and the college president are ex officio members. The majority of the board members are assigned by the government through cabinet-approved appointments.

The VCCFA takes a very active role in supporting the nomination and election of candidates for governance spots. It does not support individual candidates and makes clear throughout the process that those elected are not accountable to the union but to their constituencies and to the college as a whole. There is no special provision for the different categories of faculty. All are eligible to run for election and to vote and there has not been a need felt for nonregulars or part-timers to have separate representation.

For faculty involved in governance on the council, there has been a clear lack of resources concerning knowledge of provincial norms and best practice, as well as a lack of time available to research policy matters. This area remains a bargaining objective for the VCCFA and several faculty unions. The college administration has until very recently done little to ensure that a balance of opinion is presented. In part because of this lack of balance, the union takes a very active role in informing and advising faculty on policy issues and in presenting to and seeking to influence the governance bodies as a whole.

In 2002, there was an unfortunate but ultimately instructive instance of VCC's administration deliberately trying to bypass the education council. The case involved the college's obligation to present the changing of a department's course lengths to the education council so that it could give its formal advice on the matter to the college board. The act stipulates both that the council must give its advice and that the board must seek advice on such matters. In response to the college's intransigence, the VCCFA, with the support of FPSE, took the matter to the Supreme Court of British Columbia, where it won a stinging judgment.[10] There was no doubt in the court's mind that the college had been incorrectly trying to get around its statutory obligations. This judgment serves as an instructive precedent on ensuring that college administrations respect the processes of shared governance.

College governance also includes college committees and more routine department meetings and procedures. Assigned duty time is set aside in departmental workload profiles for such activities. With the VCCFA's pro rata approach, workload profiles apply to all faculty members regardless of their appointment status or time status.

Work on college committees generally falls under the notion of "professional responsibilities," which are not completely captured by workload profiles.[11] The collective agreement recognizes that professional responsibilities extend beyond quantifiable assigned duties but it does not compel instructors to participate in activities not directly related to their primary duty of facilitating student learning. Does the college community really want faculty on college committees who have no interest or energy for them? Everyone—new or senior, term or regular, part-time and full-time—is able to volunteer or stand for selection to committees of interest to him or her, though there is normally little or no time allowance made for such service.

Since all faculty in a department share the same workload profile, term faculty, whether full-time or part-time, are expected to attend departmental meetings. They have a vote and say on all matters, including department head elections, and they may run for such leadership positions if they wish (Article 13.4.4). In fact, if they are successful, they immediately become full-time regular faculty, a status they maintain until they retire (Article 13.1.3).

## Section 6: How Was the Vancouver Model Achieved?

In this section, I discuss seven factors that contributed to the success of the Vancouver model. I then list highlights in the rounds of bargaining held between 1988 and 2014.

### 1. Historical Circumstance
Beginning as a vocational school model has had its advantages. Through the 1950s and 1960s, there were relatively few part-timers at VCC. The normal model of work was full-time day work. It seems that without the hierarchies endemic to the academic world, it was considered reasonable to pay the few part-timers on a pro rata basis. So, when the fight for full equity began in earnest in the 1980s, the VCCFA did not have to struggle for pay equity.

### 2. Political and Social History
Canada and British Columbia in particular have long histories of union activism. Social Democrats and Socialists have sat in the provincial legislature for many decades. The first left-wing Social Democrat provincial government was elected in the early 1970s when the New Democratic Party won a majority of the seats. There have been swings between the Right and the Left since then, but the fundamental right to unionize and act as a union, while never without restrictions, has been recognized as legitimate by the courts, governments of all stripes, and society.

### 3. Union Culture
Over the years, the leaders of the VCCFA have developed a union activist culture in which they do not shy away from being unionists first—not faculty first. They have based their work on a fundamental belief that while administrators are usually fine, decent people, it is not their job or duty as employers to structure the workplace with equity as a primary value. The administrators usually prefer management flexibility. It is rather the union's duty to struggle for equity. It does not matter what a union officer's personal

job status or history is; if the officer is a unionist, he or she cannot but work to end inequity. That necessity would apply even if the leaders were starting from scratch, with the necessity of educating an uninterested group of full-time regulars as to why nonregular rights are important for all. This is in part why the VCCFA does not have designated spots on the union executive for nonregular or new instructors. It is part of the job of all union leaders to work for and to represent the nonregulars.

Working from a unionist cultural base means not shying away from using and learning to use the tools of unionism—informed argument, public advocacy, grievance, bargaining, strike votes, and strikes—to the fullest extent possible under the law. Union culture means being realistic about the political divisions within a membership, realistic about what is actually possible to achieve at a particular point in the union's work, and addressing the constant need to inform, educate, plan, and represent in order to create winning conditions for solidarity to continue to flourish.

### 4. Ending Never-Ending Probationary Status
As VCC morphed from a purely vocational school into a comprehensive community college in the 1970s, the change brought with it the realities of part-time employment for significant numbers of faculty. The conditions of never-ending probationary status and contingent employment still so rampant in North American postsecondary life in 2012 were the VCC reality as well.

### 5. Comprehensive Strategy for Inclusion
In the late 1980s, almost every group of instructors at VCC had pent-up frustrations. Pay grades were behind those of other colleges. Workloads were higher. Professional development provisions were sorely lacking. The union was able to unite its members behind bargaining agendas that had something for as many groups as possible, especially for nonregulars, and took away from no one.

This pattern has continued. In each of the ten rounds of bargaining since 1988, balanced, member-ratified bargaining packages have been put in front of management. In order to appeal to the largest possible number of faculty, packages have always included an array of proposed solutions to issues such as leave improvements for regulars, benefit and pay improvements for all, provisions focused on department heads, and non-cost and cost improvements for term instructors.

### 6. Responsible Militancy
As often happens, clumsy management has helped motivate faculty unionism, and sometimes management has helped further by being disrespectful. In the 1987 round, it served the union with a lockout notice as the semester

wound down to Christmas. When the VCCFA eventually ended up at labor board mediation, the mediator delivered a clear, hard lesson: without a strike vote, he had nothing with which to pressure management.

The VCCFA took that lesson to heart. Before the end of the collective agreement term in March 1990, its members passed a strike vote and notified VCC that if there were not a new agreement by April 1, they would be on strike: "No Contract, No Work." (Changes to provincial labor law have since prohibited that option.) That five-week strike was a watershed moment; it brought VCCFA members into the fold as equals among British Columbian postsecondary faculty. There were major advances in workload, term instructor rights, professional development, pay, benefits, and protection of faculty work. Also, the administration failed in its attempt to internally privatize parts of the college by setting up a contract arm to duplicate programs.

### 7. Making a Key Compromise

In order to address never-ending contingency—having already achieved pay equity, through the give and take of bargaining—the VCCFA agreed to modify the most directly distinguishing cost factor in attaining regular status: severance. It settled on a position that, if a person had been automatically regularized and subsequently needed to be laid off during the first three years after his or her regularization, he or she could not collect what would be the severance entitlement. For such faculty, that would normally amount to three or four months' pay. Instructors laid off after three years could collect their entitlements, and their severance accruals would be dated back to include all their service. This was felt to be a reasonable compromise because regularized faculty would gain the right to notice of at least four months and transfer possibilities in the event of layoff, as well as the other benefits and the job security of being regular. This compromise helped cement what is now a twenty-year-old practice of automatic regularization. That has meant that new VCC instructors have a clear career path from their first day of work. However, this does not mean that this compromise should continue indefinitely. If mandated by its members, the VCCFA will struggle to remove the severance restriction.

### 8. Highlights of Achievements for Nonregulars over the Past Ten Rounds

The VCCFA started prioritizing nonregular issues in the late eighties from a place of relative advantage: pro rata pay equity and an overload ban for all were already in place. Those faculty at half time or more had mandated PD days, equitable accrual of sick leave benefits, and payment by the college of 60 percent of health and dental premiums. The following highlights on improvements from that base are grouped according to the applicable round of bargaining. After each group there is an indication of the degree of militancy that was required to conclude settlement:

### 1988–1990
- The first right to automatic regularization of the person after 410 days of half-time or more work over any two-year period; the clause had retroactive application
- *Strike vote taken*

### 1990–1992
- Reduction of regularization accrual requirement to 380 days
- Right to prorated workload through workload profile system
- Evaluation required for regularization with onus on college to do it
- Protection from work going to nonunion contract arm of college
- College goes to 100 percent premium coverage for health and dental benefits
- PD funds for all terms and regulars eligible for PD time
- Workload in terms of assigned duty down to twenty-five hours per week from thirty
- *Strike of five weeks*

### 1992–1994
- Seniority accrual rate for part-time regulars equal to full-timers
- Layoff of all regulars by seniority instead of part-time regulars before full-timers
- Right to top-up term work for part-time regulars
- Right to subsequent increases in regularization level for part-time regulars
- *Strike vote taken*

### 1994–1995
- Right of the large group of term instructors in English as a Second Language division to be reappointed by seniority after their initial appointment; achieved through labor-management talks and a letter of agreement
- *No strike vote*

### 1995–1998
- The historic first round of provincial bargaining brings in a common salary scale for all BC postsecondary institutions.
- *Strike of two days*

### 1998–2001
- The second round of provincial bargaining brings wider application of the regularization of the person concept. There were no gains for VCCFA nonregulars because of their already superior provisions. An

increase in release from teaching time for department heads and coordinators brought increased work opportunities to nonregulars.
- *Strike of less than two hours*

**2001–2004**
- The right to reappointment by first refusal and seniority for terms was
  spread from the ESL division to all departments. The right takes effect
  after six months of cumulative work, and terms became subject to two
  evaluations during their probationary period.
- Standardization of hiring procedure gained through grievance process
- A new provision established that seven months of work in a year triggers
  fifteen days of PD time for terms or regulars at half time or more.
- *No strike vote*

**2004–2007**
- Laid-off regulars, full or part time, accrue full seniority after layoff for
  up to two years
- *No strike vote*

**2007–2010**
- Removal of all arbitrary caps on initial salary scale placement for all
  terms and regulars
- Through grievance, right gained to comprehensive status maintenance—benefits, regularization, and seniority accrual—for mothers and
  mothers-to-be who are term instructors at the start of their maternity
  leaves
- *No strike vote*

**2010–2012**
- Maintenance of salary placement for all auxiliary work subsequent to
  first appointment
- Right to replace department heads during vacation periods, creating
  work opportunities
- *Strike vote taken*

**2012–2014**
- Academic freedom for all faculty, regardless of status
- *No strike vote*

## Section 7: How Could Others Make Their Employment Structures More Equitable?

It is a bit risky to propose unsought-for answers to a rhetorical question.
Please take the following hopefully helpful musings as being from a place
of engagement and experience at a particular unionized community college,
which may or may not have resonance in other situations.

If the VCCFA leadership group was suddenly transported to a typical American community college—in, for example, Seattle—with the prevailing problems of contingency for many and full-time security for few, what might happen? This is purely an imaginative exercise that will certainly demonstrate my ignorance of the American reality. Apologies in advance. The use of the pronoun "we" in the following refers to an imagined union leadership group.

### 1. Extend Union Democracy

Starting with internal matters, we would seek to extend and ensure full membership and voting rights for as many college faculty as possible, no matter if they work on call or are twenty-year veterans, part time or full time. If two unions existed, one for full-timers and another for part-timers, we would seek to eventually merge them. If that did not seem fruitful or likely, we would work to make the distinction moot by closely aligning the goals and activities of the unions. Having two faculty unions at one institution working at cross purposes would be a dream for any competent college manager.

### 2. Increase Union Capacity

A union needs funds in order to buy release for at least one or two elected officers and for its bargainers in bargaining years. It is important to be able to pay for professional, experienced, union-oriented advice when needed. If necessary, we would seek to increase dues incrementally. (VCCFA dues are 2.15 percent of gross income for all members.) If not already part of a federation, some part of dues should be set aside to be pooled with like unions to build federations where more pooled financial, legal, and representative expertise can be housed. (VCCFA sends 42 percent of its dues to pool with other FPSE unions in this way.)

### 3. Set a Fair Wage Target and Policy

A fair wage, prorated for all, would be our goal. We would work to eliminate the tremendous imbalance of wages between full-timers and contingents. Given the current imbalances, achieving a fair wage for all may mean diverting some resources over time so that more could be allocated to those needing the highest boost up. This would be for a transitional period driven by the need to establish greater equity. Of course, the higher wages of incumbents would be guaranteed with whatever cost of living increases were possible. Getting to equity on salaries could take more than a decade.

### 4. Make Alliances

We would make and invest in every alliance possible with others in the labor and social justice movements, and most especially organized, progressive student groups and other unions in college and related worksites. We would get and give advice, get and offer support, work to get labor laws changed, and work to get people elected who will change laws. On the last point, our members would not take second place to political contributions. Our VCCFA constitution does not allow direct engagement in partisan activities, so we focus on education campaigns during elections. A strong union movement is one of the best, most efficient social programs possible.

### 5. Increase Political and Bargaining Clout

If we had lost the right to strike, then we would work politically to get it back. Until then, and even if that was an impossible goal in the given jurisdiction, we would be as responsibly militant as possible in every venue available. Low wage and low rights workplaces are a result of conscious policies and actions. They will not be reformed solely because of good intentions. So far, good intentions have not made for more equitable workplaces.

### 6. No Overtime and Pro Rata Workload

Setting real targets of equity for the workload of non-full-timers, along with a ban on overtime, would be a priority for us. The job of the part-timer would be prorated as closely as possible to that of the full-timer in the same area. For example, if the full-timer has office hours, then a pro rata amount for the part-timer is a necessity. Where people have through no fault of their own become dependent on overtime income, then gradual disengagement over perhaps two decades for the unit as a whole might be necessary.

### 7. Realistic Cap on Accountable Hours

We would not try to include voluntarism in workload and compensation. Every faculty member should do some college service and other nonteaching duties, but it should not be mandatory beyond certain realistic limits. Other than minimum standards, it should be voluntary. People will always work more for recognition and for personal satisfaction. Since they are the ones who want to do it, they should probably do it. Those who do not do the extra committee work would suffer no loss in status or pay or regard. In community colleges, the focus should remain on teaching.

### 8. Protect Entitlements

The rights and benefits of current full-time faculty would be protected for as long as they are working. They should not be held collectively responsible for the inequities of the current system.

### 9. Gradualism

Since the current system of inequity did not come into place overnight, dismantling it would similarly require time for significant incremental change.

Implementing revolutionary change would be a huge undertaking, the difficulty of which would be compounded by the greater resistance of governments and administrators. We would plan on the unfortunate necessity of taking several rounds of bargaining and constant engagement over perhaps a couple of decades to enshrine significant achievements. A combination of long-term goals with several intermediary steps would be mapped out.[12] In the area of benefit costs, for example, starting from wherever we found ourselves, we would go toward an array of shared benefit premiums. Our ultimate goal would be to gradually shift costs onto the employer.

### 10. Focus on Non-Cost Rights and Entitlements

As we worked on monetary fairness through a fair wage strategy, no less emphasis would be given to addressing non-cost rights issues. In fact, the non-cost area of rights might have a greater prospect of quicker success than the cost area. That would not mean it would be easy, just that resistance might yield if a campaign was strong and focused enough. Management would not be able to use the "our hands are financially tied" argument, as such issues can be easily framed as matters of fairness and justice. To the fullest extent possible, we would recreate the rights array we have in Vancouver. One system of seniority accrual, protection from harassment and bullying, the right of first refusal to term work, automatic regularization of the person, the right to top up to full-time, and full democratic rights within the union and within departments would all be short-term priorities.

### 11. Establish Credibility on Evaluation and Hiring Processes

If hiring procedures are only to be used once per individual, managements need to have confidence in the hiring procedures. It is therefore very important that they be as clear and as rigorous as necessary. We would not have a problem with management and hiring committees casting their nets as widely as possible provided the current divide between tenure and non-tenure-track was being eliminated.

In the same way, clear and fair evaluation procedures need to be mutually agreed to so that hiring decisions can be confirmed and new faculty learn what is expected of their new jobs. Students need to be confident that their instructors are accountable.

### 12. Think Union Thoughts First

All of this transformative work is going to take a long time and several generations of union leadership. While union leadership should come from the group of workers concerned, faculty who become union leaders should view their new assignments through a union-first lens. This means setting aside their relationship to management as faculty and taking on the responsibility of being a union professional, which in turn means doing the best possible for the membership as a whole and for individual members involved with some issue with management, even if as a faculty member one might be inclined to sympathize with management's side of the issue. We would not be irresponsible in this: we know the union does not get to win every case; sometimes "doing the best possible" for a member means helping the member accept that he or she is never going to work at the college again.

While most often evident in the union's interactions with management, a union-first lens also applies to relations with faculty departments. A sometimes difficult example from the VCCFA collective agreement is its language around transfer rights. In the case of a layoff caused by a decision of management to reduce offerings, our first priority as unionists is maintaining the job status of the instructors facing layoff. As part of that goal and with our members' ratification, we have established transfer (bumping) rights to other areas where one would retain his or her seniority rights to an ongoing job. Only qualified faculty may transfer, but the real question is who should judge and decide whether one can actually meet the criteria? Faculty members may say that they, as the members of the receiving department, should have the final say. As unionists, we would say no, this issue is parallel to a hiring decision; thus, it should be a grievable management decision, as currently set out by our collective agreement on the hiring process. It's ultimately a dean's decision. In the view of the VCCFA, this puts the matter in the correct forum for resolution, where the rights of the member threatened with layoff are subject to the most objective tests and procedures possible.

### 13. Think Succession and Celebrate

It is vital for current union leaders to always have their succession in mind and set about the processes of engagement, encouragement, and celebration necessary to get and keep people involved. Leaders should plan for and encourage their succession. VCCFA bylaws set a three-term cap on the union presidency, with two years per term. As vital as paid professional assistance is, it is not as good as member empowerment. Empowering members means not depending solely on professional help for leadership; appropriately sharing responsibility is key.

## Conclusion

There are alternatives to the current models of inequity in community college employment. The Vancouver model is one alternative that while imperfect and incomplete may provide some practical paths to explore. Community colleges at their best are themselves models of democratic, transforming institutions. As workplaces, they should also be models of equitable, empowering employment.

## NOTES

1. Vancouver Community College (VCC) and Vancouver Community College Faculty Association (VCCFA), *April 1, 2012–March 31, 2014 Collective Agreement*, available at *www.vccfa.ca* (under "Member Resources"). The document is composed of the collective agreement reached between VCC and the VCCFA, and the "Common Agreement," which is appended to the collective agreement and whose provisions are shared with other unions and institutions in the province. Unless otherwise noted, all citations of article numbers are from the collective agreement.
2. See Pension Corporation of British Columbia, *www.college.pensionsbc.ca*.
3. Articles 23 and 24 of the Collective Agreement and Article 2 of the Common Agreement.
4. Article 6.4 of the Common Agreement.
5. VCCFA Constitution and By-laws, *www.vccfa.ca*, under Member Resources.
6. At this writing, the 2013 seniority lists are available at *www.vccfa.ca*, under "Member Resources." The 2001 and 2008 lists are on file in the union office.
7. In 2011, to guide collective bargaining among its new university-based locals, FPSE established such a set of egalitarian principles that include bargaining for tenure separate from pay: *Policy and Principles for Bargaining in BC's Universities* can be found at *www.fpse.ca*, under "Library" (click "FPSE Publications").
8. Sections 9, 14, 23, 24 and 25 of the College and Institute Act (available at *www.bclaws.ca*).
9. Ibid., section 9.
10. See Vancouver Community College Faculty Association v. Vancouver Community College, 2005 BCSC 119 (31 January 2005), *www.courts.gov.bc.ca*.
11. From Article 6.6.1: "It is acknowledged that an instructor's professional responsibilities included more than assigned duty."
12. The author and Jack Longmate have developed such a model, the *Program for Change*; see *www.vccfa.ca*.

# Selected Bibliography
# on the Contingent Faculty Movement

*Keith Hoeller*

This selected bibliography consists of mostly books, some union policy documents, and several relevant articles on contingent faculty and the labor movement. Many more articles can be found in both the *Chronicle of Higher Education* (*chronicle.com*) and *Inside Higher Ed* (*insidehighered.com*). For a more comprehensive bibliography on adjunct faculty, see Weiss and Pankin's *Part-Time Faculty in Higher Education*.

AAUP (American Association of University Professors). *Contingent Appointments and the Academic Profession*. Washington, DC: AAUP, 2003.
———. *Looking the Other Way? Accreditation Standards and Part-Time Faculty*. Washington, DC: AAUP, 2008. *aaup.org*.
———. *Policy Documents and Reports*. 10th ed. Baltimore, MD: Johns Hopkins University Press, 2006.
———. *Recommended Institutional Regulations on Academic Freedom and Tenure*. Washington, DC: AAUP, 2006.
AFT (American Federation of Teachers). *Academic Freedom in the 21st Century College and University*. Washington, DC: AFT, 2007.
———. *Fairness and Equity: Standards of Good Practice in the Employment of Part-Time/Adjunct Faculty*. Washington, DC: AFT, 2002. *aft.org*.
———. *Standards of Good Practice in the Employment of Full-Time Nontenure-Track Faculty*. Washington, DC: AFT, 2005. *aft.org*.
———. *Standards of Good Practice in the Employment of Graduate Employees*. Washington, DC: AFT, 2004. *aft.org*.
Berrett, Dan. "Do Adjunct Votes Count?" *Inside Higher Ed*, 27 April 2011. *insidehighered.com*.
———. "A Shop Divided." *Inside Higher Ed*, 10 February 2011. *insidehighered.com*.
Berry, Joe. *Reclaiming the Ivory Tower: Organizing Adjuncts to Change Higher Education*. New York: Monthly Review Press, 2005.
Berry, Joe, and Elizabeth Hoffman. "Including Contingent Faculty in Governance." *Academe*, November-December 2008. *aaup.org*.
Berry, Joe, Beverly Stewart, and Helena Worthen. *Access to Unemployment Insurance Benefits for Contingent Faculty*. Chicago: Chicago Coalition on Contingent Academic Labor, 2008. *www.chicagococal.org*.

Bousquet, Marc. *How the University Works: Higher Education and the Low-Wage Nation*. New York: New York University Press, 2008.

Bradley, Gwen. "Contingent Faculty and the New Academic Labor System." *Academe*, January-February 2004. *aaup.org*.

———, ed. *Contingent Faculty Fighting for Equity*. Special issue, *Academe*, November-December 2008.

Brill, Steven. *Class Warfare: Inside the Fight to Fix America's Schools*. New York: Simon and Schuster, 2011.

Brown, Peter D. G. "Confessions of a Tenured Professor." *Inside Higher Ed*, 11 May 2010. *insidehighered.com*.

Buhle, Paul. *Taking Care of Business: Samuel Gompers, George Meany, Lane Kirkland and the Tragedy of American Labor*. New York: Monthly Review Press, 1999.

Burgan, Mary. *Whatever Happened to the Faculty: Drift and Decision in Higher Education*. Baltimore, MD: Johns Hopkins University Press, 2006.

Burns, Joe. *Reviving the Strike: How Working People Can Regain Power and Transform America*. Brooklyn, NY: IG Publishing, 2011.

Canadian Association of University Professors. "Policy Statement on Fairness for Contract Academic Staff," June 2010. *caut.ca*.

Cosco, Frank and Jack Longmate. "An Instructive Model of How More Equity and Equality Is Possible: The Vancouver Community College Model." In Kezar, *Embracing Non-Tenure Track Faculty*, 55–83.

Cross, John G., and Edie N. Goldenberg. *Off-Track: Nontenured Teachers in Higher Education*. Cambridge, MA: MIT Press, 2009.

Cumo, Chris, and P. D. Lesko. "A Tale of Greed and Gluttony: The California Part-Time Faculty Equity Fund Boondoggle." *Adjunct Advocate*, May-June 2004.

Curtis, John W, primary author. "Figure 1: Trends in Instructional Staff Employment Status, 1975–2009." In Saranna Thornton et al., *It's Not over Yet: The Annual Report on the Economic Status of the Profession, 2010–11*. Washington, DC: AAUP, 2011.

Curtis, John W., and Monica Jacobe. *AAUP Contingent Faculty Index 2006*. Washington, DC: AAUP, 2006.

Davis, Leonard J., Ronald G. Ehrenberg, Keith Hoeller, Daniel J. Julius, Cary Nelson, and Pamela S. Silverblatt. "Forum: The Future of Faculty Unions." *Chronicle of Higher Education*, 24 July 2011.

DeCew, Judith Wagner. *Unionization in the Academy: Visions and Realities*. Lanham, MD: Rowman and Littlefield, 2003.

DeSantis, Sylvia M. *Academic Apartheid: Waging the Adjunct War*. Newcastle upon Tyne, UK: Cambridge Scholars Publishing, 2011.

Donoghue, Frank. *The Last Professors: The Corporate University and the Fate of the Humanities*. New York: Fordham University Press, 2008.

———. "Why Academic Freedom Doesn't Matter." *South Atlantic Quarterly* 108, no. 4 (2009): 601–21.

Dray, Philip. *There Is Power in a Union: The Epic Story of Labor in America*. New York: Anchor Books, 2010.

Dubson, Michael, ed. *Ghosts in the Classroom: Stories of College Adjunct Faculty—and the Price We All Pay*. Boston: Camel's Back, 2001.

Early, Steve. *The Civil Wars in U.S. Labor: Birth of a New Workers' Movement or Death Throes of the Old?* Chicago: Haymarket Books, 2011.

———. *Embedded with Organized Labor: Journalistic Reflections on the Class War at Home.* New York: Monthly Review Press, 2009.

Euben, Donna. "Legal Contingencies for Contingent Professors." *Chronicle of Higher Education,* 16 June 2006.

Fitch, Robert. *Solidarity for Sale: How Corruption Destroyed the Labor Movement and Undermined America's Promise.* New York: Public Affairs, 2006.

Fletcher, Bill, Jr., and Fernando Gapasin. *Solidarity Divided: The Crisis in Organized Labor and a New Path toward Social Justice.* Berkeley: University of California Press, 2008.

Fountain, Wendell V. *Academic Sharecroppers: Exploitation of Adjunct Faculty and the Higher Education System.* Bloomington, IN: AuthorHouse, 2005.

FPSE (Federation of Post-Secondary Educators of British Columbia). *Policies and Principles for Bargaining in BC's Universities.* Vancouver: FPSE, 2011. *fpse.ca.*

Fuller, Robert W. *Somebodies and Nobodies: Overcoming the Abuse of Rank.* Gabriola Island, BC: New Society Publishers, 2004.

Gappa, Judith M., and David W. Leslie. *The Invisible Faculty: Improving the Status of Part-Timers in Higher Education.* San Francisco: Jossey-Bass, 1993.

Hacker, Andrew, and Claudia Dreifus. *Higher Education: How Colleges Are Wasting Our Money and Failing Our Kids—and What We Can Do About It.* New York: Times Books, 2010.

Hedrick, David W., Steven E. Henson, John M. Krieg, and Charles S. Wassell Jr. "Is There Really a Faculty Union Salary Premium?" *Industrial and Labor Relations Review* 64, no. 3 (2011). *digitalcommons.ilr.cornell.edu.*

Hess, John. "The Entrepreneurial Adjunct." *Academe,* January-February 2004.

Hoeller, Keith. "An Adjunct Bill of Rights." *Chronicle of Higher Education,* 29 November 2006.

———. "Community College Part-Timers Need Legislature's Help." *Crosscut,* 1 March 2011. *crosscut.com*

———. "Equal Pay for Equal Work." *Chronicle of Higher Education,* 22 October 2003.

———. "Equal Rights Legislation for Adjuncts." *Adjunct Advocate,* January-February 2007.

———. "The Future of the Contingent Faculty Movement." *Inside Higher Ed,* 13 November 2007. *insidehighered.com.*

———. "Neither Reasonable, Nor Assuring." *Chronicle of Higher Education,* 23 September 2004.

———. "Throwing Darts at Adjunct Activists." *Adjunct Advocate,* January-February 2008: 48–50.

———. "Union Matters." *Chronicle of Higher Education,* 13 May 2004. *chronicle.com.*

———. "We Need an Adjunct Union." *Inside Higher Ed,* 9 December 2010. *insidehighered.com.*

Hoeller, Keith, and Jack Longmate. "Some Union Members Are More Equal Than Others." *Chronicle of Higher Education,* 12 June 2011.

Jacoby, Dan. "Is Washington State an Unlikely Leader? Progress on Addressing

Contingent Work Issues in Academia." *Education Policy Analysis Archives* 9, no. 41 (8 October 2001). *epaa.asu.edu.*

Jaschik, Scott. "The Adjunct Pay Gap." *Inside Higher Ed*, 27 January 2005. *insidehighered.com.*

———. "Do Caps Help Adjuncts?" *Inside Higher Ed*, 22 April 2010. *insidehighered.com.*

———. "For Adjuncts, Progress and Complexities." *Inside Higher Ed*, 11 August 2008. *insidehighered.com.*

———. "Revolt in the Adjunct Ranks." *Inside Higher Ed*, 30 July 2008. *insidehighered.com.*

———. "Students or Employees." *Inside Higher Ed*, 24 July 2012. *insidehighered.com.*

Johnson, Benjamin, Patrick Kavanagh, and Kevin Mattson, eds. *Steal This University: The Rise of the Corporate University and the Academic Labor Movement.* New York: Routledge, 2003.

June, Audrey Williams. "Local Union Is Not Treating Part- and Full-Timers Equally, Adjunct Complains to NEA." *Chronicle of Higher Education*, 11 April 2011.

———. "A Philosopher Stirs Up the World of Adjuncts: Gadfly Takes on Colleges, Lawmakers, and Unions." *Chronicle of Higher Education*, 23 May 2008.

Kahlenberg, Richard D. "Faculty Salaries and Labor Unions." *Chronicle of Higher Education*, 12 April 2011.

———. *Tough Liberal: Albert Shanker and the Battles over Schools, Unions, Race, and Democracy.* New York: Columbia University Press, 2007.

Kezar, Adrianna, ed. *Embracing Non-Tenure Track Faculty: Changing Campuses for the New Faculty Majority.* New York: Routledge, 2012.

———. *Non-Tenure-Track Faculty in Higher Education: Theories and Tensions.* ASHE Higher Education Report 36, no. 5. Las Vegas: Association for the Study of Higher Education, 2010.

———. *Understanding the New Majority of Non-Tenure-Track Faculty in Higher Education: Demographics, Experiences, and Plans of Action.* ASHE Higher Education Report 36, no. 4. Las Vegas: Association for the Study of Higher Education, 2010.

Kudera, Alex. *Fight for Your Long Day: A Novel.* Kensington, MD: Atticus Books, 2011.

Leatherman, Courtney. "Do Accreditors Look the Other Way When Colleges Rely on Part-Timers? Adjuncts Say Agencies Ignore Their Own Rules about the Need for Full-Time Faculty Members." *Chronicle of Higher Education*, 7 November 1997.

Leslie, David W., Samuel E. Kellams, and G. Manny Gunne. *Part-Time Faculty in American Higher Education.* New York: Praeger, 1982.

Longmate, Jack. "The Overload Debate." *Community College Journal*, Fall 2010.

Longmate, Jack, and Frank Cosco. "Part-Time Instructors Deserve Equal Pay for Equal Work." *Chronicle of Higher Education*, 3 May 2002.

———. *Program for Change.* Vancouver, BC: Vancouver Community College Faculty Association, 2010. *vccfa.ca.*

Maisto, Maria. "The Adjunct's Moment of Truth." *Inside Higher Ed*, 10 September 2009. *insidehighered.com.*

Martin. James E., with Thomas D. Heetderks. *Two-Tier Compensation Structures: Their Impact on Unions, Employers and Employees.* Kalamazoo, MI: W. E. Upjohn Institute for Employment Research, 1990.

Martin, Randy, ed. "Academic Labor: An Introduction." *Social Text* 15, no. 2 (Summer 1997): 1–8.

McGee, Micki. "Hooked on Higher Education and Other Tales from Adjunct Faculty Organizing." *Social Text* 20, no. 1 (Spring 2002): 61–80.

McMartin, Joseph. *Collision Course: Ronald Reagan, the Air Traffic Controllers, and the Strike That Changed America.* New York: Oxford University Press, 2011.

Moe, Terry. *Special Interest: Teachers Unions and America's Public Schools.* Washington, DC: Brookings Institution, 2011.

Moody, Kim. *US Labor in Trouble and Transition: The Failure of Reform from Above and the Promise of Revival from Below.* London: Verso, 2007.

Moser, Richard. "The AAUP Organizes Part-Time Faculty." *Academe*, November-December 1998, 17–24.

———. *The New Academic Labor System.* Washington, DC: AAUP, 2001. *aaup.org.*

Murphy, Marjorie. *Blackboard Unions: The AFT and the NEA, 1900-1980.* Ithaca, NY: Cornell University Press, 1990.

NEA (National Education Association). *The NEA and Contingent Academic Workers in Higher Education: NBI 2004-60 Action Plan.* Washington, DC: NEA, 2004. *www.cca4me.org/part_time/contingentplan.pdf.*

———. "Part-Time Faculty: A Look at Data and Issues." *NEA Higher Education Research Center Update* 13, no. 3 (September 2007).

Nelson, Cary. "Manifesto against Contingency." *Academe*, July-August 2007.

———. *No University Is an Island.* New York: New York University Press, 2010.

———, ed. *Will Teach for Food: Academic Labor in Crisis.* Minneapolis: University of Minnesota Press, 1999.

Nocella, Anthony J., II, Steven Best, and Peter McLaren, eds. *Academic Repression: Reflections from the Academic Industrial Complex.* Oakland, CA: AK Press, 2010.

Parker, Robert E. *Flesh Peddlers and Warm Bodies: The Temporary Help Industry and Its Workers.* New Brunswick, NJ: Rutgers University Press, 1994.

Patton, Stacey. "The Ph.D. Now Comes with Food Stamps." *Chronicle of Higher Education*, 6 May 2012.

Professor X [pseud.]. *In the Basement of the Ivory Tower: Confessions of an Accidental Academic.* New York: Viking, 2011.

Rhoades, Gary. *Managed Professionals: Unionized Faculty and Restructuring Academic Labor.* Albany: State University of New York Press, 1998.

Riley, Naomi Schaefer. *The Faculty Lounges and Other Reasons Why You Won't Get the College Education You Paid For.* Chicago: Ivan R. Dee, 2011.

Ross, Andrew. "The Mental Labor Problem." *Social Text* 18, no. 2 (Summer 2000): 1–31.

Roueche, John E., Susanne D. Roueche, and Mark D. Milliron. *Strangers in Their Own Land: Part-Time Faculty in American Community Colleges.* Washington, DC: Community College Press, 1995.

Ruiz, Eddy A. "The Stone That Struck Goliath: The Part-Time Faculty Association, Washington State Community Colleges, and Class-Action Lawsuits." In *The*

*Current Landscape and Changing Perspectives of Part-Time Faculty*, special issue of *New Directions for Community Colleges* (2007, Issue 140): 49–54.

Saltzman, Gregory M. "Union Organizing and the Law: Part-Time Faculty and Graduate Teaching Assistants." In *The NEA 2000 Almanac of Higher Education*, 43–55. Washington, DC: NEA, 2000. *www.nea.org*.

Schell, Eileen. *Gypsy Academics and Mother-Teachers: Gender Contingent Labor and Writing Instruction*. Portsmouth, NH: Crosscurrents, 1998.

———. "Toward a New Labor Movement in Higher Education: Contingent Labor and Organizing for Change." *Workplace*, Issue 7 (2001).

Schmidt, Peter. "Accreditation Is Eyed as a Means to Aid Adjuncts." *Chronicle of Higher Education*, 25 March 2012.

———. "Union's Bid to Organize Georgetown U. Adjuncts Is Part of an Innovative Regional Strategy." *Chronicle of Higher Education*, 2 October 2012.

———. "Unions Confront Faultlines between Adjuncts and Full-Timers: Some Look Beyond the Big Unions for Real Improvement in Working Conditions." *Chronicle of Higher Education*, 20 November 2011.

———. "What Good Do Faculty Unions Do?" *Chronicle of Higher Education*, 1 May 2011.

Schneider, Alison. "To Many Adjunct Professors, Academic Freedom Is a Myth: As Ranks of Part-Timers Swell, They Lament How Easily Colleges Can Dump Them." *Chronicle of Higher Education*, 10 December 1999.

Schrecker, Ellen W. *The Lost Soul of Higher Education: Corporatization, the Assault on Academic Freedom, and the End of the American University*. New York: New Press, 2010.

———. *No Ivory Tower: McCarthyism and the Universities*. New York: Oxford, 1986.

Smith, Sharon. *Subterranean Fire: A History of Working-Class Radicalism in the United States*. Chicago: Haymarket Books, 2006.

Street, Steve. "Avenues for Change Adjuncts Can Believe In." *Inside Higher Ed*, 19 January 2009. *insidehighered.com*.

———. "Don't Be Kind to Adjuncts." *Chronicle of Higher Education*, 24 October 2008.

———. "Wouldn't a Progressive Era Require Faculty Equity?" *Thought and Action: The NEA Higher Education Journal* 25 (Fall 2009): 141–50.

Street, Steve, Maria Maisto, Esther Merves, and Gary Rhoades. *Who Is Professor "Staff," and How Can This Person Teach So Many Classes?* Center for the Future of Higher Education Policy Report 2, August 2012. *futureofhighered.org/research-center*.

Sweeney, Isaac. *Students Losing Out: Four Essays on Adjunct Labor in Higher Education*. Amazon Digital Services, 2011. *amazon.com*.

Tait, Vanessa. *Poor Workers' Unions: Rebuilding Labor from Below*. Cambridge, MA: South End Press, 2005.

Teeuwen, Rudolphus, and Steffen Hantke, eds. *Gypsy Scholars, Migrant Teachers, and the Global Academic Proletariat: Adjunct Labour in Higher Education*. At the Interface 40. Amsterdam: Rodopi, 2007.

Texter, Douglas W. "No Tenure, No Problem." *Chronicle of Higher Education*, 6 March 2009.

Thompson, Karen. "Piecework to Parity: Part-Timers in Action." *Thought and Action: The NEA Higher Education Journal* (Fall 2000): 53–60.

———. "The Ultimate Working Condition: Knowing Whether You Have a Job or Not." *Forum: Newsletter of the Non-Tenure-Track Faculty Special Interest Group, Conference on College Composition and Communication*, Winter 1998.

Unger, Donald N. S. "Academic Apartheid: The Predicament of Part-Time Faculty." *Thought and Action: The NEA Higher Education Journal*, Spring 1995, 117–20.

Vestal, Shawn. "Teacher Says She Lost Job for Speaking Out." *Spokane* (WA) *Spokesman-Review*, 21 February 2006. *www.spokesman.com*.

Waggoner, Jean, and Douglas Snow. *The Freeway Flier and the Life of the Mind.* Bloomington, IN: XLibris, 2011.

Weiss, Carla, and Robert Pankin. *Part-Time Faculty in Higher Education: A Selected Annotated Bibliography*. Faculty Publications, paper 276. Providence: Rhode Island College, 2011, *digitalcommons.ric.edu*.

Wilson, Robin. "Whistle-Blowing Adjunct at Binghamton U. Finds Few Allies in Local Faculty Union." *Chronicle of Higher Education*, 14 December 2010.

Wolf, Barbara. *Degrees of Shame: Part-Time Faculty; Migrant Workers of the Information Economy*. Cincinnati: Barbara Wolf Video Work, 1997.

———. *A Simple Matter of Justice: Contingent Faculty Organize*. Cincinnati: Barbara Wolf Video Work, 2001.

Zobel, Gregory. "The Adjuncts' Mandate." *Inside Higher Ed*, 5 January 2009. *insidehighered.com*.

# Appendix
## Trends in Instructional Staff Employment Status

The tables in this appendix show trends in instructional staff employment status from 1975 to 2011. The data comes from the US Department of Education, National Center for Education Statistics, IPEDS Fall Staff Survey. The tables were compiled by John Curtis, director of research and public policy at the AAUP Research Office.

**Trends in Instructional Staff Employment Status, 1975–2011** (*All institutions, national totals*)

|  | 1975 | | 1989 | | 1993 | |
|---|---|---|---|---|---|---|
| Full-time tenured faculty | 227,381 | 29.0% | 272,661 | 27.6% | 279,424 | 25.0% |
| Full-time tenure-track faculty | 126,300 | 16.1% | 112,593 | 11.4% | 114,278 | 10.2% |
| Full-time non-tenure-track faculty | 80,883 | 10.3% | 139,173 | 14.1% | 152,004 | 13.6% |
| Part-time faculty | 188,000 | 24.0% | 299,794 | 30.4% | 369,768 | 33.1% |
| Graduate student employees | 160,806 | 20.5% | 163,298 | 16.5% | 202,819 | 18.1% |
| Total instructional staff | 783,370 | 99.9% | 987,518 | 100.0% | 1,118,293 | 100.0% |
| Contingent instructional staff | 429,689 | 54.9% | 602,265 | 61.0% | 724,591 | 64.8% |

|  | 1995 | | 1999 | | 2001 | |
|---|---|---|---|---|---|---|
| Full-time tenured faculty | 284,870 | 24.8% | 281,984 | 21.8% | 278,825 | 20.3% |
| Full-time tenure-track faculty | 110,311 | 9.6% | 114,855 | 8.9% | 125,811 | 9.2% |
| Full-time non-tenure-track faculty | 155,641 | 13.6% | 196,535 | 15.2% | 213,232 | 15.5% |
| Part-time faculty | 380,884 | 33.2% | 460,377 | 35.5% | 495,315 | 36.0% |
| Graduate student employees | 215,909 | 18.8% | 242,525 | 18.7% | 261,136 | 19.0% |
| Total instructional staff | 1,147,615 | 100.0% | 1,296,276 | 100.1% | 1,374,319 | 100.0% |
| Contingent instructional staff | 752,434 | 65.6% | 899,437 | 69.4% | 969,683 | 70.6% |

|  | 2003 |  | 2005 |  | 2007 |  |
|---|---|---|---|---|---|---|
| Full-time tenured faculty | 282,429 | 19.3% | 283,434 | 17.8% | 290,581 | 17.2% |
| Full-time tenure-track faculty | 128,602 | 8.8% | 131,140 | 8.2% | 134,826 | 8.0% |
| Full-time non-tenure-track faculty | 219,388 | 15.0% | 235,171 | 14.8% | 251,361 | 14.9% |
| Part-time faculty | 543,137 | 37.0% | 624,753 | 39.3% | 684,668 | 40.5% |
| Graduate student employees | 292,801 | 20.0% | 317,146 | 19.9% | 328,979 | 19.5% |
| Total instructional staff | 1,466,357 | 100.1% | 1,591,644 | 100.0% | 1,690,415 | 100.1% |
| Contingent instructional staff | 1,055,326 | 72.0% | 1,177,070 | 74.0% | 1,265,008 | 74.8% |

|  | 2009 |  | 2011 |  |
|---|---|---|---|---|
| Full-time tenured faculty | 297,460 | 16.8% | 308,360 | 16.7% |
| Full-time tenure-track faculty | 135,250 | 7.6% | 136,320 | 7.4% |
| Full-time non-tenure-track faculty | 266,441 | 15.1% | 284,303 | 15.4% |
| Part-time faculty | 727,098 | 41.1% | 761,996 | 41.3% |
| Graduate student employees | 342,393 | 19.4% | 355,916 | 19.3% |
| Total instructional staff | 1,768,642 | 100.0% | 1,846,895 | 100.1% |
| Contingent instructional staff | 1,335,932 | 75.5% | 1,402,215 | 75.9% |

**Notes:** Figures for 2011 are estimated. Figures from 2005 have been corrected from those published in 2012. Figures are for degree-granting institutions only, but the precise category of institutions included has changed over time. Graduate student employee figure for 1975 is from 1976. Percentages may not add to 100 due to rounding.

**Trends in Instructional Staff Employment Status, 1975–2011** *(All institutions, national totals)*

| | Rate of Growth, by Time Period | | | | | | |
|---|---|---|---|---|---|---|---|
| | 1975–1989 | 1989–1995 | 1995–2001 | 2001–2007 | 2007–2011 | 1975–2011 | 2001–2011 |
| Full-time tenured faculty | 19.9% | 4.5% | -2.1% | 4.2% | 6.1% | 35.6% | 10.6% |
| Full-time tenure-track faculty | -10.9% | -2.0% | 14.1% | 7.2% | 1.1% | 7.9% | 8.4% |
| Full-time non-tenure-track faculty | 72.1% | 11.8% | 37.0% | 17.9% | 13.1% | 251.5% | 33.3% |
| Part-time faculty | 59.5% | 27.0% | 30.0% | 38.2% | 11.3% | 305.3% | 53.8% |
| Graduate student employees | 1.5% | 32.2% | 20.9% | 26.0% | 8.2% | 121.3% | 36.3% |
| Total instructional staff | 26.1% | 16.2% | 19.8% | 23.0% | 9.3% | 135.8% | 34.4% |
| Contingent instructional staff | 40.2% | 24.9% | 28.9% | 30.5% | 10.8% | 226.3% | 44.6% |
| Tenured/tenure-track faculty | 8.9% | 2.6% | 2.4% | 5.1% | 4.5% | 25.7% | 9.9% |
| Proportion of total growth attributable to contingent positions | 84.5% | 93.8% | 95.8% | 93.4% | 87.7% | 91.4% | 91.5% |

*See full trend data table for explanatory notes and source information.*

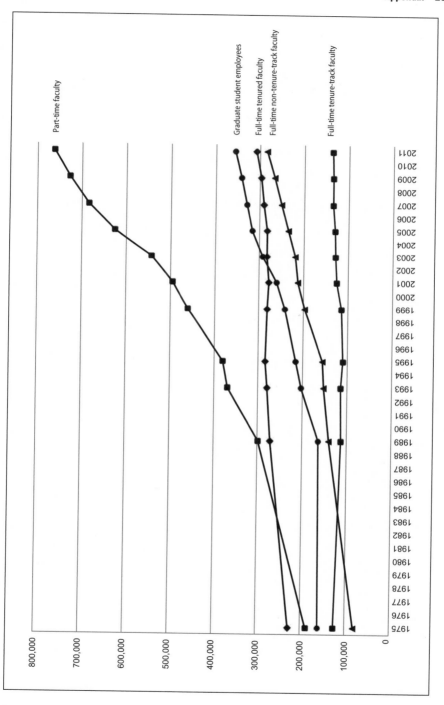

# Acknowledgments

I would like to thank several people for their help with this book and with the contingent faculty movement in general.

I wish to express my gratitude to Terry Knudsen, who joined me in co-founding the Washington Part-Time Faculty Association in 1997. She has shown incredible insight and courage, and lost her teaching job for speaking out about our exploitation.

I also want to thank the other members of the steering committee of the Washington Part-Time Faculty Association; they all deserve mention for contributing to one of the most successful adjunct groups in the country, having initiated and helped to settle two class-action lawsuits on retirement and health care benefits for $12 million each, providing sick leave and regular incremental raises for all part-timers in the community colleges, and leading the charge to secure $60 million in raises: Doug Collins, Jack Longmate, Wally Marquardt, Dana Rush, and Ron Swift.

All of the contributors of this book deserve credit for their willingness to share their ideas with others: Frank Cosco, Frank Donoghue, Don Eron, John Hess, Elizabeth Hoffman, Jack Longmate, Dougal MacDonald, Rich Moser, Natalie Sharpe, and Lantz Simpson.

My special appreciation goes to Michael Ames, director of Vanderbilt University Press, for his support of this project at every stage. It has been a pleasure working with someone who understands higher education as much as he does.

Thanks as well to Joell Smith-Borne, managing editor for Vanderbilt; Peg Duthie, copyeditor; Dariel Mayer, production manager; and Sue Havlish, marketing manager.

My philosophy colleague Jeffner Allen was immensely helpful with constructive advice and editing tips throughout every stage of this project. Her expertise with academic publishing was extremely helpful in putting this book together. Labor journalist Steve Early offered helpful advice throughout the project and immense support through his writings on unions. The late Robert Fitch, labor historian and adjunct professor of political science at

LaGuardia Community College, offered insightful advice into the history of unions. Jack Longmate deserves thanks for help with the proofs and providing the index.

My wife, Renee Barton, deserves recognition not only for her twenty-five years of devotion to a maverick such as myself, but for the myriad sacrifices she has made being married to an adjunct professor. Without her influence, I would have become a much different, and lesser, person. Thank goodness even poor adjuncts can find life-mates and ride their bicycles together into the rainy Seattle sunset.

# Contributors

**Frank Cosco** served as president of the Vancouver Community College Faculty Association, British Columbia. He has contributed through many roles in the union as bargainer, executive member, leader, and steward. He has taught English as a Second or Additional Language to adults in Canada, Italy, and Japan for over thirty years. He is also a vice president of the Federation of Post-Secondary Educators of British Columbia, a federation of faculty unions from ten colleges, six universities, and two institutes in the public sector and a federated local from five private training schools.

**Frank Donoghue** is professor of English at the Ohio State University. He is the author of *The Fame Machine: Book Reviewing and Eighteenth-Century Literary Careers* and *The Last Professors: The Corporate University and the Fate of the Humanities.*

**Don Eron** is senior instructor in the Program for Writing and Rhetoric at the University of Colorado (CU), Boulder. He is the architect, with Suzanne Hudson, of the Instructor Tenure Project (ITP), which has led to significant changes in Colorado state law. He is the principal author of the AAUP Colorado Conference's "Report on the Termination of Phil Mitchell," as well as "Report on the Termination of Ward Churchill" (in *AAUP Journal of Academic Freedom* 3). With Suzanne Hudson, he was the recipient of the AAUP's 2012 Tacey Award. He is a member of the AAUP's Committee A on Academic Freedom and Tenure.

**John Hess** has taught film studies in contingent positions at Sonoma State University (Rohnert Park, California) and San Francisco State University, where he became an activist in the faculty union. In the early 1990s, he taught as associate professor at Ithaca College in New York State, then returned to California and was hired by the California Faculty Association to serve as an organizer of the contingent faculty. He has written widely about film and is one of the founding coeditors of *Jump Cut: A Review of Contemporary Film.*

**Keith Hoeller** is an adjunct professor of philosophy at Green River Community College, where he became the first adjunct to win the college's Distinguished Faculty Award (2012). He received the 2012 John and Suanne Roueche Excellence Award from the League for Innovation in the Community College. He was also the first adjunct to win the AAUP's Georgina Smith Award (2002) for improving the status of women and advancing collective bargaining. He is the cofounder of the Washington Part-Time Faculty Association and helped to organize the New Faculty Majority. He has published more than two dozen opinion articles on adjunct faculty in newspapers throughout Washington and in the *Chronicle of Higher Education* and *Inside Higher Ed*. He initiated two successful class-action lawsuits to recover health care and retirement benefits for adjuncts, drafted successful Washington legislation to give sick leave to adjuncts, and helped to pass a budget amendment to extend incremental step raises to all community college adjuncts.

**Elizabeth Hoffman** is lecturer in English at California State University, Long Beach. Hoffman served ten years as a statewide officer of the California Faculty Association (CFA); she has also been a member of four CFA bargaining teams. She served two terms on the National Council of the AAUP, and served on the AAUP committee that developed the AAUP policy statement *Contingent Appointments and the Academic Profession*.

**Jack Longmate** is an adjunct English instructor at Olympic College (Bremerton, WA), where he has taught for twenty years. As a member of TESOL (Teachers of English to Speakers of Other Languages), he chaired its caucus on part-time employment concerns and its employment issues committee. He is a founder and former board member of the New Faculty Majority. With Frank Cosco, he drafted *The Program for Change*, which is a roadmap to convert the two-tiered American system into a single tier.

**Dougal MacDonald** is an online tutor (instructor) at Athabasca University, Alberta, where he teaches Introduction to the Profession of Teaching. He has also been an award-winning sessional (contract) instructor at the University of Alberta in Edmonton for the last thirteen years and an intermittent contract instructor at Northern Lakes College, Alberta, and Yellowhead Tribal College in Edmonton. In 2005 he coauthored a textbook for elementary science teaching methods that is now in its second edition.

**Richard Moser** was associate professor of American history at Middle Tennessee State University. He is author of *The New Winter Soldiers: GI and Veteran Dissent during the Vietnam Era* and is coeditor with Van Gosse of *The World the Sixties Made: Politics and Culture in Recent America*. Moser was national field representative for the AAUP from 1998 to 2004 and was the first chair of Campus Equity Week. He was senior staff representative at the Rutgers Council of AAUP-AFT Chapters from 2004 to 2013, where he specialized in membership recruitment and contingent faculty issues. He is currently an independent scholar.

**Natalie Sharpe** has taught courses in anthropology, sociology, labor studies, and alternate dispute resolution for First Nations colleges, traditional universities, and distance education universities since the mid-1970s. She has also been a university ombudsperson for twenty-seven years, and is currently involved in a four-year study of cyberbullying at Canadian postsecondary institutions; the study is being funded by Canada's Social Sciences and Humanities Research Council. Sharpe has worked as an editor-researcher for a Canadian encyclopedia and as a Metis land claims research director. Sharpe has served as a grievance officer and cochair for CUPE Local 3911, the educational local for Athabasca University part-timers. Sharpe has presented at several COCAL conferences.

**Lantz Simpson** is professor of English at Santa Monica College, where he was president of the Santa Monica College Faculty Association for nine years. He was one of the original founders of the California Part-Time Faculty Association. He has written numerous articles and essays on faculty issues, as well as participating in many conferences and workshops on these issues. He was temporary part-time faculty for fifteen years.

# Index